The Unkindest Cuts

The Unkindest Cuts

The Scissors and the Cinema

DOUG McCLELLAND

South Brunswick and New York: A. S. Barnes and Company
London: Thomas Yoseloff Ltd

Library of Congress Catalogue Card Number: 72-146767

A. S. Barnes and Co., Inc.
Cranbury, New Jersey 08512

Thomas Yoseloff Ltd
108 New Bond Street
London W1Y OQX, England

ISBN 0-498-07825-6
Printed in the United States of America

CONTENTS

ACKNOWLEDGMENTS

My gratitude for their help to—besides the sources mentioned in the text and therewith thanked—Donald Deschner, Charlie Earle, Dave Finkle, Peter Levinson, Joseph Longo, Leonard Maltin, Alvin H. Marill, Gloria Martin, Jim Meyer, James Robert Parish, Gene Ringgold, Joel Rudikoff, Gladys Shelley, Eve Siegel, George Simon, Bea Smith, John Springer, Jeanne Stein, and Bill Weeden. Plus, the staff and Theater Collection, Library and Museum of Performing Arts, Lincoln Center; Memory Shop; and Movie Star News, along with film company employees (anonymous by their will, and sometimes even unknowing of their assistance) and countless newspapers, magazines, and books.

D. McC., N.Y.C.

The Unkindest Cuts

1. THE OSCAR AND THE IMPORT

"The Picture with Something to Offend Everyone."

That's the way English director Tony Richardson advertised his film *The Loved One* with uncharacteristic restraint for a Hollywood production. It offended not only discriminating audiences with its bizarre, uncreative, calculated-to-shock treatment of the American way of death, but also many of its cast "names" by cutting them out of the finished picture. While many viewers considered these actors well out of it, the performers themselves would undoubtedly have welcomed the exposure this much-talked-about black comedy afforded.

Richardson had been a mighty busy fellow slashing away at his five-hour funereal orgy until it was down to two. Released about a year after completion, the picture looked it, too. *Loved One* may hold the record for important players who wound up completely edited out of a single film.

Among the first to go was Ruth Gordon, distinguished lady of the theater celebrating her 50th year in show business at the time of *Loved One,* which also marked her first film appearance in more than 20 years. She played Mrs. Bradley, who insisted that her dog be disinterred and relocated because the Happier Hunting Grounds had buried a cat next to it. ("Personally, I don't mind cats myself, but Stoutman loathed them, and would go well out of his way to simply kill a cat. Please put him alongside some nice doggie-dogs . . .") Miss Gordon's play, *A Very Rich Woman,* opened around the same time as *Loved One* in the fall of 1965, and she still listed the latter in *Playbill* as one of her films.

Keenan Wynn's entire role as heaven-knows-what was soon interred; and director Richardson even tried to bury executive producer Martin Ransohoff's bit as a studio boss' son-in-law (what the hell, why not offend him, too?), but Ransohoff overrode him and *his* flash appearance stayed in. Having no shame, Richardson then omitted Jayne Mansfield's part(s) as the traveler's-aid girl.

Just before one of the last pre-opening MGM screenings of *Loved One,* I wandered into the company's New York Advertising, Publicity, and Exploitation offices for one reason or other and discovered that star-snipping was still the name of the game. As I was leaving with an invitation to the screening and a black-bordered credit sheet for the picture, a female employee, worn-down blue pencil poised, came rushing after me to cross off Barbara Nichols' name.

Miss Nichols had taken the role originally announced for Kim Stanley yet, that of Sadie Blodgett, the stripteaser widow of America's first astronaut. She got to take it off, play a scene or two with the film's leading—man?—Robert Morse, and then turned up in widow's weeds for her husband's blastoff burial "in an orbit of eternal grace." But Miss Nichols was not completely out of *Loved One.* She still got billing in the picture and was visible as an extra (veiled, no lines to speak) when her deceased husband was fired into space at the end—"Resurrection Now!" (Actually, there'd been a switch and the self-embalmed, young female mortuary cosmetician had secretly replaced Capt. Todd Blodgett, USAF. . . .)

The reviews ranged from the equivocal "A failure of excess but worth seeing" (Judith Crist) and "A triumphant disaster" (Pauline Kael) to a one-half star rating (the New York *Daily News*) and a "Burn it!" (Hedda Hopper, only a few months away from her own demise). The latter, considering the subject matter of the picture, seemed the most appropriate critique.

The movies cry about the threat of television, dwindling box-office returns, and such. But in some ways the motion picture industry's unkindest cuts are self-inflicted.

For instance—in *this* instance—the cutting of scenes. Not necessarily that routine area of toil in which the studio's film editor whacks, definitely not the one in which the censor frowns, but essentially the arbitrary cutting that too many times is done at the request of an "expert" producer, or even inexpert director, or even on some occasions at the insistence of a powerful leading player who has been overshadowed by the expertise of another player in the film. The motion picture exhibitor is also influential perhaps as never before. This kind of cutting, the kind that usually occurs after the picture has been finished, to all intents and purposes, sometimes even trade-shown and sometimes even after the public has had glimpses, fleeting and not so, of the "superfluous" celluloid.

All this can be very serious to a film's welfare, artistically and commercially. It can fascinate and infuriate the buff, and can also gripe hell out of a plain old moviegoer. Critics, too, are getting wise. Early in 1965 former New York *Times* reviewer Bosley Crowther took out after "a practice that has become much too frequent for patient endurance by the critical tribe. This is the practice of cutting whole sequences or scenes out of films after they have been reviewed by the critics, without notice that they have been cut. . . . This sort of thing becomes an offense to the public and eventually to posterity, which must depend for judgment of a picture on what the critics have said. . . . It seems to be a tactic of producers and distributors to try to conceal the 'editing' they do on their expanded pictures after they have got their reviews. Evidently there is no protection against this for critics, except eternal vigilance."

In his autobiography, *Fun in a Chinese Laundry,* the director-discoverer of Marlene Dietrich, Josef von Sternberg, said that the trouble began earlier than the preview, although his own peculiar experiences may have colored his view more than somewhat. "The finished product is not finished when the actor is; the work is completed by a pair of shears," he wrote. "These go into action when the stage has gone dark, and are often wielded by someone who has little knowledge (sometimes none whatsoever) of the original intention. He can remove the most precious sentence or word from the mouth of the actor and eliminate his most treasured expression. This operator, known as the cutter, literally cuts the actor's face and words. Few directors, strangely enough, have even the privilege of sitting in on this process. . . . Not only does the cutter cut, but everyone who can manage to put his hands on the film, including the distributor and the exhibitor, who often alters the film between the afternoon and evening performance, waters at the mouth at this opportunity to improve a film. Actually, were everyone permitted to apply his genius to make a film fit for exhibition, nothing would be left but the title, and that, too, is strongly debated until the morning of the day when the film is taken out of its container."

Today—unlike the '20s–'30s prime of von Sternberg—the director enjoys much more creative freedom (the film medium now is frequently called "a director's medium"). But, except for a handful of mighties like Federico Fellini, William Wyler, George Stevens, Alfred Hitchcock, and Stanley Kubrick (and even they take their chances with exhibitors, and outside their own countries anything can happen), he is still subject to an override by studio chiefs (or powers-that-be).

Early in 1965 *Variety* printed: "Film showmen point to the inevitability of cutting overlong films which should have been edited fundamentally rather than post-premiere when captious comment forced such editings. *Lawrence of Arabia, Cleopatra, Exodus* and *Greatest Story Ever Told* are cited although *Ben-Hur* and *Ten Commandments,* also in the three-hour-plus category, were not. Instances are cited where the producer-director calls the shots too literally and the distributor-bankrollers find themselves contractually hamstrung since any and all editing rests with the actual filmmakers. George Stevens' *Greatest Story* and Richard Brooks' *Lord Jim* are recent instances where dominant authority rested with the individuals and not the distributing ocmpany."

In 1966 an infrequent filmmaker from television named Fielder Cook, who had a success with a little film called *A Big Hand for the Little Lady,* starring Henry Fonda, Joanne Woodward, and Jason Robards, Jr., said: "They call the movies a director's medium. It is, about one-tenth of the time. It is also the producer's medium. It is the studio's medium. The medium belongs to the one who has the power. On this picture I was director, producer and I was Eden Productions, which joined with Warner Brothers in producing."

Yet Cook admitted he did not have the last word. "If the studio didn't like my final cut, Jack Warner could take it and cut it. If you want my personal opinion, he could make it better."

Asked if he were buttering up the boss, Cook replied, "He did make some cuts at the very beginning. Three minutes. It was where the hearse was racing. When I saw it, the improvement was tremendous. . . . But I *do* like to say something nice."

Director Irvin Kershner, who directed another Joanne Woodward vehicle for the Warner company the same year, *A Fine Madness* (with Sean Connery), was not so anxious to please: "That wasn't my cut you saw. Jack Warner saw it and re-edited it. The script was edited in New York, you see, and he hadn't read it. You know what he said when he saw it? 'It's anti-social!' Can you imagine? That's only the point!"

Fred Zinnemann, Academy Awarded Best Director for the 1953 Best Picture, *From Here to Eternity,* recently revealed: "I rather liked Harry Cohn (the late head of Columbia Pictures) even though he could be a monster. He insisted a movie should never be more than two hours long. He cut one of my favorite scenes in *From Here to Eternity,* in which Montgomery Clift composed a blues number on the bugle."

Bob Thomas discussed the *Eternity* cutting in more detail in his Cohn biography, *King Cohn.* "The two-hour limit pained Zinnemann," he wrote. "He was forced to abandon two prized scenes: one in which Clift believed the Pearl Harbor attackers were Germans; another in which half a dozen soldiers in the barracks improvised a blues number, which Zinnemann wanted to use as a theme similar to the *High Noon* ballad.

"Cohn remained adamant, and Zinnemann cut the film to its final 118 minutes. He permitted no interference in his right under the Directors Guild contract to edit the first cut himself. When Cohn surrepititiously edited a scene before Zinnemann had reviewed it, the two men had another confrontation of power. This time it was Cohn who relented; he restored the edited scene to its original condition."

Russian film master V. I. Pudovkin once wrote: "Editing is the foundation of the film art." Few will deny that the precept still goes today, perhaps even more than ever.

Most of us at one time or another have stood outside a movie theater and perused the photo stills from the show we'd just seen, exclaiming, "Hey, that wasn't in the picture! That neither . . . nor that . . . we were cheated!" This especially applied to the halcyon days of the old movie palaces, when we didn't have that much money and wanted to make sure we got its worth, or even more especially when we were kids, forgetting as we stood there crabbing that we were already 14 and had gotten into the theater for children's price.

(Time was in films when a still photographer was always present on the set and actually made these photographs. Now this happens less frequently and most stills, even for major productions, are taken directly from the film footage.)

Cheated we were. Many of the scenes we spotted outside—it became a game—were not to be found inside. Some, of course, were specially posed publicity stills by the stars, usually distinguishable by plain backdrops (but occasionally made against the film's settings) or static groupings. Often, though, they were scenes that had been excised from the picture, and, despite the technically expert excisers, not to the picture's advantage. As a wise man once said: holes, like smoke, elephants and pregnancy, have a way of showing.

And when the film buff discovers there is some film around on any of his favorites to which he is not privy, he becomes just what the word fan is derived from until he (1) gets to see the mysterious film *somehow;* and/or (2) gets all the particulars on it.

In 1954 Judy Garland's expensive, highly touted, and troubled return to the screen after a couple of years' hiatus, *A Star is Born,* opened to favorable reviews, running a little more than three hours. However, Warner Brothers decided it would do better by *Born* if a half hour or more were cut, allowing more audience turnover. So Judy's exciting tour de force was butchered. Out went much of her courtship with James Mason and several musical numbers (including her big "Lose That Long Face"), which just about destroyed the picture. So when Mason took that suicidal walk into the surf at the end, audiences thought "So what?" because all the scenes in which he had been humanized, where they should have been getting to know and understand and sympathize with Mason, were gone with the Warners. It should have been retitled *Excerpts from A Star is Born* or *A Star is Shorn.*

The film was one of Mason's big disappointments: "It was shot at ludicrous marathon length, with superfluous musical numbers thrown in at all the wrong times. Then it was cut unmercifully, and some of Judy Garland's best scenes were gone and some of her most dramatic ones—not all good—were kept. Also, we never really had a producer. Sid Luft [Judy's husband] was an amateur. There was nobody to check on or discipline Judy or George Cukor [the director]. As for Moss Hart, he just turned in the script, dealt very severely with anyone who criticized it and packed up and went back to New York. Recently Portland [Mason's daughter] and I were taking a long walk near my home in Switzerland and we came across a mountain cafe where *Star* was playing on TV. There I was, dubbed in French, and I rather liked it. That long, disturbing 'Born in a Trunk' number had been cut and the movie seemed much better."

Cukor had more to say on the matter. "When the story was finished they dropped in a great big divertissement called 'Born in a Trunk,' which tells the story all over again and which I didn't shoot. Partly to accommodate this they made cuts, including some charming songs, some very funny scenes between Judy Garland and James Mason, little episodes building up the relationship between them. There were scenes when they meet again when she is living in a very shabby boarding house downtown in Los Angeles; a scene on the way to the film premiere, when she's so nervous that she jumps out of the car and is sick, all among oil derricks; and a scene I was very fond of when they play a love scene on the sound stage, with a live microphone going so that the whole thing is played back to them."

Cukor went on: "If they thought it was too long there were other ways of shortening it besides chopping out vital bits. Had we been allowed, Moss Hart and I could have sweated out 20 minutes which would have been imperceptible to the audience. That's something which I can't understand. Producers spend millions of dollars to do pictures and then suddenly, right out of the blue, they say: 'Let's chop this out, then that . . .' In what other business does this happen? I'm sure at Ford they don't make models of some car and then just throw them out.

"It's very painful, all this. Fanny Brice, who was a wonderful woman and a great friend of mine, once said, 'The older we get, kid, the less you can brush off them knocks.' And she was right. But there are some things I won't stand for, old or not. For example, when you're filming and there comes a moment of indecision—the people around you say: 'O.K., let's do it both ways . . . do the scene both ways, and you can't go wrong.' I refuse point blank and say that there is only one way to do it: let's decide what is the correct way and after there will be no alternatives. There is a right way and a wrong way—that's all. Mind you, I'm not always right, don't think that by any means. I've miscalculated a great many things. Very often you imagine certain things and then the audience tells you differently. You must never underestimate the audience. The audience is, after all, always right. Sometimes they react the way you don't want them to and sometimes there are a lot of kids in the house and they laugh at the wrong place. But the audience is always right. You must not be hysterical, though; you must interpret their reactions calmly and correctly. You must know cause and effect. If you had a bad laugh in the fourth reel that doesn't mean the line is bad. It simply means that what preceded, what came before the line, is all off . . . that the preparation for the line is wrong. You must be detached and look at your children from a distance. You must be patient and loving."

A critic admirer of the uncut *Star* observed in '54 that the cut version "almost falls apart. The 'Lose That Long Face' cut robs Judy Garland's superb preceding dressing room scene of much of its dramatic impact. The proposal scene, and its accompanying song, were also dropped. So was the fabulous sequence in which Mason gives Judy first-hand advice on what to expect at her first premiere. Worst of all was the removal of the large section when Judy leaves Tommy Noonan's room after informing him she has decided to quit the band. About 15 minutes were scissored and we next see Judy making up for her screen test."

In his autobiography, *My First Hundred Years in Hollywood,* Jack L. Warner spent several pages characterizing *Star* producer Sid Luft as a despicable deadbeat.

"I wanted Judy Garland for the lead, but in order to get her I had to take her husband . . . and bill him as the producer. A charming fellow, Sid. He's one of the original guys who promised his parents he'd never work a day in his life—and made good," wrote Warner, who later was sued for six million dollars for these words by Luft, who charged libel.

Luft, "who could make Judy go home just by snapping his fingers," allegedly forced Warner to hire James Mason for the male lead when Warner wanted contract player Humphrey Bogart. And among other things about Luft and the *Star* shooting Warner remembered with rancor were the periodic—and successful—touches Luft put on Warner, "which were never repaid."

What Warner *didn't* remember to mention in his book was the stupefying, notorious cutting of *A Star is Born;* but he did boast that he has had a hand in editing all Warner films.

Judy herself told me that executive producer of the movie Jack Warner was to blame for the cuts, and that she would love to get a theater somewhere, "anywhere!", to show her uncut *A Star is Born* for an extended special run. Later, of Harry Warner, one of the founding brothers and at the time of the cutting in his 70s, she said, "They didn't cut the picture. Harry gummed it to death."

She got an Oscar nomination for Best Actress out of the whole thing, and many feel Judy might have won the statuette if her performance had not been tampered with, if her *Star* hadn't been spliced.

Something like that happened a couple of years later with *The King and I* as filmed by 20th Century-Fox with Deborah Kerr and Yul Brynner. Deborah's singing was done for her by "ghostess with the mostes'" Marni Nixon, but Deborah did have one piece that she was allowed to talk-sing for the most part by herself. It was the amusing "Shall I Tell You What I Think of You?" in which a fed-up Mrs. Anna told off the absent King. It was the kind of strong personal moment that would have given Deborah a firmer hold on the picture. But Fox cut the scene, which helped throw the film to Brynner, who walked off with the Best Actor award for 1956. Deborah got an Oscar nomination, but many feel that the inclusion of her big number might have swung audience reaction and voters more solidly in her favor.

Just before the final editing of *King and I,* music supervisor Alfred Newman (who, with Ken Darby, picked up an Oscar for this chore) stated: "We discovered that Miss Kerr has a pleasing singing voice, which you shall hear in Anna's soliloquy, 'Shall I Tell You What I Think of You?' But because of the extreme range of many of the other songs, Miss Kerr agreed with us that a voice-double should be used. We discovered Marni Nixon's voice matched Miss Kerr's."

Talking with Miss Nixon (who also sang for Natalie Wood in *West Side Story* and Audrey Hepburn in *My Fair Lady*), I asked why that number had been cut. She said, "Fox felt it made Anna too bitchy, I think, and they wanted her to be more sympathetic." Well, it was not too bitchy for inclusion in Gertrude Lawrence's winning Broadway interpretation, countless stock presentations, and the extraordinary number of about a half-dozen different full cast album recordings of the show (the Kerr solo *was* left in the Capitol Records soundtrack LP). Interestingly, in the original Broadway billing, Lawrence received star billing above the title and Brynner—the male lead then, too—a "*with* Yul Brynner" below.

(Mind, I'm talking about the United States. Overseas, where musicals are usually notsohot boxoffice, *The King and I* has been stripped of *all* musical numbers in some locations!)

The stills released from Miss Kerr's *The Night of the Iguana* in which she gave another matchlessly sensitive performance as the cool itinerant philosopher, Hannah Jelkes, indicated some more strange goings-on. Miss Kerr was shown in several of them, including the scene in which she removed glass from the feet of "fever"-flippy Richard Burton, in a checkered dress. She wore no such dress in the film, although the action portrayed in the stills was in the picture. If these were rehearsal shots, why did Metro-Goldwyn-Mayer release the stills (with captions) everywhere as scenes from the movie? Very odd. (Miss Kerr did not get even an Academy *nomination* for what columnist Robert Sylvester called "just about the best acting I've seen on or off stage or screen." Incensed Academy members who fought the exclusion that year—'64—of Audrey Hepburn's stick of a *Fair Lady* from the Best Actress nominee list and started an unsuccessful write-in drive for her would have had a worthier cause in Miss Kerr's Hannah.)

Peculiar, too, was the omission of the closing sequence in Miss Kerr's 1961 *The Innocents,* a film formidable critic Pauline Kael called "the best ghost movie I've ever seen . . . and maybe Deborah Kerr's performance should really be called great. Kerr's performance is in the grand manner—as modulated and controlled, and yet as flamboyant, as almost anything you'll see on the stage. And it's a tribute to Miss Kerr's beauty and dramatic powers that, after 20 years in the movies—years of constant overexposure—she is more exciting than ever. Perhaps she *is* a demon." There are stills showing Miss Kerr after the tragic climax (at which point the released version ended), dressed in black traveling clothes and wandering through the rooms of the country estate where everything was covered with white sheets. *The Innocents* was always a visual treat, and these stills indicate that this epilogue was no less so. (P.S. Another outstanding Kerr portrayal which the Academy did not even recognize with a Best Actress nomination.)

More understandable was the cutting of a dream scene from Miss Kerr's *Heaven Knows, Mr. Allison* (1957) in which she, a nun, and Robert Mitchum, a Marine, were marooned on a Japaneseinfested South Pacific island during World War II. Mitchum dreamed he and Kerr were in civvies having a romantic fling, and the bit, if left in, might have offended, although never a Kerrdiac like myself.

Miss Kerr's troubles with the British-made *The Life and Death of Colonel Blimp,* however, had historical relevance. On June 13th, 1947, the Federal Trade Commission accused Charlie Chaplin, Mary Pickford, David O. Selznick, and Edward C. Rafferty, President and General Manager of United Artists, of showing a cut version of *Blimp* as the complete film, the first time a film company had been called on the carpet by the FTC. Indeed, an hour had been cut from this highly praised saga of a professional soldier, Roger Livesey, and the three women in various stages of his life, all played by Kerr, by the time it played neighborhood theaters. Hearings began in '49, but it was too late to do the movie—made in '43—any good then.

Reviewer Steven H. Scheuer noted: "In full-length form, *Blimp* is a magnificent, large-scale portrait of a windbag, ironic, witty, superbly done. A shortened, drastically cut version destroys all the sense and impact of the film."

Poor Deborah Kerr. There is no finer actress today. Some feel the Scottish-born redhead with the eloquent, quiveringly sensitive hands is the most consistent supplier of quality acting of any leading lady in the history of films. She has received many Academy Award nominations, and not often enough, but no Oscar. Surely no actress working in leads has done more during increasingly sensational movie times to provide subtlety, dignity, and refinement in a medium that today needs all the class it can get. I could not be so bitchy as to cut a Deborah Kerr scene, I'm afraid.

Recalling the problems with *Colonel Blimp,* film historian William K. Everson—sometimes called the Father of Film Buffery—once wrote: "British product, on the whole, suffers more at the hands of the American distributors than at those of the U.S. censors. When *Secret People* was released here, it was shortened considerably and sold as an action picture. To tighten it up, most of the early Audrey Hepburn footage was removed. But along came *Roman Holiday* to boost Miss Hepburn, and so back went all her deleted scenes. In order to keep the same running time, however, another cut had to be made, and consequently the entire ending of the film was hacked off. The picture now concludes—almost in the middle of a sentence.

"There is also the occasional need to shorten a film allegedly far too long for the market in which it now finds itself. For instance, *Dead of Night* was put out with two complete stories missing (despite the confusion this created in the climactic nightmare sequence)."

Nineteen forty-four's *Journey Together,* a semi-documentary feature produced by the RAF film unit, was relieved of Rex Harrison's entire appearance in the states. Featured players Cyril Fletcher and Fay Compton (as the Mantolinis) also were cut from American prints of their '47 *Nicholas Nickleby.*

H. G. Wells' *Things to Come* (1936), produced in England with Sir Ralph Richardson and Sir Cedric Hardwicke, and a major science fiction film effort of all time, lost 15 minutes of running time en route to America. This may have been because in '36 English films were far from popular over here—it would be 10 to 15 years before they would become fashionable in the U. S. The differences between Hollywood and British film-making were so marked at the time (Hollywood, of the glittering sheen; Britain, of the grainy, slightly stodgy approach—how the latter has changed!) that it may have been some of these English differences that were purposely lost in transit.

Even before the United Kingdom got to see *Things,* Hardwicke later divulged: "Wells invited me to replace a distinguished English actor whose performance, already completely filmed, had not been to Wells' liking. The voice of this actor needed more *vox humana,* the author held, and my actor's instinct would not permit me to disagree with him. . . . My work in *Things to Come* was completed with such speed and lack of ceremony that the actor I had replaced had no idea that his entire performance lay on the cutting room floor. He arrived with a party of expectant friends at the London premiere, an exceedingly fashionable gathering. After his disappointment, I remained pleasantly surprised that he did not become my enemy for life."

A few years later, England produced the even more acclaimed *The Stars Look Down,* a mining story involving a couple of other

"Sirs," Michael Redgrave (star), and Carol Reed (director). When it arrived in North America in the early '40s, the original ending, in which Redgrave left his family home for the last time for London to continue working for the miners in the political realm, had been replaced by a narrator's wrap-up. Also chucked: a love scene between Redgrave and Margaret Lockwood, as two raindrops coursed down their windowpane toward each other, eventually merging into one.

An Italian film generally conceded to have been saved by the trip here was the Alessandro Blasetti-directed *Fabiola,* starring Michèle Morgan and presented in the states in '51 by Jules Levey. Originally a three-hour bore, *Fabiola* was chopped in half by Levey and thus greatly improved.

This kind of thing happens with our pictures overseas, too. Early in '65 *Daily Variety's* man in Japan reported: "A scissored version of *Halls of Montezuma,* 20th-Fox oldie, is doing big biz in early situations outside Tokyo and looms likely to earn a fat $180,000 before it goes back into the vaults. That would make 20th's third heftiest Japan coiner within the past year, behind *Cleopatra* and *The Leopard.* The 1951-made Pacific War film starring Richard Widmark and Jack Palance was never before released in this country. Scenes that might have been offensive to Japanese viewers have been snipped."

But it was nothing new. Nineteen twenty-eight's *The Godless Girl,* directed by Cecil B. DeMille, was the story of a high school atheist club and a "godless girl," Lina Basquette, who was redeemed in the final reel, and the picture was called shocking and brutal by many at the time. When DeMille visited Russia in '31 he found that the film was very popular there and that he was almost a national hero because of it. This confused him, because he couldn't understand how a girl's redemption by gaining faith in God could be so appealing to Communists—until near the end of his visit when he learned that "The Russians simply did not screen the last redeeming reel, but played the rest of the picture as a document of American police brutality and the glorious spreading of atheism among American youth."

A 1965 communiqué from Paris informed me that the previously always-shortened 1939 French classic from director Jean Renoir,

Rules of the Game, had been restored to within a minute of its original 113 minutes and was revived to unanimously favorable reviews. Only one shot could not be found.

This reconstitution prompted Henri Langlois, head of the French Film Museum, La Cinémathèque Française, to grudgingly admit that some film people around the world do try to preserve pictures, but most do not care and usually do away with the negative for storage space or even to recoup film for use again or get the bit of silver in it. Langlois advocated the laws that will make it mandatory for all negatives to be kept for future archive needs.

Director Renoir, one of several directors whose careers have managed to shine despite consistent unauthorized (by them) cutting of their work (and more about him and them later), is yet to see his 1934 *Madame Bovary* restored.

A report from Spain suggested that the Latin temperament may be the ideal one to deal with harmful cutting. It covered the peculiar story of Madrid showings of Alfred Hitchcock's *Marnie* (1964), which came close to being redeemed as a picture by Diane Baker's just-right secondary minx but was ultimately damned by Hitchcock's colorless protégée Tippi Hedren in the demanding title role originally meant for Grace Kelly.

"After its premiere," our Spanish correspondent said, "*Marnie* was cut by 15 minutes. When the massacre was discovered, a group of 15 to 20 people—editors, friends, sympathizers—along with a member of the Censor Board, went one evening to the cinema where the film was showing. When the first cut came—the horse racing sequence—everyone began to protest vigorously, explaining to neighboring spectators what was happening, that they'd been robbed, etc. Of course this caused quite a bit of noise, the cinema attendant came up, and, after a short conference, he and the member of the Censor Board went out to talk to the cinema manager. The projection of the film went on and when the second cut was reached, the missing piece was there! Since then, the film has always been shown completely uncut."

"While this affair was amusing," José Luis Guarner of *Movie* magazine went on, "I thought it important to relate because the cutting of films has become quite a habit in Madrid. For example, I saw in a second-run cinema well-equipped with 70mm. a version of *Exodus* cut by a good half-hour, including important sequences such as Sal Mineo's confession before the Irgun. Also, after its first run, *Man's Favorite Sport?* was shown without the sequence in the revolving bar and without the trains which accompany the kisses between Rock Hudson and Paula Prentiss. At present, even on their first run, films suffer much damage, so the success of Operation Marnie will perhaps put an end to such iniquities."

Major Barbara, much of which was shot in the Empire during the Battle of Britain (the summer of 1940), introduced Deborah Kerr and was further distinguished by a prologue with George Bernard Shaw that was deleted in England in which Shaw joked: "I am sending you my old plays, just as you are sending us your old battleships."

Switching from his topic of the desecration of the British film, William K. Everson continued: "These [cutting] troubles occasionally descend also upon American releases. After lying on the shelf for over a year and a half in New York, John Ford's *The Sun Shines Bright* was clipped down to 65 minutes and sent out as a second feature to the uncut British *Trent's Last Case.*

"The practice of cutting has produced some confusing results in its time. For the creation of unnecessary chaos, though, no one has perhaps equalled the Herculean efforts of one company in editing a 15-episode serial, *The Secret of Treasure Island,* down to a 12-episode serial, retitled *Hidden Treasure.* This task was performed without the loss of a single frame of footage or the re-recording of any spoken forewords, with the result that episode six would open with the narrator explaining that 'last week in episode seven we saw . . . ', and describing events that had not yet taken place!"

A couple of the best serials ever made, Universal's *Flash Gordon* (1936) and *Flash Gordon's Trip to Mars* (1938), were cut down to feature length with paradoxical results. The former condensation of the costly original serial ran 72 minutes and was called *Rocket Ship* in some re-issues. It was much less confusing and jerky than the 70-minute version of *Flash Gordon's Trip to Mars,* which was retitled *Mars Attacks the World* and rush-released as a feature within two weeks after Orson Welles' famed *War of the Worlds* radio broadcast in '38. Oddly, *Rocket Ship* had been inferior to *Mars Attacks* in their original serial form.

Cutting serials down to regular feature-film length is a trick as old as serials themselves. Jack Warner made a circus serial around 1920 titled *A Dangerous Adventure,* which proved to be just that in more ways than one. A real circus was leased for the serial, animals and all, and the ensuing mishaps included an escaped lion that had to be shot; the near-fatal attack on a Warner employee by a tiger; the fatal attack on a young stagehand by a leopard; an elephant gone amuck; the resignation of three directors (Warner took over); a demanding leading lady who tantrumed herself out of the script by being eaten by a lion (in the story only); and a pair of leading men who, after completing six of the 15 episodes, claimed illness and bedded up in a hotel suite for two weeks—with around-the-clock "nurses."

The serial barely made back its cost. Two years later its 30 reels were cut down to a single seven-reel feature with the same title and made a lot of money this time.

In 1968, Ricardo Montalban said: "I've been in the business over 25 years, and in that time only two roles have I considered meaningful. One was *Sayonara* in which my role was cut very badly. And now my dream role in *Blue*—it's been emasculated!" Montalban wished there were some way actors could protect themselves in the cutting room clinches.

Actors have been known to get the scissors and still go on to win the Award. There's Patricia Neal, whose life has been marked by incredible personal sorrow: an ill-fated love affair with a married Gary Cooper; the sudden death of her small daughter; the near-fatal accident that could permanently impair her little boy's mind; and her own near-fatal, three partially paralyzing strokes in 1965 (during the early months of a pregnancy and after she had filmed a couple of scenes of *Seven Women*), from which she may never completely recover. Neal's Best Actress Oscar for her warm emoting as the knocked-around housekeeper in *Hud* (1963) was a deserved one, although many claimed her part was in the supporting category: she was third-billed, her name below the title. (Even Miss Neal said, "I'm surprised, because it was a part with no high moments.") Actually, she was the main female in the picture, in and out throughout the length, so much criticism seemed unfair. But there probably would have been less doubt about Miss Neal belonging in the starring category if her favorite scene had not been cut from the finished film.

She told an interviewer, "My best bit, and the thing I loved the most about Alma, hit the cutting room floor. It was a scene where the young boy, played by Brandon de Wilde, comes out to her cabin and asks Alma what life is all about anyway. 'Honey,' she tells him, 'you'll just have to ask somebody else.' "

There have been hints—denied by all—that this deletion had something to do with the fact that Paul Newman, the star (billed alone above the title), and director Martin Ritt were partners.

More extraordinary than this, though, was Miss Neal's experience soon after *Hud* with a "cameo" she filmed for the British movie, *The Third Secret* (1964). She was *completely* cut from the released picture, even though she had just won the Oscar and the publicity might have helped *Secret,* a dud, to make some money.

The greatest of artists are not above a little green-eyed scissor-wielding, and Orson Welles tells this one about Charlie Chaplin: "In *Limelight* there was a scene between Chaplin and Buster Keaton that was 10 minutes long. Chaplin was excellent and Keaton sensational. It was the most successful thing Keaton had done in the course of his career. Chaplin cut almost the entire scene, because he understood who, of the two, had completely dominated it."

In early 1967, ten years after his last film had opened (*A King in New York*), Chaplin's Marlon Brando-Sophia Loren starrer, *A Countess from Hong Kong,* opened in England, where it had been made, to critical jeers. It was dated 1930s fluff, the press felt, and Chaplin should have stayed retired. Sheilah Graham was quick to flash: "Someone who worked with Chaplin on *The Great Dictator* [1940] told me no one dared suggest he make any cuts. Well, before *A Countess from Hong Kong* comes to the states, the Universal powers-that-be will cut 20 minutes from the now one hour and 55-minute picture."

Many years before, Chaplin shot and edited four additional reels for his silent *Shoulder Arms* that were not used in the picture. When his 1925 production of *The Gold Rush*—which some have called Chaplin's finest achievement—was reissued in 1942, some scenes had been cut and some previously unused ones inserted, along with a soundtrack and a narration written and spoken by Chaplin. James Field received an Academy Award nomination for his sound recording, Max Terr for scoring.

Talking about the European filming of Welles' *The Trial* (1963), Tony Perkins recalled: "We used to call each other the 'Ever-Ready Players' because we never really knew what scenes we were going to be shooting due to financial difficulties, difficulties with sets, or with actors stuck in Zurich overnight. So I memorized the entire script which was so thick that it was written in two volumes—it is the only script I have ever known that was in two separate books. We cut a lot, including Katina Paxinou's entire role. That is one of the great mysteries of that picture. When Welles announced that Katina Paxinou was one of the players, some people went back and paid another admission to see if they could find her."

Welles, who has called the far from well-received *Trial* "the best film I have ever made," explained Paxinou's exit this way: "There was a long scene with her that lasted 10 minutes and that, moreover, I cut on the eve of the Paris premiere. It should have been the best scene in the film and it wasn't. Something went wrong, I guess. I don't know why, but it didn't succeed. The subject of that scene was free will. It was stained with *comédie noire.*"

The Greek Miss Paxinou, of course, is 1943's Best Supporting Actress Oscar holder for her role in *For Whom the Bell Tolls,* whose politics have made her unpopular in the U.S. She had played a scientist in *The Trial.*

Luise Rainer, the Viennese star who won Best Actress Oscars for 1936's *The Great Ziegfeld* and 1937's *The Good Earth* and then practically disappeared from the film scene, once traced a good deal of her problems to studio head Louis B. Mayer who told her in '38: "We made you and we're going to kill you." Miss Rainer, who was still collecting only $250 weekly on *Good Earth,* replied: "God made me."

She later confided that Mayer had not wanted her for *Ziegfeld,* which started one of their early battles. She finally talked him into it; but found upon completion of the picture that her big moment—the highly emotional scene in which Anna Held (Miss Rainer) telephoned her ex-husband, Florenz Ziegfeld (William Powell), to congratulate him on his forthcoming marriage—had been cut.

"The only reason we got it back was because the picture suddenly ended short," she remembered, "and that was the easiest thing to put back." This celebrated piece of ham on Rainer's part wrapped up the Academy Award for her. She has reprised the scene many times ("Hello, Flo? . . .") and years later even did it on the Ed Sullivan show.

A specific movie scene that also proved to be rather a boon to Buster Keaton came close to being vetoed for his second MGM vehicle, 1929's *Spite Marriage,* following a string of independent successes. The precarious scene that producer Lawrence Weingarten nixed ("I don't like that type of thing in *my* pictures!") and that Keaton had to beg him to retain was described by Rudi Blesh in his biography, *Keaton,* as "the one in which Buster struggles to put his bride to bed, both of them equally full of wedding champagne. The scene made the picture—both because of Keaton's famous way with props and because it was an especially pretty prop. It proved, too, to be a long-lived bit of foolery. Almost 25 years later, Gregory Peck tried his hand at it with Audrey Hepburn in *Roman Holiday.*" Donald O'Connor tackled the project more legitimately when portraying Keaton with Ann Blyth in Paramount's *The Buster Keaton Story,* a shabby 1957 biographical "tribute" to a great artist. Buster and various female partners have performed the almost-wasn't routine in many media over the years as well.

When *The Philadelphia Story* (1940) was finished, scored, and ready for previewing, it was discovered to be overlong by about 30 minutes. Lengthy viewing sessions were then held by the studio to determine what should be left in and what removed. And during this period it is rumored that there were several nasty real scenes with various members of the cast, which was headed by Cary Grant, Katharine Hepburn, and James Stewart, who felt that their best reel scenes were in danger of being left on the cutting room floor. But when the half-hour shorter film opened, it was a great success. Story has since become a minor classic (despite its rather talky, static treatment), has remained one of Grant's favorite films, revitalized Hepburn's career after she had been labeled "box-office poison," and won Stewart his Best Actor Academy Award.

The next year, Alfred Hitchcock, to whom words and actors (to hear him tell it) have always rated behind visual organization, was dismayed to find a part of Joan Fontaine's starring performance in the thriller *Suspicion* garnering unwanted laughs at its Pasadena preview. Joan had found a letter she was not supposed to read. It told her husband, Cary Grant, that he would be paid the insurance only on the occasion of his wife's death. Fontaine's eyes rose and she looked into the camera, thinking—provoking, Hitchcock recalled, "Belly laughs!" The director still can't figure out why the audience laughed, but he didn't wait to try it out elsewhere. All Fontaine did in the released version was read the letter, and there were no more belly laughs. There was, however, a Best Actress Oscar for the lady that year.

Following a violently negative sneak preview, United Artists was sure it had a flop in the 1952 western, *High Noon,* made by producer Stanley Kramer mainly to fulfill a six-picture commitment to the company. It was too long and lacked dramatic urgency. One show doctor suggested that they throw away approximately half the footage, bridging the deleted portions with a ballad in the Western idiom. Since no other solution was forthcoming, the producers scattered celluloid and hired Dimitri Tiomkin to provide the melody for the ballad, Ned Washington the words, and veteran cowboy Tex Ritter to sing it.

Thus, a classic Western film was born, with Oscars to star Gary Cooper, film editors Elmo Williams and Harry Gerstad, and Tiomkin, one for Best Score and one for Best Song, the latter shared with Washington. It was the first title tune ever to win an Academy Award.

For over a decade now, foreign filmmakers, when in doubt, have found it extremely profitable to be vague and, in more than a few cases—such as the French film *Last Year at Marienbad* (1962), directed by Alain Resnais—downright incomprehensible. Critics, and thus the audience for foreign films, too often mistake dimness for depth.

In the fall of 1966 when the Ingmar Bergman-directed film *Persona* opened in Sweden, it was, as always, an event. Mr. Bergman picked up his usual critical accolades for a tale (the first half already scrapped and remade) found "one of his simplest, freest, most powerful." The story, that of a psyche-induced mute actress, would have been even simpler, etc., if it had kept the original conclusion, which saw the lady returning rehabilitated to the stage. Bergman dropped that one (a little too simple?) for the more inconclusive (but more provocatively "arty"?) ending that left no indication whether or not the actress would ever speak again.

8½, a long, seemingly extemporaneous, and definitely pretentious film with a brilliant technical sheen but little sensible content (although it was basically Italian director Federico Fellini's too subjective autobiography), won the 1963 Best Foreign Language Film Academy Award. Its filming (and cutting) was diaried in Deena Boyer's book, *The Two Hundred Days of 8½*. (Suggested alternate title: *The 200 Days of Eight and a Half*.)

"November 10 [1962]: Screening of the preliminary version of the picture," wrote Miss Boyer at about 7¾. "The fantasy of Claudia with her bicycle in the hotel corridor, almost all of Pace's speech on the bench in the steam room, Guido's line during the nightclub dinner ('You want to know what political party I belong to? So do I. I've been wondering for ten years'), Agostini's dance on the theater runway—all have been eliminated, as well as other scenes. This version has the first ending, in the dining car."

When asked why he had cut Guido's speech about political parties and Agostini's dance, Fellini replied: "Too complacent. To say at Guido's age that one has spent ten years wondering what party one belonged to, with that smug manner. . . . As for the dance, it was too obvious, too easy."

According to *Sight and Sound:* "Two weeks before *8½* opened in Rome Fellini still hadn't made up his mind how to end it." The dining car sequence with all the characters assembled in striking white dress (Miss Boyer's book contained a still of this grouping) was ultimately dropped in favor of the second filmed ending in which the fanciful leading character, Guido (Marcello Mastroianni), brought on all the people in his life for a dream dance around an outdoor circus arena. Why this ending? Only Fellini knows the answer—if there is one. Perhaps it parallels the reason for the picture's title—Fellini: "I haven't found a title, so I'll simply designate the film by number."

Four of Italy's top-ranking, most fashionable directors worked on the naughty 1962 moneymaker, *Boccaccio '70*, including Fellini, who did the first episode, "The Temptation of Dr. Antonio," with Sweden's Anita Ekberg; Luchino Visconti, "The Job," with Germany's Romy Schneider; Vittorio De Sica, "The Raffle," with Italy's Sophia Loren; and Mario Monicelli (soon responsible for the much-praised feature, *The Organizer,* with Mastroianni), the fourth segment, which had no stars comparable to the other three and dealt with a couple working in a plant where employees were forbidden to marry.

The concluding Monicelli part was considered by producer Carlo Ponti, Loren's husband, and distributor Joseph E. Levine, who brought you *Hercules,* to be "less sophisticated" than the preceding stories and was discarded. When *Boccaccio '70* was released, it was Signora Ponti's end the art house audiences saw.

2. IN A CLASS BY HERSELF

When we had tea early in 1967, England's Ethel Griffies, then on the New York stage and about to turn 89, was being called the oldest working actress in the English-speaking theater. With her imperious Empire manner, voice, and aquiline profile, Miss Griffies had been Hollywood's sharpest battle-axe in residence from around 1930 until 1947. Then, working only a few weeks that last year as Maureen O'Hara's Bostonian aunt in *The Homestretch* ("They get to know your face too well out there, and then you're finished"), she left for Broadway and a successful new career in such as *The Druid Circle* and *Write Me a Murder,* and, off-Broadway, *Billy Liar,* as the senile grandmother, a part she created on the London stage and in the movie, too.

I found her to be a luv.

This player in more than 100 films, who arrived in America in 1924 for theater work, had been living for a few years in a West 70s Manhattan hotel on what appeared to be Geriatrics Row. "How's the weather?", asked the still brightly blue-eyed, smooth-skinned old trouper. (*"Please,* what ever you do, don't be like so many others and write that I was carried on stage by my parents in *East Lynne* when I was a child! It's not true! In the first place, the character I played is four years old and walks on under his own steam.

And in the second, do I look like someone who would allow herself to be carried?") Drapes covered her living room windows. "All you can see from there," the widowed actress instructed, pointing the finger that had cautioned screen stars from George Arliss, Will Rogers, Garbo, and Bing Crosby to Orson Welles, Jack Benny, Chevalier and Ann-Margret, "is a nursing home. I don't look out much."

She was married twice, says she was relieved when the first husband died, less so when the second, Edward Cooper, whom she liked, passed on in 1956 during her only attempt at retirement. "He played butlers a great deal, but Arthur Treacher got the cream of that crop. Mr. Treacher had a more colorful film personality."

Miss Griffies insisted that her memory was failing ("I'm weary of making excuses for it"), yet she had no trouble whizzing back 23 years to a disappointing but hardly discouraging career epoch on 20th Century-Fox's *The Keys of the Kingdom,* Gregory Peck's second movie and his first Oscar nomination.

"The film was about a Scotch missionary's life, and he was played as a boy by Roddy McDowall and as a man by Mr. Peck," the lady recalled. "There was a sequence in the cottage of the boy's grandparents, where he had gone after his parents' tragic deaths. I was his dour old grandmother who sent him off to work in the nearby shipyard and pocketed his few shillings pay. Poor Roddy was soon suffering physically from neglect. There were a half-dozen of us or more in this part of the picture, I forget who they all were now—some, like myself, only in this section—and we worked about eight days on it, including Saturdays. They worked Saturdays then.

"When I saw the film, I expected to see us all come along right after the scene where little Roddy cried over the drowning of his parents. To my amazement, the next thing I saw was a very large Gregory Peck sitting in a cart. We had all been cut from the movie!"

So was Mary Anderson, who shortly before had scored on Broadway as the treacherous *Guest in the House.* Miss Anderson played the girl Peck gave up for the church. After she had completed her role, she was replaced in the final print by Jane Ball, apparently because the fair Miss Ball more closely resembled blonde Peggy

Ann Garner—the child actress Fox was grooming and who played Peck's sweetheart as a child—than the brunette Miss Anderson did.

Miss Griffies' eyes twinkled when she noted that "At least we cut-outs still get paid."

This kind of thing happened to her friend and countrywoman, the lovely Dame Gladys Cooper, on a 1941 Fox picture in which they supported Tyrone Power and Betty Grable, *A Yank in the RAF.* Miss Griffies portrayed Lady Fitzhugh, a bossy, mannish army nurse whom Power jokingly asked for a date.

"Or was it *A Yank at Oxford?* I was in that as well, happened to be back in England visiting when MGM came over to make it. No, it had to be *A Yank in the RAF.* When my husband and I sat down to watch this one, I was surprised to find that Gladys' name was not listed. I sometimes went unbilled, but Gladys had been a really celebrated stage star here and abroad. I remembered from the script that she'd had a good scene as a woman whose flyer son had been killed. We soon discovered that her whole appearance had been cut out."

She mused: "There is a strange thing about Gladys. She has become an excellent actress, although she was first known more as a beauty. Still, for some reason, there is an unpleasant streak that shows up in all her acting, no matter what kind of role it is. And this unpleasantness in *not* in Gladys herself at all. Very strange indeed."

Miss Griffies' memory did not desert her, either, when it came to recollecting the remarkable story surrounding her single scene in *Saratoga Trunk* at Warners—where she not only often acted but "made myself available for other duties such as conducting private speech classes for foreign actresses." (She also did not mind letting the interviewer know when *his* pronunciation was not up to snuff.) Her part was the domineering Saratoga society mother, Mme. Clarissa Van Steed, implacable enemy of adventuress Ingrid Bergman. "The director, Sam Wood, saw me for the part, and said no," she admitted. "So they put someone else in, and got the film in the can, as they say. Then they decided they didn't like her in it, so they filmed someone else in the role. Once again they didn't like their Mrs. Van Steed and got still *someone else.* Didn't like her footage, either! Finally, they said, 'Get Griffies!' That's how they did things out there."

I remembered Miss Griffies pleasantly from another mid-1940s Warner production, *Devotion,* the story of the Brontë geniuses. "Yes, that was a nice one," agreed the actress who had played their grim Aunt Bramwell, "but it was highly romanticized as biography. Did you ever see a picture of the *real* Brontë house on the moors? It was little more than a shack. And the film showed Emily, Charlotte and Anne Brontë arriving in a splendid carriage for a splendid ball accompanied by the young curate they were all after—without a chaperone! Ida Lupino, who was Emily, and Olivia de Havilland, who was Charlotte, had daggers drawn for each other throughout the shooting, although it was all kept very quiet."

In his recent book, *Horror!,* Drake Douglas lauded the lady's 1935 *Werewolf of London,* going on to write: "In the scenes involving the tipsy landlady, superbly played by Ethel Griffies, we have probably the finest comedy relief ever provided in a horror film." Miss Griffies noted that, no doubt due to its frequent television appearances, more people comment to her on this relatively minor production than any of her other movies.

"I never really enjoyed filming, you know," she maintained. "I think of myself as a theater person, so I have no real favorite picture role . . . *Between Us Girls* in 1942 afforded me a good part as an Irish maid. Universal handed the star, Diana Barrymore, one of the greatest roles for a woman I'd ever seen in this. She got to masquerade as a little girl, play Sadie Thompson, Queen Victoria and Joan of Arc, had a crying scene, a laughing scene, got the glamour treatment, everything. They gave Miss Barrymore, who was just starting in pictures, every chance, but she just wasn't up to it. By the time they got to popping her into Joan's armor, the girl's knees were knocking so the clang was deafening. She was a *very* difficult young lady, too . . . I remember the first time I ever laid eyes on her father, John Barrymore. We were both having our hair done at the RKO beauty salon for a couple of films around 1940. I was doing *Vigil in the Night* with Carole Lombard or *Stranger on the Third Floor* with Peter Lorre or *Irene* with Anna Neagle, one of those things, maybe even all *three* of them. Barrymore was having his hair crimped—marcelled; you know. I paid absolutely no attention to him, wouldn't even *look* at him. It made him furious. Imagine, getting peevish because a woman who was in her 60s wouldn't look at him. But that was Barrymore. In spite of my age, I was still *a woman* . . . Lionel Barrymore—I had a very good part as a busybody with him in *Return of Peter Grimm*—was the best actor of the bunch. I never cared for Ethel very much. And she could be unkind to the 'small people' around her.

"Oh, yes, I also did something called *Man at Large,* in 1941, I should think, which was an inexpensive Fox second feature, but I liked it as well as any screen performance I've given. I played the manageress in an *American's* conception of a cheap London music hall. I worked two days on it: all day Saturday until 12 midnight and the same hours again on Monday."

Too, she is warmly disposed towards a more recent effort, Hitchcock's *The Birds,* in which, said *Time,* "Veteran Ethel Griffies, as a sensible-shoed bird-lover, provides a deft and daft counterpoint to the bird-damning villagers."

As for other people's movies, Miss Griffies today gets about as adventurous as *Born Free,* which she adored—"I fell in love with lions, wanted to have one in the hotel. They could certainly use one here!" She does not endorse the rampant sex in contemporary films and has her movies "thoroughly investigated by reliable friends before I give up any of my now more-valuable-than-ever time. At my age, they can't give away any secrets, anyway."

At the time, Miss Griffies was enjoying a new kind of fame as a guest on talk-television, a contraption she also has acted on in such as *The Nurses* but which she herself would not think of owning because of the commercial interruptions. Slightly deaf, she is nevertheless very sensitive to noise—"I never go to musical shows," she brags, even though she was stopping one nightly in her early 70s when she sang "Only for Americans" in Irving Berlin's *Miss Liberty.*

"Griff," as some dare to call her, sprang up to pour more tea (dislodging a half-read *Jalna* book at her side) and chortled: "People are always recognizing me now from that machine and stopping me in the streets to bestow blessings upon me!"

In 1966, before I met Ethel Griffies, I saw her with Sir John Gielgud and Vivien Leigh in Gielgud's adaptation of Chekhov's *Ivanov* on Broadway. She portrayed the marriage broker (and recorded her performance with the rest of the cast for the RCA Victor Records album), and I had occasion to mention to Arthur Treacher that she ran away with the very long evening.

"Not surprising," he deadpanned. "The old girl is probably the only one who knows what the hell it's all about."

3. A MOTHER'S HISSES

What if it were 1951 and *you* woke up one day and heard your mother taking the Fifth Amendment before the House Un-American Activities Committee?

Back in the 1940s, when I was literally growing up in the movies and my mother was necessarily a working lady, character actress Anne Revere seemed as much a mother to me as anyone else. God knows she was a mother to damned near everyone else: Jennifer Jones in *The Song of Bernadette,* Elizabeth Taylor in *National Velvet,* Gregory Peck in *Gentleman's Agreement,* John Garfield in *Body and Soul;* she was even Lon McCallister's stepmother in *Scudda Hoo! Scudda Hay!,* not to mention Linda Darnell's Mother Red-Cap in *Forever Amber.*

For *Bernadette* and *Agreement* Miss Revere won Best Supporting Actress Oscar nominations, and for 1945's channel swimmer mom in *National Velvet,* which even Elizabeth Taylor will concede contains Miss Taylor's best screen performance, Miss Revere won the statuette. ("It came as a surprise, really. The odds were all against me. I was under contract to Fox, but the picture was MGM's, and MGM wasn't terribly interested in promoting an award for another studio's contract player. Nor was Fox anxious to push a picture made at Metro. Little Ann Blyth was the favorite for her performance in Warners' *Mildred Pierce.* My winning was such an upset, some of the papers the next day were still dazed and wrote things like, 'Anne Revere, who played the troublesome teen-ager in *Mildred Pierce,* won the Best Supporting Actress Academy Award last night. . . .' I was very surprised.")

Sometimes she was a bad mother, but more often she was a good one; sometimes, as in *You're My Everything* ("This role was written for me"), she was a mother-figure aunt (to Anne Baxter), or, as in *Secret Beyond the Door,* a mother-figure sister (to Michael Redgrave). She was *always* believable. There was something about Anne Revere—her long Yankee face, her rigid, even stern stoicism that was not without a certain humor, her golden silences, the repressed emotion only a nick beneath the surface, her seeming familiarity with that thin individual rattling in the closet, her air of knowing just what to do until the doctor arrived, her strength, her presence. Miss Revere could fasten down the flightiest screenplay, toss security blankets to an entire audience.

Now here it was 1951, and on May 31st, the New York *Times* noted: "Anne Revere, actress, who refused on April 17 on grounds of self-incrimination to answer questions of the House Un-American Activities Committee regarding her alleged Communist affiliations, has resigned from the board of directors of the Screen Actors Guild. . . . The announcement made no mention of Miss Revere's stand during the House hearings and gave no reason for her resignation. It is understood, however, that she resigned on her own motion, because she believed that she could no longer work in the film industry."

Miss Revere, to believe a recent article in *After Dark* magazine, had been named to the HUAC by her old "friend," actor Lee J. Cobb. She ultimately maintained she took the "Fifth" because she knew the Committee would insist on her naming names, which she could not do since, she averred, she did not know anyone guilty of un-American activities. She stated that she had signed a United States loyalty oath in 1948, and had not changed her ideology, further claiming that the unsigned photocopy of her alleged Communist Party registration card was "a plant."

Sixteen years later, Richard Lamparski, host and creator of the *What Ever Became Of . . . ?* radio series, said: "Anne Revere's name was one of the 300 that appeared on the Hollywood blacklist. Although, unlike her friend and neighbor, Gale Sondergaard, she has been able to find occasional TV work and parts in Broadway plays, the actress who was once one of the highest paid and most respected character people in films is still *personna non grata* in Hollywood."

A few months after Miss Revere quit the Screen Actors Guild in '51, her then last released feature opened, *A Place in the Sun.* I was dismayed to find when I saw this much-lauded, now classic film that

Miss Revere's role as Montgomery Clift's mother, despite the actress' good billing, was a bit she quite literally phoned in, and partly superimposed over other scenes at that.

Again, 16 years later: talking with Miss Revere myself, I at last confirmed my suspicions on *A Place in the Sun,* and—as I had suspected—there was a sizable scissor in the haystack. In fact, and begging Miss Revere's pardon, it turned out to be more like a sickle.

"My last *three* movies were irreparably damaged by cutting," Miss Revere showed no hesitancy in testifying, "including *Deep Waters* and *The Great Missouri Raid. A Place in the Sun* was the most tragic, for several reasons. When director George Stevens first asked me to do it, I wasn't too keen on it. I wanted to get away from playing mothers. But this mother was different. She ran a soup kitchen, was a strong influence in the life of the ambitious protagonist, played by Montgomery Clift without the necessary drive, I thought, and she was actually a villainess. She had to carry a great deal of weight in relatively little footage. I took the part, at a reduction in salary, I might add. The film was a labor of love for Stevens, who had to convince Paramount to let him make it. Filming started in 1948.

"Between 1948 and 1951 things happened in Hollywood. There was the invasion of television. And there was the blacklist which started in '47 with the Hollywood 10, followed by a kind of truce after they threw the 10 to the wolves.

"I finished my part in a little less than two weeks. Stevens shoots with three cameras, incidentally, which adds up to an enormous amount of film used.

"By 1951, however, Paramount had gotten itself in a state over the picture because of the blacklist and because the film criticized the American way of life and because the studio hadn't wanted to do it in the first place. After the picture opened (I still hadn't seen it), a friend who had said, 'What happened to you in it?!' I went to see the film and was appalled, long before I got to my stuff. The thing bore absolutely no resemblance to the film Stevens and I had talked about.

"As for my role—my two best scenes had been cut. One scene that made you gasp was when this mother comes to her son in prison as he awaits the electric chair and begs him to write a letter to the youth of America exonerating her of any blame for his downfall. The other—and this part even visibly moved the crew when we did it—was also in the prison. The mother has finally caught a glimpse of what she has helped to do, and says to her boy, 'God bless you, my boy. God forgive me if I've failed you.' They kept this last speech in—you only hear me saying it over a big close-up of Mr. Clift.

"They were two long scenes. It took me five hours to see the rushes of them. There was one head-on shot both Stevens and I were particularly proud of which showed the essence of this woman. This was removed, too. Stevens fought for me, but his hands were tied, contractually."

"Before the cutting, my part in *A Place in the Sun* was the best work I'd ever done in Hollywood," opined Miss Revere.

And this was the same film Stevens went to court in 1966 to keep from being cut or ruined by commercial interruptions when premiered on television. It had won the Academy awards for direction; writing, screenplay (Michael Wilson, Harry Brown); black and white photography (William C. Mellor); music score (Franz Waxman); black and white costume design (Edith Head); and—film editing (William Hornbeck).

The Great Missouri Raid, also at Paramount, was the last picture Miss Revere made then, although it was released next-to-last, in 1950. "The script was by Western authority Frank Gruber, who wanted to tell the story of Jesse and Frank James closer to the facts. They weren't out-and-out villains; they were driven to it. I played their mother; and Wendell Corey and Macdonald Carey were Frank and Jesse, respectively. There was a narration which went something like 'This is the story of Frank and Jesse James, who were not born bad. . . . ' After the picture was finished, I got a call for retakes. To my surprise, when I got there I found I was the only one called. Just the cutter was present, I think, with a narration for me to read. I couldn't believe my eyes. The narration now said 'This is the story of Frank and Jesse James, who were born bad. . . . ' I said no! The cutter said the Breen Office [Joseph I. Breen was then the movies' chief censor] wouldn't let it go through any other way. Now, the studio had bought all the rights from the James estate, so there was no problem there. I was told if I didn't do the narration they'd junk the whole thing. So I did it. Naturally, since the picture no longer fit the narration they had to scrap much of the footage, quite a bit of my work with it."

In '48, Fox's *Deep Waters* also promised more than it delivered, due, Miss Revere feels, to cutting. It was her third film with director Henry King—they had done *Bernadette* and *Remember the Day.* "The heart of the picture" was a scene between Jean Peters, in only her second movie, as the welfare officer ("A portrayal as exciting as in *Captain from Castile*" said the ads!), and Miss Revere as the gruff but soft-hearted widow who, having raised her own family, housed "state kid" Dean Stockwell. She recalls: "The story was from a best-seller called *Spoonhandle* and was set in Maine, where we locationed. Jean, who was being given a big build-up at the studio, was really still a little midwestern schoolteacher at heart. She was madly in love with Howard Hughes at the time"—she married him ten years later, although, interestingly, she had another marriage in the interim—"and was on the phone long-distance to Hughes much of the time we were in Maine. In our scene, I was shelling lobsters, without any make-up, while Jean and I unravelled the plot. Now Henry talks a lot while directing and is often unintelligible. This can be very frightening, at least to actors, and poor Jean looked completely at sea in the scene. Later I asked Henry, 'How's the scene?' He said, 'She looks like your mother in it!' We did the thing once more. Again, it proved bad. I thought if I had a few closeups it might alleviate the problem, but Henry said no. So our scene was just cut. Consequently, you never really know what the story is about."

Before these three encounters with the cutting room floor, Miss Revere said she had not suffered excessively from cutting. "My husband"—Samuel Rosen, the writer-director-coach she married in '35 while she was starring on Broadway in *The Children's Hour*—"and I always had eyes for parts that were functional, vital to the film." Had he ever directed her in a film? "My husband has directed me in practically everything I've ever done, really," she smiled in that familiar three-quarter way that was always the more valuable because it had not come cheaply.

Miss Revere, born in 1903, 1906, or 1907, and a Wellesley graduate, first came to Hollywood in '34 to recreate her stage role in *Double Door* at Paramount. She returned to New York for more theater work, but moved to the West Coast seven years later and, starting with *The Howards of Virginia,* made about 40 movies. She is now a Manhattan resident.

"I was out there for the last seven years of what they call the

Golden Age of the Movies," she continued. "In '47, everything fell apart in Hollywood."

Aside from her more celebrated films, Miss Revere—warm and friendly, not at all the Anne "Severe" her roles had led me to expect—liked *Remember the Day,* disliked *Fallen Angel,* didn't see *H. M. Pulham, Esq.,* wasn't aware that Marilyn Monroe had a bit in *Scudda Hoo! Scudda Hay!* and was surprisingly enthusiastic about Paramount's all-star 1942 mélange, *Star Spangled Rhythm.* "Did you see it? Wasn't that a wonderful picture? And wasn't Betty Hutton something? Do you remember that scene where she's trying to get over the movie studio wall? That was so funny."

Like myself, Miss Revere was especially fond of a modest but thoroughly beguiling family-type entertainment released in 1944 called *Sunday Dinner for a Soldier,* with Anne Baxter as the fanciful poor girl who invited lonely serviceman Jack Hodiak to dinner on her ramshackle houseboat, and Miss Revere as the indispensable owner of a nearby poultry farm. "Anne and John met when we worked on this one," Miss Revere reminisced. Miss Baxter, the granddaughter of architect Frank Lloyd Wright, and the late Hodiak, the son of Ukrainian immigrants, soon wed, extending the tenuous fairytale spell of their movie into real life. Sadly, divorce is a fact of real life—and so is death.

Two unrealized film projects from literary classics that could have brought classic Revere mothers were *The Yearling* and *Little Women.* She was signed for both. In '42, Miss Revere, co-star Spencer Tracy (with whom she had shared her one brief scene in *Men of Boys' Town* as a mother whose son was beaten to death in reform school), director Victor Fleming, and crew set out for Florida to start *The Yearling,* which told of a family's hardships in the scrub country there years ago.

"We were in Florida for about ten days," Miss Revere related. "I don't know that we shot any real scenes. We did a lot of testing. Spence was to play 'Penny' Baxter, who was called that because he was small. Remember, these were poor people to whom a little spilled milk was a tragedy. I recall they put Spence on a huge horse that looked like it could win the Preakness, hoping the animal's size would make Spence seem smaller. They got me up in lifts and big bosoms. Oh, it was all terrible! I'm glad the filming didn't go on. I wasn't ready to play Ma Baxter then. After I did

Velvet under his direction in '45, Clarence Brown tested me for the *Yearling* he was preparing now. I was ready then. But they wanted someone sexy to appear opposite the rising young actor Gregory Peck, who already had risen over six feet in height—so they got Jane Wyman and took all the sexiness out of her! I didn't especially like the movie. It was too pretty."

She said the *Little Women* film, which was to have been re-made in '46 by David Selznick with Jennifer Jones as the tomboy Jo and Miss Revere as Marmee, "never got off the ground. I think Jennifer was afraid of it." The re-make was made three years later by other hands with Mary Astor as Marmee, a brunette June Allyson as Jo, and a blonde Elizabeth Taylor as Amy.

When we talked, the still slender actress looked little different than she had in films 20 years before, although, she remarked, "A young man I recently acted with saw me in *Dragonwyck* on TV the other night and told me I looked 20 years older in it than I do now!"

Miss Revere found occasion, as she chatted, to imitate affectionately some of the celebrities she had known, such as the gentle, lisping Boris Karloff, with whom she had tried to raise the dead in 1941's *The Devil Commands* ("Why do I keep making thith kind of movie? Well . . ."); and the heavily Teutonic Otto Preminger, who directed her in several flops on both stage and screen and was the first to give her film work after the 1951 blacklisting in 1970's *Tell Me That You Love Me, Junie Moon* ("Now Anna, let's try it zis vay . . .").

In 1960, Miss Revere picked up a Best Supporting Actress Antoinette Perry Award for her work in *Toys in the Attic* on Broadway. Since then, she has done some lesser plays like off-Broadway's *Night of the Dunce* and some ditto television, including the soap operas *The Edge of Night* and *Search for Tomorrow.* She considers her 1960s performance as *Mother Courage,* which she gave on college stages, her best in any medium.

"You know, I was *that* close to getting the role of Thomas Wolfe's mother that Jo Van Fleet played on the stage in *Look Homeward, Angel,*" she informed me. "I didn't even get the replacement. There also was my own TV series—I was to play a woman judge—that was practically set when the blacklisting happened and ruined everything. I've been getting some nibbles from some of the big nighttime programs in recent years, but have always been doing something that tied me up when they came. I hope to be able to do some of them now."

In the mid-1960s she worked for many months as a doctor's mother on the daytime serial, *A Time for Us,* and told an interviewer then who questioned her on the blacklisting: "I've talked about it until I am tired of hearing myself, and I expect those listening are tired, too. I am very glad to be back working and hope to continue."

Certainly this is little to ask for a mother, who in real life never became one.

4. THE SECOND TIME AROUND

George Stevens' *The Greatest Story Ever Told*—a vulgarly tasteful, static, practically immovable re-telling with everyone arranged in muted tableaux while *audiences* prayed futilely for a tasteless DeMille dancing girl around the next rock—took almost as long to get made, released, and, at first, run off as it did for the Subject to Come. Soon after its 1965 premiere, United Artists (or the director) began carving away at its big turkey and looked to continue the chore until television could take over. In the spring of 1967, it was revealed that the still-playing film, at last estimate, had been abridged from its 225 minutes opening time to 141. The considerable celluloid dropped included the whole "cameos" of leper Shelley Winters and centurion John Wayne, although both names were still being used to sell the epic. Asked if this greatest story ever told would ever make back its cost, a UA executive sighed, "Never."

Nothing's sacred to the snip-happy. . . .

Not Walt Disney, whose *Fantasia* (1940) was more extensively cut—and more often—than any other Disney feature.

The producer's most ambitious film at the time, it is considered the medium's outstanding attempt to interest the masses in classical music. But it did not recoup its cost—$2,250,000—until the fifth reissue in '63.

The completed film ran 120 minutes, not counting the intermission, and consisted of seven animated sequences illustrating eight musical selections. Each sequence began with the Philadelphia Orchestra tuning up, Deems Taylor speaking a short commentary, and conductor Leopold Stokowski mounting the podium, and a kind of stereophonic sound called Fantasound was used.

After its disappointing 57-week boxoffice at New York's Broadway Theater, Disney's bankers demanded the film be cut and put into general release instead of road-shown. Against his will, Disney shortened *Fantasia* to 82 minutes (the first part, Bach's "Toccata and Fugue in D Minor," was omitted, and all the numbers, except the Dukas, were shortened), and prints supplied to theaters had only a single soundtrack.

But business was still unsatisfactory. *Fantasia* was reissued in '44, '46, and '48. Finally, in '56 and '63, Disney felt the world was ready for his intellectual cartoon feature and re-released it again, restoring all but five minutes of the original footage—a Deems Taylor prologue to the second half and some shots of the orchestra were left out.

In the beginning, ironically, Disney had planned to send the picture on tour annually, like an opera, with one or more new sequences *added* from time to time. . . .

Not even old *King Kong* (1933), who was revived in '38, '42, and '52 with a bit more cut each time.

Most seriously damaged was the scene in the native village after giant gorilla Kong broke through the gate in the great wall. One of the more harrowing New York sequences also has been cut. However, the most regrettable cut from several viewpoints was the scene on the cliff where Kong sat to admire the captive Fay Wray and pulled off part of her dress. Chief special effects technician Willis O'Brien declared that this had been the most difficult scene in the picture, that it had required the use of seven separate composites.

It appears, however, that old Kong will enjoy a happy ending after all. In March 1966, the New York *Times* wrote that Janus Films, a New York-based independent distributor, had acquired the theatrical release rights to *King Kong* and 19 other American film classics "as the nucleus of a future repertory of such productions, both domestic and foreign."

Continued the *Times:* "In an interesting footnote to history [Saul J.] Turell (a partner in Janus) revealed that when *King Kong* is next released, it will include three short scenes, adding up to about six minutes of running time, never used in earlier showing here. He describes one as revealing more of Fay Wray than the censors previously thought decent, and another as a scene in which the giant ape expresses an unmistakable affection for the leading lady."

With *Lost Horizon,* the Ronald Colman (remember when actors —and actresses—had voices?) film from James Hilton's best seller, there was no happy ending for the trouble in Paradise. This has a history of cuts that stands alone.

First of all, the important role of the High Lama initially was filmed with two different actors: Walter Connolly, who had just played the Chinese uncle in *The Good Earth,* and Sam Jaffe. Director Frank Capra had a tough time deciding between the two characterizations, but, of course, eventually chose Jaffe, who made it one of his two most famous film parts (the other: the title role in *Gunga Din* a few years later). Henry B. Walthall, the original choice to play the High Lama, died before he could get a crack at it.

In production at the Columbia studios for about 100 days in 1936, with a great amount of film exposed at a cost of the then exorbitant two million dollars (half the entire cost of the studio product for a year), *Lost Horizon* was cut to 16 reels by Capra and editors Gene Havlick and Gene Milford, and the last named pair ultimately got the Oscar for their efforts.

However, at the preview, director Capra—who had devoted two years of his life to the project—said: "The audience started laughing five minutes after it began and kept on laughing through all three hours of it. *Lost Horizon* was the most important movie I'd made—and it had turned out absolutely unshowable! I walked for three hours trying to think why. At last I concluded the first two reels were wrong. We discarded them and when we showed *Lost Horizon* beginning with what had been the third reel, nobody laughed." (Capra eventually had assistants go to previews and tape-record reactions.)

Minus the prologue, which set the stage for the flashback-told story of Shangri-La, the resulting 14-reel version—130 minutes long—was roadshown in the spring of 1937, and was commended by the critics. The film then went into general release on Sept. 1st,

1937, inexplicably minus 12 minutes of footage that rendered meaningless and confusing several scenes and story points.

Edward Connor listed the early cuts in *Screen Facts:* (1) a conversation between Colman and John Howard on the place; (2) H. B. Warner's solicitude for Isabel Jewell the first evening at Shangri-La; (3) the discussion of religion (i.e. the principle of moderation that governed the lamasery) between Warner and Colman; (4) the scene in the aviary between Jane Wyatt and Colman; and (5) Edward Everett Horton's venture into the Valley of the Blue Moon, where several thousand Tibetans lived under the rule of Shangri-La lamas.

Explained O'Connor: "Audiences must have been most puzzled by the first cut, wondering why the Conway brothers are talking so excitedly and happily one moment and then are brooding and silent the next. The heart of their conversation, in which Bob (Colman) disclaims any praise for saving a handful of white people at Baskul while leaving thousands of natives to die, is now missing, and with it a valuable early insight into Conway's character.

"On the first occasions when Conway sees Sondra (Miss Wyatt) he is curious about a strange sound he hears overhead. After he has met her and asked about the phenomenon she takes him to the aviary and shows him doves with flutes attached to their tails who follow her wherever she goes. Omission of this sequence naturally means that audiences never got to see Conway's curiosity satisfied.

"Cutting the scene of Lovett's (Horton's) visit to the valley and his delight with what he finds there leaves unexplained his subsequent change of heart towards Shangri-La."

(Sometimes an actor can be completely indifferent to what happens to his handiwork after it's gotten on film, and Horton, to hear him tell it, is among these rare birds. In a mid-'60s interview on TV, host Merv Griffin—a charming, talented fellow who deserved to make it in movies but didn't—told guest Horton that *Lost Horizon* was a film he never tired of seeing over and over again. To which Horton replied he had never even seen the picture once: it upset him to watch himself on the screen.)

In 1942, after Doolittle's planes had bombed Japan, President Roosevelt was asked where the planes had come from, and he answered, "Shangri-La," which aroused new interest in the movie and caused Capra to prepare it for re-release. Although admirers of the story hoped the cut footage would be returned—maybe even previously publicized but not used film, such as the scene of Margo and Miss Wyatt playing violin and piano and the scenes involving the Western monk, Montaigne, played by real-life ex-monk John Tettemer—the picture reappeared as *Lost Horizon of Shangri-La,* and the local Baskul revolution of the plot was changed to the Sino-Japanese war. And more scenes were cut, including Horton's near-missing the plane at the beginning. Ten years later it was reissued again, this time scissored even more senselessly. Featured player Isabel Jewell had almost disappeared. Scenes and conversations were trimmed, and completely omitted was the scene near the end in which the porters shot at Colman, Margo, and Howard and precipitated the avalanche that now appeared to be nature's doing, plus the long view of the Tibetan children going swimming.

It is the latter version of *Lost Horizon* that is shown on television today. Needless to say, this one, too, has been ruthlessly slashed to fit TV show time slots. A classic movie never had it so bad.

The biggest change, however, could not be blamed on film cuts: Isabel Jewell's character had been converted from a missionary in the book to a consumptive prostitute in the screenplay.

Another scandalously treated reissue was *The Long Voyage Home,* released by Argosy Pictures and United Artists in 1940 and nominated for Best Picture. Eight years later it was brought out again by Masterpiece Productions with scarcely a sequence escaping the scissors. Seven scenes completely disappeared and many others were cut to the bone. Some years later distributors, perhaps smarting over complaints, reissued the film (based on four one-act Eugene O'Neill plays) minus the *Moon of the Carribees* section.

About the time World War II ended, Warner Brothers trooped out a bunch of reissues for double feature use in theaters. Some of the pictures were shortened; and it appears that no one at Warners bothered to save the original negative, for these films play on television in the cut versions.

One of these hacked jobs was *City for Conquest,* a sentimental but warm and appealing 1940 drama filmed in Hollywood but which managed to capture the pulsebeat of Manhattan more vividly than the score of pictures locationed there nowadays for "realism."

It concerned a tough New Yorker (James Cagney) who boxed to allow his kid brother (Arthur Kennedy) to study music, and the film was shockingly cut for theater and TV reissue. Scenes showing Cagney, Kennedy, and Ann Sheridan as children on the New York streets were cut; and Frank Craven, as the old-timer who told the story (à la his earlier *Our Town* success), was cut so much that only the viewer who'd seen it originally would know why Craven meaninglessly wandered in and out of the film: to be able to sit down at the beginning in Times Square, warm his hands over a fire, and tell the story—and have this whole section cut out.

More films that got the axe when reissued (some Warners') were: *City Lights* (1931), *Public Enemy* (1931), *Call of the Wild* (1935), *Follow the Fleet* (1936), *Beau Geste* (1939), *So Ends Our Night* (1941), and *The Sea Wolf* (1941). James Cagney's *G-Men* (1936) broke the monotony when it was re-released by Warners in the 1940s by *adding* a prologue in which David Brian told a class of FBI students that while the clothes, etc., in the film they were about to see would be dated, the story was still an exciting and valid look at the Bureau's beginnings.

When Cecil B. DeMille's 1932 production of *The Sign of the Cross* was sent out again by Paramount ten years later, it was re-edited and also included a prologue showing an American air-force leaflet raid on Rome during World War II. Along for the ride were a couple of clergymen, played by Stanley Ridges and Arthur Shields, and a gunner called "Hoboken," essayed by Tom Tully. Prior to the leaflet dropping and the ensuing air battle over the Eternal City, all discussed the glory that was Rome. When the Italian capital appeared, Father Shields cried, "It's gorgeous!" Soon we were drifting down through the clouds and watching a putty-nosed Charles Laughton as Nero in the midst of the familiar '32-filmed while-Rome-burned business. But the best was saved for last. As the Roman warrior Fredric March and his Christian sweetheart Elissa Landi entered the arena to be devoured by Nero's lions, the camera moved back up through the clouds for a last shot of the American planes returning home after their mission. Anyone who had missed the modern prologue might well have pondered if the Lord had not turned those Christian martyrs into great steel doves who were now winging their way to Him.

Universal's *Spartacus,* considered one of the more intelligent of the expensive ancient spectacles when it premiered in 1960, was cut from 183 minutes to 161 when it was reissued seven years later. Among the missing were: scenes showing the training of the gladiators; the growing friendship between fellow Roman slaves Kirk Douglas and Woody Strode; a conversation on the steps of the Roman Senate between Charles Laughton and John Gavin; the refusal of revolutionary Douglas' comrades to betray him to victorious general Laurence Olivier; and parts of the last scene showing Jean Simmons saying "Oh please die my darling" to Douglas as he writhed in agony on a cross—the impression given in the reissue print was that he was already dead.

Much-cut prints of D. W. Griffith's *The Birth of a Nation* (1915) have been playing around for years, sometimes more cut than at others, to the confusion of even the players. Bessie Love has denied she was in this landmark, but it has been said that the actress (then just starting, under director Griffith's Svengaliship) was visible in one scene as "a Piedmont girl" who, with a group, looked out of a window at the triumphant parade of the Klansmen. A possible reason for all the uncertainty may be that this sequence *was* eliminated from the emasculated version of the picture reissued in the '30s and again in the '50s in England, where Miss Love has lived for years.

Birth of a Nation was first shown in Los Angeles on Feb. 15th at Clune's Auditorium under its original title, *The Clansman,* and ran about three hours. A month later it opened at New York's Liberty Theater under its new title, *The Birth of a Nation.* For general release, about 15 minutes were removed and this was the version then shown around the world. In the ensuing years many illegal prints were duped; and, as motion picture collector Samuel A. Peeples has explained: "These prints were often faded, chopped and worn, yet still more prints were duped and re-duped from them, and it is these sad remnants that are most usually shown publicly. The careful editing, direction and photography of the original were obliterated, or so muted that the qualities of the original film could not possibly be appreciated. Very few people have seen a good copy of the original release print of *The Birth of a Nation.*"

In his "Films on TV" feature in *Films in Review,* Don Miller wrote in 1962: "The involved case of *All Quiet on the Western Front* has become notorious in film circles. When it was planned to reissue that film a decade or so ago, the negative was discovered to be so deteriorated it was unusable. Enough prints were found, however, for an acceptable version. Furthermore, the imperfections in the prints from which the negative was made were noticeable in the reissue prints, and are noticeable in the TV prints, since what you see on TV today is the incomplete reissue version of *All Quiet.*"

Universal re-released *All Quiet* for the first time in '39, adding a narration that superfluously stressed the horrors of war and detracted from the picture's effectiveness.

All Quiet already had undergone considerable scissoring before it was released the first time in 1930. The first showing for studio officials ran 20 reels, from nine one morning until 2:30 the following; and the second ran nine reels, which still took most of a day to view. The third showing was a sneak preview at San Bernardino for the now 16,500-foot-long production, which was more like it. But studio executives were still apprehensive and thought it too downbeat. One asked director Lewis Milestone if he couldn't provide a happier ending. Replied Milestone: "Well, we could have the Germans win the war."

The late fluttery comedienne ZaSu Pitts had played a tragic mother role in *All Quiet* up through early previews; but audiences had been conditioned by then to laugh at Miss Pitts, and their snickers caused her to be replaced by Beryl Mercer in the official release.

George Stevens' *The Diary of Anne Frank* (1959), which was shown first-run on a reserved-seat basis, was then sliced up and released to second-run houses. Among the more harmful deletions were the opening shot of Otto Frank (Joseph Schildkraut) crying as he held the scarf given him by his Nazi-murdered daughter, Anne (Millie Perkins), which helped establish the film's whole mood; and the sequence at the end, which revealed the fate of the refugees.

With movies now generally longer than ever before in history, the cutting of films after first-run engagements, usually to fit on double bills, naturally has worsened. Where once only the hard-ticket, special engagement presentation (and they were rare) occasionally was cut to fit the demands of the double feature in second-run locations, today even a regular engagement feature gets snipped when it retires to the neighborhoods.

In a 1965 grouse in the British publication, *Sight and Sound,* the writer known as "Arkadin" admitted that it was hard to be concerned over the loss of 12 minutes a piece from *Tammy and the Doctor* and *Those Calloways* or the paring down of *Ride the Wild Surf* from 101 minutes to 68. But he *was* concerned about the quality films that were being hacked up in Britain, sometimes losing more and more footage as they traveled away from their first West End appearances.

Arkadin went on: "What can you expect if you try to fit, say *Youngblood Hawke* (136 minutes) and *Kisses for My President* (113 minutes) into one bill? The answer is, cuts totalling nearly an hour—and largely unrecorded cuts, since *Youngblood* was shown to the critics complete and *Kisses* was not shown to them at all."

"Now things are moving on a stage further," he reported. "They are even showing the critics drastically cut versions of films. The excellent *Robinson Crusoe on Mars* as shown over here had lost 29 minutes, some of them very obviously; and *Dear Heart,* minus 18 minutes, even had glaring cuts in the middle of scenes, suggesting that director Delbert Mann had suddenly, improbably acquired a New Wave taste for jump-cuts. No doubt some of the blame for all this must be laid at the door of the filmmakers themselves: we always seem to be saying that films these days are too long, and maybe some of the shortened films would have benefitted by further editing earlier. But last-minute cutting merely to facilitate programming is very different."

The thing is, the average audience may not always *know* what's missing from a film, may not even *care,* but it does *sense* a loss, and the picture is often diminished by it. Word of mouth can be as deadly as critical brickbats, especially with motion pictures.

5. YOU CAN QUOTE ME

How the author (or even screenwriter) feels on the occasion of most celluloid cuts is not hard to imagine.

There was *The Actress* (1953), an MGM translation of the Ruth

Gordon play about her New England girlhood, *Years Ago,* with Miss Gordon doing the screenplay and Jean Simmons doing Miss Gordon. To believe director George Cukor, though, producer Lawrence Weingarten pretty much did them all in. "The producer made some minor cuts and they had an *enormous* effect on the picture. Ruth was very pained by it because they changed the whole sense of film. Jean had the willfulness, the slight ruthlessness of an actress. But in the cutting, slight as it was, her strength was mitigated—her character was completely changed. Ruth was very pained by the slices and I agree with her," Cukor recounted.

Ernest Hemingway, who was never very happy about the filmings of his works (yet was not above making a quick anonymous appearance in the 1958 movie of his *The Old Man and the Sea*), had one of his closest calls with the 1933 film of *A Farewell to Arms,* though he bore up well. Paramount made an alternate ending in which Catherine Barkley (Helen Hayes) did not die, and when the studio offered to send Hemingway prints of the film with the different endings, he replied, "Use your imagination as to where to put the two prints but do not send them here." Catherine died, as she had in his book. (In the '50s Paramount reissued Hemingway's *For Whom the Bell Tolls*—which had originally begun filming with toe-dancer Vera Zorina as the forlorn Maria, mascot of a Spanish guerrilla band, and finished with Ingrid Bergman replacing her—in abridged form. Supporting actors George Coulouris and Konstantin Shayne were cut the second time around. Hemingway had not been consulted this time. The omission of Shayne's performance, which James Agee in '43 found "the best use of a bit in years," may have had something to do with the fact that the script was very politically oriented and Shayne had had to utter such lines as "I come from Stalin.")

When *A Farewell to Arms* was remade in 1958 by David O. Selznick and director Charles Vidor (after John Huston had quit over a disagreement with Selznick in how to direct the story), it was overdone, oversexed, and overlong and was trimmed down from its extreme initial length for later playdates.

Robert Penn Warren, who wrote the book from which director-scenarist Robert Rossen fashioned the 1949 Oscar-winning Best Picture, *All the King's Men,* for Columbia, and which won Broderick Crawford and Mercedes McCambridge their Best Actor and

Best Suppoting Actress honors, said he thought Rossen had turned out "an extraordinarily good movie. I can praise it, because it seems to me that when a movie is made from a novel the novel is merely raw material, the movie is a new creation, and the novelist can properly attract neither praise nor blame for it. The movie, as a matter of fact, does not 'mean' what I think my book meant. It is Bob's movie. On this point I may tell a tale. When the editing of the film was being done, Bob, out of courtesy, invited me in. He ran off several different endings, then asked me which I liked best. I said the second, or third, or whatever it was, but added that none of the endings had a meaning like my novel—this said in the friendliest way. And Bob replied: 'Son, in dealing with American movies when you get to the end you can forget anything like what you call irony—then it's cops and robbers, cowboys and Indians."

The Nun's Story is an instance when an author did not become riled—even politely—at cuts in the film made from her book. In '59 *Life* reported that Gabrielle Van Der Mal, whose story Kathryn Hulme had turned into a bestseller, was living with her Boswell and both were delighted with the way director Fred Zinnemann, star Audrey Hepburn, and the others had filmed their tale of the young Belgian who had spent 17 years trying to be a good nun when her calling really had been a desire to nurse.

They first saw an uncut version that ran almost four hours. When released, it ran two and a half. "It was too overwhelming," sighed Lou—an abbreviation for Sister Luke. She had seen it three times since, in various versions. "I'm never going to see it again," she vowed, "because if I do I'm going to run right back to the convent. When you see the chapel, all those nuns . . . I could just sit there and cry my eyes out, not with regret or anything, but because of the beauty of it. It is a beautiful life, the religious life, if you are really a religious person. If you can accept it without murmuring all the time. People say I didn't fail in leaving the convent. They don't understand. So many women stay in that life. They can take it. I couldn't take it and I failed."

In his rave for both picture and title performance (to me, Audrey Hepburn seemed too cool for a girl experiencing so much inner and outer turmoil), Henry Hart said: "Walter Thompson's editing is full of rhythms, both fast and slow. There are also a few untidinesses. E.g., Dr. van der Mal (Dean Jagger) still says, 'I ordered a table for one o'clock,' though the luncheon scene it refers to was cut (in its present form *The Nun's Story* runs 149 minutes and could run about 30 minutes more.)" And it *had* run 30 minutes longer, until after the first preview when producer Henry Blanke insisted on the excision of not only the luncheon but a sequence of postulant self-questioning.

That same year, columnist Sheilah Graham—like the lady now known as Lou—cried, too, when she saw the debacle Fox had made of her eminently filmable best-selling autobiography, *Beloved Infidel,* about the Cockney-born Lily Sheil's short but tempestuous affair with F. Scott Fitzgerald. A bit numb after her first viewing of the picture (in which Deborah Kerr as Lily-Sheilah went down doing her damnedest with an abominable script), Miss Graham could only suggest to director Henry King that maybe it dragged a bit and might be improved if he would cut a half-hour. But King, she reported, loved every minute of his unspeakable footage and said no.

No casual cuthound, King.

While more at home directing Americana such as *Tol'able David, In Old Chicago, Wilson, Margie, I'd Climb the Highest Mountain,* and *The Gunfighter,* Henry King has observed in a byline article: "The 'inscrutable Oriental' isn't as apart from us as some have thought. In Hong Kong, while scouting locations for *Love Is a Many-Splendored Thing* in 1955, I met a personable young bank clerk who, like any aspiring actor in the U.S. 'temporarily' tied down to a commercial career, approached me for a bit part in the picture. Months later I mailed him the film clip in which he fleetingly appeared, which, alas, I had recovered, so to speak, from the cutting room floor. I probably didn't make an actor of him but I certainly made a friend—judging from the letter of profuse thanks I subsequenttly received."

In '56, the charming film about Quakers in the midst of war, *Friendly Persuasion,* came out, and the following year Jessamyn West, who had written the novel on which it was based, wrote a book detailing her experiences with the film version, *To See the Dream.* She told of a continuous struggle with director William Wyler, who thought the character Gary Cooper portrayed should give up his Quaker opposition to war and fight. So did Cooper, who said: "There comes a time when the people who see me in a picture expect me to do something—deliver a blow, fist or bullet. Or sword. They expect it. They feel let down without it."

According to a review of *To See the Dream:* "Miss West convinced Cooper there was positive action in resisting the temptation to fight, and Wyler finally compromised by inserting a scene in which Cooper drives an abandoned Confederate cannon between the two remaining Confederate cannons and knocks them out, thus winning the battle without firing a shot. But even this was too militant for Miss West and it was later edited out."

Nine years later Columbia Pictures and producer-director Stanley Kramer filmed Katherine Anne Porter's *Ship of Fools,* a *Grand Hotel*ish book set on a German passenger freighter in 1933. It had taken the authoress almost half a lifetime to write her novel. The movie, while a commercial and, largely, critical hit, was a one-dimensional, gabby seagoing soporific with only the late Vivien Leigh's dying swan grace as a bitter 46-year-old divorceé and Lee Marvin's slack-jawed, aging ballplayer to recommend it. For some reason it was decided to concentrate on the rather unlikely romance between the boyish ship's doctor (Oskar Werner) and the blowsy, drug-addicted ex-mistress of a Spanish dictator (a fat, anchor-ankled Simone Signoret), in the film as well as in the publicity for the picture, and significant Leigh footage was excised. The two-time Best Actress Academy Award winner was reduced to supporting player status in her last film—a magazine biographer of hers at the time went so far as to call Leigh's leavings a "cameo," and the *Film Daily* poll chose Leigh as 1965's Best *Supporting* Actress—but she retained top billing.

Very important to fully establish the rather silly and self-centered side of Miss Leigh's character were scenes in which she and her cabinmate, the buxom Nazi romancer Christiane Schmidtmer, prepared for sleep. As seen only in stills released by the studio, Miss Leigh's vain nocturnal cosmetic preparations, as well as her girlish nightwear, helped point up her immature nature. And when Schmidtmer had a young German removed from the captain's table because his wife was Jewish, Miss Leigh told another voyager, "Oh, it's my fault. I told that dreadful Brunhilde his wife was Jewish to keep her from chattering so." The audience never saw the scene to which Miss Leigh referred and the dialogue was not adequate to cover an obvious missing chunk of film. Presumably, the vital scene in which Miss Leigh had betrayed the German husband's confidence had been one of her cut bedtime tête-à-têtes with Schmidtmer.

Also, presumably, authoress Porter had no say in the filming. You could say that Kramer's *Ship of Fools* was half a lifetime's work thrown in the drink.

Advertising and trailers (or "Prevues of Coming Attractions"), even the credits of a film, therefore, frequently can be chockful of nuggets the viewer never gets to see in the finished (off?) product. In '58 the credits of Spencer Tracy's *The Last Hurrah* were shown over background shots taken from the movie itself, scenes that popped up as the story unfolded. One of the background shots, however, was of a fight ring that was not seen later because the sequence was edited out. Ads for *I Take This Woman,* a 1940 Tracy-Hedy Lamarr co-starrer, featured the names of Ina Claire and Walter Pidgeon even though they were replaced in the final print by Verree Teasdale and Kent Taylor. "In" groups kiddingly referred to this one as *I Re-take This Woman.* Paramount Pictures advertised two arias by Kirsten Flagstad in *The Big Broadcast of 1938*, but only one was shown in the picture—the trailer gave a flash of the other. And the trailer for *An American Romance* (1944) showed star Brian Donlevy watching a candlelight procession that was not glimpsed in the movie.

An American Romance, as initially conceived by veteran producer-director King Vidor, MGM and lead actors Donlevy and lovely Australian actress Ann Richards, was a most promising panorama of America first titled *America.*

Vidor read extensively about the lives of immigrants who came to this country penniless and through democratic opportunity worked their way to the top. Related Vidor: "I would have the immigrant Stephen marry a schoolteacher in Minnesota, who would bear his children when they moved to Chicago. These children would go to high schools, colleges, play football. Then their children would say: 'My grandfather came from the old country, but my father was born in America.' This is what I believe has made America strong, this constant process of rebirth and refining of its cruder basic ores. I would attempt to make metals and men analogous.

"We opened the picture in Cincinnati after a big build-up over a radio station that covered three states. All were highly enthusiastic and seemed to appreciate the values I had tried to get into the film. The only adverse criticism was that there may have been too many technological scenes for their non-technological minds. The show ran about two hours and 15 minutes. I felt that if this criticism proved general through a week's run, it would be well to do some editing on the mechanical sequences. However, an order came from the New York office of the company to cut half an hour out of the film. I went to New York and talked it over; they pointed out that with a shorter version they could get in two shows during the advantageous evening hours, while they could only show the long picture once."

Vidor accepted the inevitable, and was told he could supervise the necessary editing. "Yet a few days later," he continued, "when I passed through Chicago on my way home, I visited the office of MGM and there in the projection room was the shortened version of the film being screened for the sales force. Some eager minor executive at the studio had been unable to await my return and had edited the film, taking advantage of neither my familiarity with it nor the knowledge I had gained at its first showings. They had cut the human elements of the story instead of the documentary sections. They explained later that this was the only way a half hour could be taken out without complications in the musical soundtrack."

In other words, the picture had been cut according to the soundtrack with no respect to the inherent story values. At the lowest emotional level Vidor had reached since he arrived in Hollywood, he went to his office, packed his belongings, and moved out of the studio.

The film was not a boxoffice success, Vidor lamented, adding that many of the inhabitants of Beverly Hills and Hollywood never saw the movie and many do not even know it was made. He spent 20 years preparing the project and MGM spent close to three million dollars. Since they were both still in business, he guessed there was no time for tears.

Cecil B. DeMille's 1927 production of *The King of Kings,* starring H. B. Warner, was shortened to fit a new policy after general release. In his book, *Yes, Mr. DeMille,* which was about the great showman-director, author Phil Koury reported: "Most of Ernest

Torrence's portrayal of Peter was cut out. This grieved DeMille, as he considered it almost superior to Warner's handling of the Christ role. His feelings were close to shock when the Cinema people lopped off virtually all of the opening episodes containing the affair between Mary Magdalene and Judas. After this, neither Magdalene nor Judas made much sense to him as characters. He viewed it as unlikely that a man would betray a King for 'a lousy 30 pieces of silver. There must have been a dame in the background,' he told us in a tone of finality."

DeMille's latest film before his death was *The Ten Commandments* (1956), which ran about three hours and 40 minutes minus one of the most unusual cut sequences ever: the plague of the frogs, which DeMille shot and then decided against using.

Haunted by guilt (I like to think) at its penchant for cutting, Hollywood often will proclaim throughout an ad campaign—especially for the release of an epic—that the film is "Uncut! Original Full-Length Version!" This has been especially true of that oft-reissued peak of Hollywood movie-making, *Gone with the Wind,* which they don't fool around with (in the U.S., anyway) and had better not. In England in a more innocent time, censors have removed the part in which Clark Gable told his unhappily pregnant wife, Vivien Leigh, something like, "Cheer up, Scarlett, there's always time for you to have an accident."

In the strictest sense, though, the cries of "Uncut!" were not entirely true in the last *GwtW* outing (1968). For the first time, the letters which originally and so atmospherically swept across the screen letter by letter to form the main title were replaced by static letters which spelled out the words on a single frame. Wide-screen had set in, too, and to stretch out the now old-fashioned postage stamp film to the wider new width, the top and bottom of the picture were lost. For instance, Olivia de Havilland, horizontal across the bottom of the screen, had to play much of her moving deathbed scene with her loved ones mournfully gathered around only her very expressive vertical nose. Miss de Havilland was lucky—her nose was equipped to pull it off.

The producer of *GwtW,* David Selznick, once remarked, "There was not one re-take, and there was not one scene that wasn't used. There were only two previews. The first ran four hours and 20 minutes. Nick Schenck begged me not to cut a foot. I took 40 minutes out without losing a scene." The record shows that one scene did go by the boards, however: the wedding of Rhett and Scarlett.

Samuel Goldwyn's beloved story of returning war veterans, *The Best Years of Our Lives,* was apparently in even better shape for the first "sneak" in October of 1946. After shooting for more than 100 days, director William Wyler had edited the resulting 400 reels of film to 16 reels—two hours and 40 minutes of screen time—and the preview audience was so receptive no further editing was done.

However, professional advice is not always all it's cracked up to be. Producer Goldwyn has said that he once kept a careful tally about the advice given him by his own experienced friends for *Best Years.* After each screening he took notes on the scene each friend wanted him to cut from the film. "If I'd listened to them all," said Goldwyn, "the only thing left would have been the credits."

Most epics are not as lucky as *GwtW* and *TBYoOL.* Elizabeth Taylor has been in a couple, *Raintree County* and *Cleopatra,* from which enough footage was cut—before and after release—to provide at least two more movies, although *County* and *Cleo* have proved more than enough.

Early in 1957 Metro held some previews of *Raintree County,* its sumptuous answer to *Gone with the Wind,* but the reactions were not enthusiastic. So Miss Taylor's boyfriend Mike Todd, hot from his *Around the World in 80 Days,* took a look and advised: "This picture is too damned long. Sure, there's miles of local color and tons of subtlety, but who needs it? Actually the picture has just one asset, and I am not saying that because I am in love with this little broad. But you cut it to where it's almost all Liz, and you don't have to preview it to see what happens. I can tell you right now. The picture will be a hit, and Liz will get an Academy nomination as the result." MGM agreed; but Todd was only half right: the picture was terrible and Liz won an Oscar nomination. Next to *nothing,* Liz's assets had looked fine indeed.

Of her *Cleopatra* (1963), which came to a particularly ignominious end, one reviewer wrote: "Elizabeth Taylor is the first Cleopatra to sail down the Nile to Las Vegas."

Director Joseph L. Mankiewicz originally had planned to show the film in two parts on two successive evenings. From its initial release time of four hours and five minutes (plus intermission), it was cut down to three hours and four minutes. A notable cut was the scene between Cleopatra and Caesar at Alexander's tomb. This was the part in which the queen of Egypt told the consul of Rome her one-world dream; without it, the whole motivation disappeared.

Roddy McDowell squealed that his portrayal of Octavian—probably his most important film role since *Lassie Come Home* child star days—suffered from a scissorian soon after the opening. A seven-and-a-half minute speech of Roddy's already had been whittled down to two minutes.

Young character actor Martin Landau, who later landed his own hit television series, *Mission: Impossible,* claims some of the most cutting experiences of all on *Cleopatra.* "I spent a year of my life on *Cleopatra,*" he has moaned, "and I was sick when I saw only fragments of my role in the finished product.

"But some good came of it. Director Mankiewicz showed some of the cut footage of Roddy McDowall to director George Stevens who was casting *The Greatest Story Ever Told.* I happened to be in this footage, too, so Stevens hired me along with Roddy." Landau had the second largest role in *Greatest Story,* actually, but again was cut severely, this time down to a bit.

"An actor's at the mercy of the director, the producer, the head of the studio, the film cutter, musicians and even some of the stars who want to throw their weight around," Landau said.

"You have no artistic control yourself. If a star is big enough he can demand that his scenes remain uncut, or if a supporting actor looks too good in a scene the star can have him lopped out."

Portraying Liz' lover before and after the suits of Rex Harrison and Richard Burton, Italian actor Cesare Danova filed his complaint, too: "I knew they were going to cut a lot out of *Cleopatra.* But when I went to see the picture in Rome I had no idea they had perpetrated murder on me! All of my romantic interludes with Miss Taylor were scissored. I came out looking like some supernumerary who wasn't even carrying a spear!"

The veteran Hume Cronyn took a much cooler view of his co-starring role as Sosigenes, Cleo's counselor. About three years after its release, he told a TV audience: "The film originally ran about six hours and a half long, although none of the information available on this film is really reliable. I was filming in Italy almost 11 months—I was originally supposed to be there about four. Since I was neither in the battle nor boudoir scenes, when the picture had to be cut down to showable length, most of my part went—at least, that's what I'm told: I still haven't seen the film."

(Cronyn, you may recall, upon being informed that his last scene finally had been shot, cried, "Jess, here I come!"—meaning wife Jessica Tandy—and jumped into the nearby Mediterranean, costume and all.)

According to reviewer Alan Branigan, who saw *Cleopatra* before and after she sailed out into the world: "Most cuts have been made in the second part, in which Burton has the misfortune to portray Mark Antony, whom the film presents to us as a fumbler, a loser and something of an idiot. As an example of the cuts, we might mention a long sequence following upon Caesar's assassination. This portion, in which Antony reads the will of Caesar and goes ahead with the foolish idea of making Octavian the successor, has hit the cutting room floor, and now the move—the play's turning point—is covered in a line from Cleopatra. This omission and the loss of some succeeding bridge passages make the action murky and cause Antony's already unfocused character to become more elusive."

While the million-dollar salary offered her had prompted Liz to do *Cleopatra,* Burton (nowhere near that salary league *then*) had accepted the Mark Antony role, it says here, because it originally afforded him a three-dimensional characterization of a man who worshipped Caesar and tried to emulate him in every way, including taking up with his woman. After the cuts, though, most of what remained found Cleopatra and Antony lolling around within bedding distance, and as many reviewers pointed out, the sack scenes were curiously unexciting.

Milady Liz passed on her reactions. "I'm afraid *Cleopatra* may have been rather a low point. The only thing I was proud of in *Cleopatra* Fox cut out with unerring accuracy—that is, the core of the characterization. I never would have gone to see it ever, but the British Embassy trapped me. I was in London and they asked me to take the Bolshoi Ballet as my guests to a screening of *Cleopatra.* Afterwards I raced back to the Dorchester Hotel and just made it to the downstairs lavatory and I vomited," detailed the actress with the royal sensitiveness.

In her autobiography, affectionately titled *Elizabeth Taylor,* she added: "Richard's part built marvelously from a very strong man with a flaw until you could see him disintegrate. They cut the film so all you see is him drunk and shouting all the time, and you never know what in his character led up to it. He just looks like a drunken sot on campus."

And before it ever reached any paying audience, *Cleopatra* had at least one well-publicized scene cut. That was the one where Burton and Liz and Liz's child (oops—Antony and Cleopatra and Cleopatra's child) were frolicking about on the ground and one of Liz's "amples" slipped out of Irene Sharaff's zippered Caesarian gilding. Wirephotos of as much of this funning as possible made newspapers and magazines around the world. There was a re-take, of course, but the scene later was deemed extraneous, anyhow.

As some of the photo caption writers summed up the last incident: "That's our Liz—all over."

6. THE WARNER BROTHERS WAY

Not even volatile types like Bette Davis are exempt from shear madness. In her autobiography, *The Lonely Life,* Bette gave Sir Alec Guinness a boot in his bag of beards for having many of her scenes cut from their co-starring film, *The Scapegoat* (1959), in which her part as a dope-addicted crone was no Scarlett O'Hara to begin with. (In this pre-*What Ever Happened to Baby Jane?* time, two-time Oscar winner Davis admittedly was having trouble getting the quality jobs she once drew.) But, cracked Bette, not *that* dopey and no scapegoat, Guinness, "an actor who plays by himself, unto himself," played a dual role in *Scapegoat,* which at least gave him "the privilege of playing with himself."

"The competition with a male star is unbelievable," wrote Bette, about to chronicle a trying time during early Warner Brothers days.

"*Juarez,* for instance, was peculiarly constructed. The antagonists never meet. The part of the film in which Brian Aherne and I appeared as Maximilian and Carlotta was shot and assembled before Mr. Paul Muni as Juarez ever stepped before a camera. He saw our part of the picture in the projection room and his wife, Bella, observed that it was 'a complete picture without ever seeing Juarez.' It was true. Mr. Muni brought with him 50 additional pages of script that he wanted added to his part. He was that powerful and the studio allowed it.

"The length of any picture must be limited. When the Juarez part of the film was finished, we were in trouble lengthwise. Something had to go. Brian's and my part of the film received the cuts. Although it was a good picture, the film, before cutting destroyed it in the abattoir, was a great one. Mr. Muni's seniority proved our downfall."

Davis also told the story of an unpleasant encounter as a summer stock ingenue in Massachusetts early in her career with that grande dame of the theater (later movie character woman) Laura Hope Crews, whose most well-known film performance is probably the scatterbrained Aunt Pittypat in *Gone with the Wind.*

Madame Crews, directing as well as starring in a production of *Mr. Pim Passes By,* didn't think Davis, just promoted from usher at the playhouse, was right for the English girl in the play, and made it difficult for her. Crews told Davis she used her hands too much and even slapped her on the wrist during dress rehearsal. Davis was a hit, anyway. Many years later (1941) when Davis was starring at Warners in *The Man Who Came to Dinner,* Crews turned up to play a small role in the picture. When her part was finished, Crews, ostensibly as a belated apology, presented Davis with a watch that a forgiving Davis said she still cherishes. What Davis neglected to tell in her book was that Crews' entire role was cut from the released version of that unsurpassed film comedy.

Bette lives in a jungle where self is perhaps more important than anywhere else—except the jungle—and from necessity she is not above pulling rank herself. Right after *Dinner,* Bette and pal Olivia de Havilland were co-starring as the sisters Stanley and Roy, respectively, in a John Huston film called *In This Our Life.* Bette had the meatier role as the bad sister but Olivia had director Huston as her escort in those days; and, according to reports, Olivia was getting an awful lot of flattering closeups. When Davis saw

Patricia Neal's first film after Hud *was* The Third Secret, *but her role was completely excised when the picture was released. Here is a Neal–Stephen Boyd scene the public never saw in* Secret.

An unknown actor with Jessica Tandy and Peggy Cummins in Forever Amber, *which was stopped after several weeks and ultimately made with Linda Darnell replacing much-touted English import Peggy Cummins in the sexy title role. Miss Tandy was retained.*

Romantic leads Betty Grable and Dale Robertson in the musical dream sequence cut from The Farmer Takes a Wife. *In the chorus, seated, are two future stars: Julie Newmar, at far right, and Gwen Verdon, at Robertson's feet.*

Although she was a lead in many films by then, Audrey Totter's entire role was excised from Tenth Avenue Angel. *Shown above from left: Totter, Margaret O'Brien, and George Murphy.*

Anne Revere, whose alleged Communist affiliations brought her some of the unkindest cuts of all, shells lobsters and straightens out the plot with Jean Peters (Mrs. Howard Hughes) in this scene "lifted" from Deep Waters, *leaving the film to make little sense, Miss Revere feels.*

From left: Robert Sterling, Eleanor Parker, Tuesday Weld, Gunnar Hellstrom, Carol Lynley, and (behind Miss Lynley) the late Jeff Chandler enjoying the burning of Mary Astor's house in Return to Peyton Place. *The audience wasn't as lucky—the fire and all reference to it was cut.*

The actual confrontation scene from Surrender, *if anyone should ask, had Vera (Hruba) Ralston and Maria Palmer both on their feet for the blow-out.*

Shirley MacLaine's praised Apache dance from Can-Can *was cut out of the picture for second-run engagements.*

Susan Hayward was a doomed party girl in Stolen Hours, *and this still shows her partying. The scene, however, was doomed to be cut.*

Veteran player of flighty matrons (and "Lovey" in the TV series Gilligan's Island*) Natalie Schafer was completely cut from the much-hacked* Bus Riley's Back in Town. *Miss Schafer is seen above in one of the missing scenes with male lead Michael Parks.*

Robert Montgomery was replaced in the final version of the Greer Garson vehicle, Desire Me, *by newcomer Richard Hart.*

I, Claudius, *started in 1936 in England with Charles Laughton and Flora Robson, was shut down after about a month's shooting and never completed or released.*

When a good part of Bus Riley's Back in Town *was remade, the above scene with Larry Storch (co-star of TV's* F Troop*) and Ann-Margret was among the first to go.*

The flop of the much-cut, expensive Arch of Triumph *helped finish off the Enterprise Studios. And Ruth Warrick's important role was cut to one meaningless scene. Above, Miss Warrick with Charles Boyer and Louis Calhern in a missing moment from the picture.*

the rushes she demanded many of the scenes re-shot in her (Davis') favor and long-time pal de Havilland was kept in her second-billed place.

But Davis and de Havilland, practically raised together at the Warner studios, have remained close friends through the years—Olivia, a two-time Oscar winner like Bette, has called the slightly older actress her idol, as well as referred to the pair of them as "Maxine and Laverne." And when in the summer of '64 Joan Crawford became ill and had to relinquish *Hush . . . Hush, Sweet Charlotte,* her co-star, Bette, always distant to Joan, recommended Olivia take her place. With Pepsi Cola queen Joan departed (and several weeks' Crawford footage scrapped), Bette and Olivia toasted the new beginning of *Hush* with Coca Cola.

As for John Huston—the cuts in his 1951 *The Red Badge of Courage,* which saw the film go from 78 minutes up to 88, and down to its release time of 69, are fabled.

The film might not be such a well-known victim of "big studio shears" if it weren't for Lillian Ross, a *New Yorker* magazine staff writer who was assigned to write articles on the filming of *Red Badge* from outset to conclusion. This she did, to the celebration of the New York theatrical scene and the chagrin of Hollywood, and then assembled her pieces in a book called *Picture,* likewise devoted entirely to the shooting—and shearing—of *Badge.*

It was not an easy film to get going. Based on Stephen Crane's classic novel of the Civil War and a Youth's resurrection from cowardice, the script had no love interest and, according to producer Gottfried Reinhardt toward the finish, "no story, because we do not show what the Youth is thinking. It is not in the script. John said he would put it on the screen. It is not on the screen." Although Reinhardt and Dore Schary, then vice president in charge of production at MGM, had championed the production from the beginning—along with Huston, of course, who also did the screen treatment—L. B. Mayer, vice president in charge of the studio and crusader for "clean and wholesome" entertainment, thought the idea stank. Agreeing with him (at first) was the powerful New York-based Nick Schenck, the president of Loew's, Inc. ("the ruler of the rulers"), not to mention Mrs. Reinhardt.

Aside from the archly demeaning portrait of Hollywood movie-making machinations offered in *Picture,* the book (today a bit tame) is notable for two (still) fresh peeks at two outstanding movieland figures: Louis B. Mayer and John Huston. Now that the initial shock of finding out that the boss of stars from Mickey Rooney to Esther Williams was not the High Lama of Shangri-La, the MGM chief re-reads as an amusing, colorful, and above all instinctively wise showman (the old rascal seemed right most of the time to me, anyway, regardless of Miss Ross' intent). But Huston, long canonized as *one* Hollywood movie-maker of integrity who is greatly gifted at the work that he takes with dead seriousness, stays characterized as an indifferent movie-maker but dedicated horse player-breeder-rider who crusaded to get *Red Badge* on film and then, instead of staying with his specious project to the end, took off for darkest Africa on another movie-making jaunt. Huston cabled his reply to Reinhardt's long, tear-stained, soul-searching, conscience-stricken letter apologizing for the cuts the studio insisted be made: "JUST GOT YOUR LETTER. KNOW YOU FOUGHT GOOD FIGHT. HOPE YOU NOT TOO BLOODY MY ACCOUNT. LET'S MAKE NEXT ONE REINHARDT NOT A HUSTON PICTURE. JOHN." If one were to believe authoress Ross, Huston was shockingly disinterested in the picture which, after the first preview, he had said was his best.

In a 1967 TV interview, the director stated: "The audience completely rejected the film at the preview—I never saw so many people leave a theater. I thought it was a good film. There were things done to it then that I didn't approve of, but I still think it's a good film."

A clue to the reason for Huston's apparent diffidence concerning *Red Badge* may be found in a quote he gave writer Ezra Goodman during the filming: "Assistants do all the work and the director gets all the glory." Goodman noted that Huston's assistant, Reggie Callow, was too busy at the time to hear the compliment.

In '65 Reinhardt called Miss Ross' work "true, but a caricature" and affirmed that *Courage* had been important to Metro not in itself, but as a pawn in the power struggle between Schary and Mayer. He said that after Miss Ross' stories appeared, he called up MGM and asked for the discarded footage, so that the film could be pieced together again close to its original form. The footage had been destroyed.

On the subject of producers and directors gaining their independence from the all-powerful studios, Reinhardt had this to say: "The situation has changed, but things like that still happen. I know of two very recent pictures, made by highly reputable producers, and immensely respected directors, that were cut to ribbons by the studio. Oh, some people have deals to protect them, but in most cases, as long as it's the studio's money, they can take the picture away from you and do what they want with it."

Mayer's argument to Huston and Reinhardt against filming *Courage,* Reinhardt recalled, was a "six-hour monologue," including such lines from Mayer to Huston as "Does your wife go to the toilet? If she goes to the toilet during a party, does she keep the door open while she's taking a weewee, or does she keep it shut?" Intimidated, Huston and Reinhardt told Schary they would cancel preparations for the film, since Mayer was so dead set against it. Schary, however, was now bent on filming it.

"I learned something from it all," said Reinhardt. "Don't try to force a picture down their throats! And that's when I decided to become a director; I determined I'd never go through that again for anybody else!"

But the cuts:

MGM's executive film editor, Margaret Booth, had worked with Reinhardt in rough-cutting *Red Badge* while Huston was off on location finishing the production. "A lot of stuff can go," she said. It did, with Booth and Schary, as well as Reinhardt, getting their licks in.

To quote Miss Ross on the final version: "The Tattered Man's death scene had definitely been cut out, and most of the other changes that Reinhardt had seen at Schary's house had now been made permanent. The battle sequences added up to an entirely different war from the one that had been fought and photographed at Huston's ranch in the San Fernando Valley. The elimination of scenes accounted for part of the difference. The old man with the lined face who was digging was gone, the ragged veterans gibing at the recruits both before and after a battle were gone. Many small touches—brief glimpses of the men at war—had been trimmed, including a close-up of a wounded man berating an officer for 'small wounds and big talk.' The last shot in the picture—of the Youth's regiment marching away from the battlefield—which

Huston had wanted to run long, had been cut to run short. (Reinhardt had succeeded in getting Schary to restore the wounded man singing 'John Brown's Body' and part of the scene of the Youth shouting to the artillerymen.) The revision had some odd results. For one thing, the two main battles became one. Audie Murphy, who played the Youth, was seen wearing a bandage on his head at the start of the charge, was seen without it in the middle, then had it on again at the end. A narration with quotes from the novel also was dropped in at the last minute (spoken by James Whitmore).

Years later William F. Nolan noted in his biography of Huston, *King Rebel:* "Mayer, angry with the New York office and feeling they were unjustly favoring Schary, resigned from Metro, leaving the studio in late August. He had been firmly opposed to releasing *Red Badge* in any form—but within a month after Mayer's withdrawal Schary brought the film out in New York."

. . . Where Huston's apparently half-hearted battle ended, appropriately enough, not with a bang but with a thud—at the box-office.

Another veteran of the Hollywood wars, Rosalind Russell, has had her share of problems on the cutting room floor, too, in recent years. Both her *A Majority of One,* a hit on stage with Gertrude Berg, and *Gypsy,* Ethel Merman's Broadway triumph, had important scenes that were *in* for press and trade showings by Warners, but *out* for general release.

A fabulous comedienne *without* TV, Miss Russell's elevated image was chipped by these two film adaptations (although *Gypsy* was a moneymaker) and the monstrous filmization of the play *Five Finger Exercise,* which completed her early '60s trilogy known as the Big Russell Stage Rustle. Giving rise to such rather "inside" anti-Hollywood (and anti-Russell) jokes as: "They're going to film *My Fair Lady* and Rosalind Russell will probably play Henry Higgins." In one of the unlikeliest castings in years, Roz was a middle-aged Jewish widow in love with a Japanese businessman (Alec Guinness); and, soon afterward and more realistically, she was the aggressive stage mother of the young Gypsy Rose Lee (another unlikely casting—Natalie Wood, whose measurements hadn't changed *that* much since she was the small Santa Claus knocker in 1947's *Miracle on 34th Street*).

For a time it looked as if Russell's *Gypsy* and *Majority* (and *Exercise*) might at least curtail the wholesale practice of filming Broadway plays with movie stars taking the leads first played by stage stars. But *My Fair Lady* was waiting in Warners' wings with not Roz but Rex Harrison repeating as Higgins and Audrey Hepburn getting to do Julie Andrews' original role. It's well known the furor, bad Warner public relations, and, more importantly, boxoffice fall-off into which Jack Warner outsmarted himself when he "played it safe" by paying Audrey (whose singing was dubbed) a million dollars to play Eliza and bypassing the stage's "untried" Julie, whose *Mary Poppins* (co-starring Dick Van Dyke, who did not get nearly the credit due him), had helped her become the Sweetheart of the Movies at just about the time *My Fair Lady* was opening.

As for La Russell's movie mothers from, respectively, burlesque and Brooklyn. . . .

In *Gypsy* Miss Russell was helped in the singing department by Lisa Kirk. When I asked Lisa how much of the vocalizing she had done for Russell, she said: "All of it, except for the 'Mr. Goldstone' number. The whole thing turned out to be a drag. Warners contacted me to do it three days before I was to leave for England, offering me a piece of the soundtrack album, too. And I begged them to let me sing it 'up,' but I had to sing the whole thing in her key, which was lower than mine." However, the one number in which Roz really *seemed* to be doing her own warbling—and the liveliest in the film, superior to its rendering on the stage—was "Together," which she did with Natalie Wood and Karl Malden. It rated applause from previewers. When the film bowed at Radio City Music Hall in New York, it did so minus this delightful interlude—along with a little dance done by Russell and Malden in a Chinese restaurant. This footage was not to reappear for subsequent engagements, either. The film, and Russell's performance, had been deprived of considerable steam.

A few years later on her TV interview series, Gypsy Rose Lee mentioned to guest Ethel Merman that "one of my favorite numbers from the show was cut from the movie—'Together.' " Merman—perhaps because she had not seen the movie?—seemed surprised to hear this.

In *Majority* something even stranger happened, although it wasn't as damaging to the film. The opening scene, in which Russell, working in a dress shop, outfitted bride-to-be Sharon Hugueny, was cut for general release. Miss Hugueny, who had only this one scene but received good billing, remained in the credits of the picture, too. You can't get much better billing than that.

Pity the bit player when the scissors flash. Barbara Pepper, a blonde floozie player from the 1930s who was still at her blowsy specialty in 1964's Warner production, *My Fair Lady* (she did some stepping with Stanley Holloway in the "Get Me to the Church on Time" number), and as Doris Ziffel in the Eddie Albert–Eva Gabor TV series, *Green Acres,* was cut from at least two major Warner productions of the 1950s, *A Star is Born* and *Auntie Mame.* She was a fat Hotel Lancaster neighbor of Judy Garland's during Judy's courtship by James Mason, and an equally ample hillbilly in a deleted scene with Rosalind Russell in *Mame.* Veda Ann Borg, although she was still in her teens (she says) when contracted by Warners in '37, got started playing blonde broads, too, a genre in which she is still most at home; and while Miss Borg has never attained star status (indeed it's a good day when she gets a supporting role and not a walk-on), she is perhaps better known than Barbara Pepper. In 1960 Borg had one of her best showings in John Wayne's *The Alamo* cast against type as Blind Nell. The part was reduced in the final editing to a glorified bit, but viewers still remember her big scene, which remained intact: when she told her husband to stay and help defend the fort.

Another hardy "pro," the wonderfully wise-cracking Ruth Donnelly, has said that more often than not her best Hollywood work wound up on the cutting room floor. As a nun and Ingrid Bergman's shadow in RKO's *The Bells of St. Mary's* (1945), Donnelly danced an Irish jig to which she was very partial, but it was cut. "They want you to be good, but not too good," she winked that *Snake Pit* wink not long ago. "Marie Dressler told me about the heartbreaks she had, and I thought of her words often as I looked in vain for a bit or a scene that took years of experience."

In '33 Warners had planned *Footlight Parade* for Dick Powell, but he was having trouble with his throat and was replaced by Stanley Smith opposite Ruby Keeler. When their scenes were wrapped, Powell recovered and the studio, anxious to promote

Powell and Keeler as a team, scrapped all Smith's footage, and put Powell in the picture. Smith's career declined.

In the early '40s *Motion Picture* ran a Fredda Dudley piece on the occasion of veteran (but still young) Warner bit player John Ridgely's cardinal success with a substantial role in *Air Force.* The piece was called "Success—On the 125th Try."

Related Miss Dudley: "John recalls with a grim chuckle that he was working one morning at the Warner ranch near Castiac when he received a call to the effect that he was imperatively needed by a company shooting at Santa Monica. John finished his morning appearance in one picture and catapulted to the beach city, where he spoke several lines for a menace part. Then he was notified that he had been requisitioned by the Burbank lot to work that night. He was kept busy until nearly dawn by his scenes in his third picture in 24 hours."

"As these films were released in Pasadena, where John lives, he went to see them," continued the writer in her story on the one-time stand-in. "He caught no sight of himself in the first opus. Nor, several weeks later, in the second. Nor, several months later, in the third. Apparently he landed on the cutting room floor."

Many a comeback has been quelled by cuts, notably late-silents, early-talkies star Nancy Carroll. She told her long-time admirer, press agent John Springer, that her return to pictures in '38 following a three-year lay-off, for United Artists' *There Goes My Heart,* with Fredric March, just about broke her heart. Says Springer: "She had a lesser, but good, comedy second lead, but it was so cut she emerged just a vengeful girl who is nasty to the heroine." It was the late Carroll's next-to-last film.

In January 1967, columnist Radie Harris covered a Warner Brothers junket to the Eden Roc Hotel in Miami Beach to see a movie about a New Orleans hotel titled *Hotel,* starring, among several, Rod Taylor and Merle Oberon. Noted Radie: "*Hotel* is Merle's first Hollywood-made film in several years [apart from a guest star bit in *The Oscar*] and the reason that producer-writer Wendell Mayes was able to uproot her from her magnificent home in Acapulco and world travels with her wealthy industrialist husband, Bruno Pagliai, was two-fold. First, the role of the Duchess, as it appeared in the original script, intrigued her with its possibility of a rich characterization, and secondly, her salary would go to her pet charity—a home for impoverished Mexican children. . . . She sat with director Richard Quine and saw the film for the first time. Unfortunately, some of her best scenes were left on the cutting room floor (Hollywood moves in a mysterious way, its editing to perform!)."

Richard Conte, a contemporary of Oberon's, was dealt a worse blow shortly before by the brothers Warner. Work being a precious thing for aging leading men, too, Conte grabbed at the supporting part offered him in *Act One* (1963), the Moss Hart story. When the last curtain had fallen, so had Conte's entire appearance in the production. Ditto Vera Miles' feminine lead in *The Green Berets* (1968), also a Warner release.

Ten years after Diane Varsi had been nominated for 1957's supporting actress Academy honors for *Peyton Place,* and several years after she had voluntarily quit the screen because the roles and the life seemed superficial to the intense young woman, Miss Varsi found a comeback vehicle. The Philadelphia-New York filmed *Sweet Love, Bitter,* also featuring a couple of other causists named Don Murray and Dick Gregory, was the movie Miss Varsi thought she could do and still live with herself. It dealt with Negro-white relationships. When the picture opened, it was more the story of a single jazz musician (Gregory) than of the interrelationships of the four leading characters (including Robert Hooks) due, claimed director-writer Herbert Danska and producer-writer Lewis Jacobs, to the considerable cutting of the film by executive producers Robert Ferman and Gerald Kleppel. The latter pair said that the movie as originally completed had lacked a direction and story line. Most of the reviewers felt, however, that the characters and their motivation in the project to which Danska had devoted four years of his life had been made entirely too sketchy by the cutting.

Warned Danska: "When you got a dream, you better make sure you got a key to the cutting room."

Following poor business in initial bookings, the dream was retitled *Black Love, White Love.*

Much the same was the experience of one-time child actress and Shirley Temple tormentor Jane Withers when she turned to adult characterization in *Giant* (1956). Before this epic story of Texas living was completed, word was osmosing that Jane's comic, good-naturedly gauche Vashti Snythe was practically stealing the film from Elizabeth Taylor, Rock Hudson, and James Dean. A supporting actress Oscar was even being mentioned as a possibility. But this Warner film was hardly dry when Dean was killed in an auto accident. It was written that director George Stevens, in a bit of monumentally senseless over-concern, decided that many of the laughs in his already marathon picture would now be in questionable taste. Consequently, most of Jane's jollies were deleted and the resulting effect was not unlike that of a comedian's routine deprived of its punch lines.

Shirley had her own troubles when it came time to swap her Mary Janes for wedgees back in the late '40s. For her first grown-up role, she co-starred with Ronald Reagan in a Warner embarrassment called *That Hagen Girl,* the shooting screenplay for which was in its fifth revision. Reagan vainly tried to force a sixth—for he was playing not only Shirley's love interest but also the man towns-people suspected of being her father, and he felt the public "was not ready to give up the *young* Shirley Temple, particularly to a man old enough to be her father." And who might *be* her father, an even stickier proposition.

Reagan continued: "I won the argument at the sneak preview, but it didn't make me happy. Came the moment on screen when I said to Shirley, 'I love you,' and the entire audience en masse cried, 'Oh, no!' I sat huddled in the darkness until I was sure the lobby would be empty. You couldn't have gotten me to face that audience for a million bucks. Before release the line was edited out of the picture, leaving us with a kind of oddball finish in which we climb on a train—Shirley carrying a bouquet—and leave town. You are left to guess as to whether we are married, just traveling together, or did I adopt her."

More than one actor has gotten the surprise of his celluloid life at a premiere of his picture, but the case of comedian Paul Lynde, of the voracious smile and the ability to wrench laughs whether his material deserves them or not, may be said to be *cat*astrophic.

During the filming of Columbia's *Under the Yum-Yum Tree* (1963), in which Lynde was featured, he had one line that presented more trouble than anything else he had to do in the movie. Producer Freddie Brisson (Rosalind Russell's husband) frequently was heard to say variations of "No, Paul, that doesn't sound exactly like the Lynde delivery, and it is important that this be so individual —as only Paul Lynde could do it. This is a line that is to smack right at the funny button of those Lynde buffs."

They spent half a day shooting and re-shooting, getting different angles, completely changing set-ups, etc., in an effort to get it right. When the premiere rolled around, Lynde discovered that the scene containing his delivery of the troublesome line had been cut, although the line eventually turned up—delivered at the end of the picture, in his own voice, through the mouth of a cat!

Less degrading but even more irritating is the story Margaret Lindsay tells about her 1930s days as one of the fillies in the Warner Brothers stable. She had wrapped up a '36 picture with Humphrey Bogart (one he always claimed he couldn't remember making) and took off for Hawaii on an ocean liner for one of those well-deserved vacations. When Lindsay docked, she received a message from the studio requesting her immediate return for one additional line of dialogue. It was a five-day trip in those days, but she complied—and ruined her vacation. When the picture opened, it was without that costly line of dialogue. The line had been cut. Appropriately, the film's title was *Isle of Fury.*

Ann Sheridan, whose publicity as the "oomph" girl got her out of the Warner stable and in the running (Walter Winchell had remarked that she had plenty of "umph," and from there—with the studio's help—it evolved naturally enough to "OOmph"), and whose cynical approach to a line gave '30s, '40s, and even '50s pictures a delicious bite, started a trouble-beset remake of *The Animal Kingdom* in '44 that was not released until '46.

Remembered Sheridan, shortly before her death early in 1967: "We worked for five weeks on it. Then Mr. Warner found out that Barney Glazier, the producer, hadn't even had it OK'd by the Johnson Office. So they closed the picture because it had no Johnson Seal and couldn't be released. Irving Rapper was the first director on it. So there was a whole rewrite done. Dane Clark was written out. They closed it and I came to New York, stayed six weeks, went back, did *Shine On, Harvest Moon,* then went back and finished this with the rewrite. They put Peter Godfrey on as the new director. It was released as *One More Tomorrow,* with Dennis Morgan, Jack Carson, Jane Wyman, Alexis Smith—the Warner stock company. You can tell the difference in the scenes between the things

Rapper had done and what Godfrey did. It was one of the most horrible things I'd ever seen in my life! They bought Mr. Glazier's contract, paid him off $150,000 and sent him for—so they told the papers—a rest in South America."

After the initial release of Warner Brothers' *The Private Lives of Elizabeth and Essex* (1939), Errol Flynn's entire execution scene was cut.

Pretty sneaky pool on the part of the studio(s) is what much of the cutting up can't help looking like, with the critics and trade members, in many cases, seeing the whole lovely film(s), and the public—they're only paying—seeing slapdash abbreviations. Warners is an habitual offender at this, and late in 1964 the company pulled off another of its annoying swindles with John Ford's *Cheyenne Autumn.* But this time critic Bosley Crowther—only a quarter of a century on the job—caught them and said so.

In the version shown to reviewers, *Cheyenne Autumn* contained a half-hour segment dropped into the middle of this story of an Indian tribe's exodus, circa 1878, from its southwest reservation to more fertile land in the north. Suddenly, the scene was no longer the desert but a Dodge City saloon, and Wyatt Earp (James Stewart) was exposing three cowboys as the murderers of a starving Cheyenne, a feat Earp accomplished via a seemingly extraneous comic poker game. There then should have followed a scene in which the poker players and townspeople rode out to jeer the passing Indians and were dispersed by a Cheyenne scout.

As Bosley Crowther put it, "This whole segment of the picture emerged as an obviously nonessential but eventually bold and meaningful thrust of significantly sardonic comment on the callousness of the frontier white man into the solemn body of the film.

"So, what was our amazement and annoyance to discover just the other day that the whole last part of this segment—the sequence of the people riding out and making their brief contact with the Indians—has been completely cut from the film . . . and the encounter in the saloon has been left dangling as though it were a sequence from another film!

"The explanations for the cut have been elaborate, now that we have inquired: the segment was too long, it fell athwart the intermission, its basic point of the white man's disposition toward the

Indian is made in the scene in the saloon. But there was no explanation of why the critics were not informed after they had been compelled by the exigencies of the pre-Christmas rush of pictures to see the film in a solitary preview several weeks before the opening."

Crowther would have been even more disturbed if he had known parts of this cut action were turning up in both theater and TV trailers for the picture.

The incident of Marilyn Monroe's first film, Fox's *Scudda Hoo! Scudda Hay!,* in 1948, is ironic and worthy of note for other reasons beside the well-known one that Miss Monroe's part was cut to such excess that many claim they can't find her in it. She originally had something of a running part as Betty, one of star June Haver's girlfriends, but wound up with one line, "Hi, Rad," directed at Miss Haver as they left church one Sunday morning. There is also a shot of MM and co-starlet Colleen Townsend in a rowboat, although it was made from afar and their faces are not really visible. The irony is in the pairing of these two diverse screen newcomers: the doomed Marilyn, who was to become one of the world's all-time great sex symbols, and Colleen, who a few years later quit a promising Hollywood career to become a Protestant minister.

Marilyn later said her *Scudda Hoo!* role had been snipped "because they said it was too confusing with two blondes in the picture," the other being star Haver, of course. (It was said, too, that studio chief Darryl F. Zanuck thought MM too "trampy looking.") Almost a decade later Marilyn could pull rank on blonde newcomer Hope Lange in *Bus Stop* and make her darken her blonde hair.

Marilyn and brunette Jane Russell also were seen in stills from a much-publicized musical number in *Gentlemen Prefer Blondes* (1953), in which the gals wore tights (a huge flower on each huge seat) and exaggerated Napoleonic headgear; but the scene, while glimpsed in the trailer (the two healthies seemed to be climbing a ladder to a quarter-moon in the shadow of the Eiffel Tower) and used extensively in the advertising (even for TV showings), never appeared in the picture. Another *Blondes* production number with Monroe and Russell, "When the Wild Wild Women Go Swimmin' Down in the Swimmin' Hole," has been reported as filmed and missing, although this song conceivably could be the one the gals sang as they tackled that ladder.

The experience of the radiant Joan Hackett with her first film might have disheartened a less philosophic girl than Joan, a marvelous actress with a case of galloping integrity, a virus especially prevalent on the New York theatrical scene. After a few years of extraordinary success on television and the straw hat circuit, plus several off-Broadway awards for her performance in *Call Me by My Rightful Name,* Joan finally was lured to Hollywood in 1963 (after 18 invitations) as George Maharis' leading lady in his first starring movie, *The Satan Bug* (1964).

"It wasn't a very good part, really," Joan told me, "and I'd wanted my first flick to be important, but I thought I'd get my feet wet. Well, it was a mess. We locationed on the desert and I was allergic to something there—not the sun, exactly, but a combination of sun and dryness, I think. I looked awful in the picture. And they'd tried to glamourize me, too. After four days of filming, I asked to be released from the picture, and was, with no arguments. I think George thought I was just putting up a front and would cry all the way back to New York, but I was really glad to be out of it."

Anne Francis, whose whole part as the prostitute in the earlier *Hemingway's Adventures of a Young Man* was cut, replaced Joan in this *Bug* bomb. It's a small cutting room floor, as further substantiated by the cuts in Hackett's first film, *The Group* (1966), in which Candice Bergen, too, made her much-publicized film debut as "Lakey" the lesbo. Bergen's part, the smallest of the eight Depression Vassar grads the picture observed, was shortened even more by post-filming cuts that also deprived Polish actress Lidia Prochnicka (as Lakey's baroness) of all save one line of dialogue.

When *The Group* was first screened for the cast, six of the eight leading gals of novelist Mary McCarthy's invention (?) were present—along with reporter recruits who could record the girls' reactions to the event. Most of the group had never appeared in a film before. Afterward, novice Mary-Robin Redd observed that "our best moments were on the cutting room floor. I didn't think it was possible for anything of mine to be cut—the part was so small anyway—but they managed."

Allan Jones originally was to co-star with Jeanette MacDonald in

1935's *Naughty Marietta* at Metro, but couldn't get a release in time from his contract with Broadway's Shubert brothers, thereby paving the way for Nelson Eddy to step in and become a screen immortal as one half of the medium's most successful singing duo. Jones finally got his freedom and started at MGM in the operatic sequence from 1936's *Rose Marie,* with Jeanette and Nelson starring. Solo, Jones did the prison scene from *Tosca,* singing the aria "E lucevan le stelle," and then with Jeanette the death scene from *Romeo and Juliet.* Only Jones' work with Jeanette was kept in.

Almost 30 years later, MGM's *Honeymoon Hotel,* the first of several bomb movies for tyro Robert Goulet, needn't have been such a trend-setter, according to the Oscar and Emmy-winning composers Sammy Cahn and Jimmy Van Heusen. The fellows wrote five songs for the picture, but only one turned up, the title number sung by Goulet behind the credits. "After the first preview of the film, which was originally called *His and His,* the head of the studio said, 'Take out four songs!' It was a terrible flop. How can you have a picture with Goulet without songs?", asked Van Heusen.

Gordon MacRae told me that his oldest child, the pretty Meredith, who was to achieve continuity on television's *Petticoat Junction* as one of Bea Benaderet's three daughters, got her first movie roles in two of her dad's films: *By the Light of the Silvery Moon* at Warners and Fox's *Carousel.* "Mairzy was just a little girl then," MacRae remembered, "and she was quite thrilled about her two small parts in those pictures. She memorized her lines and all. But everything was cut except a couple of glimpses of her, at the beginning of *Carousel* on the merry-go-round and during an ice-skating scene in *Silvery Moon.*"

Even the late James Dean was a first-time loser. The actor who was to die in 1955 at 24 and become a legend made his film debut in a '51 Dean Martin-Jerry Lewis vehicle, *Sailor Beware,* as an eager seaman. His three lines of dialogue disappeared from the picture by the time it was shown, and Jimmy was merely one of a gaggle of gobs in the background of a few scenes.

Jane Wyman is perhaps the most versatile leading lady ever developed by motion pictures, an artist who could win a Best Actress Oscar for her deaf-mute in *Johnny Belinda* (1948) and then have "In the Cool, Cool, Cool of the Evening," the song she sang with Bing Crosby in *Here Comes the Groom* (1951), win that year's

Best Song Academy honor. But Wyman, starting out as a Warner Brothers contract player, was years working her way up from walk-ons (some even unbilled) to First Lady status. Universal's *My Man Godfrey*, the enduring 1936-made comedy starring William Powell (whose kind of mature suavity is absolutely extinct, sadly, among today's men, except for Cary Grant, who is hardly *of* today) and Carole Lombard, is generally listed (erroneously) as Wyman's first movie. Yet Wyman has said that her whole part—a bit very important to the girl who had been trying to make it in Hollywood for some time—was cut.

Martha Vickers, the third Mrs. Mickey Rooney and mother of Teddy Rooney, made several films, the most notable probably *Time, the Place and the Girl* and *The Big Sleep* (both 1946 Warner releases). She is remembered, especially, for her bad-girl role in the latter Bogart-Bacall opus (her first click), which enjoys continuous theater and television revival and is a favorite of the Bogie cultists. A couple of seasons before *Sleep,* as Martha MacVicar, ex-model, she had what has been called (again erroneously) her cinematic initiation in Pat O'Brien's *Marine Raiders* at RKO. Reported an early biographer: "The part she won was a goodly hunk of script pages. But on the screen it came out just one brief but potent scene in a voice recording booth! Lost: Somewhere between the sound stage and the theater, one promising career." Moaned Martha: "And me with 11 friends at the preview! I could have cried for a week, except that it struck me so darned funny!"

Eleanor Parker, one of Hollywood's most classically handsome and gifted ladies, made her bow technically in a 1941 Errol Flynn-Olivia de Havilland number called *They Died with Their Boots On.* As Parker recalls it: "I was very new at Warners and was visiting the *Boots* set one day. The director decided he needed a young thing to kiss Gig Young off to war, so I was drafted to do it. People who look for me in it can't find me for the very good reason that I was cut out of the final print." The story that some of Young's false mustache adhered to Parker's upper lip and ruined things is only hearsay. Long called Hollywood's most neglected star talent, Parker was initiated prophetically on a career of second-class stardom by the *Boots* bigwigs who cut her out of her first film.

Twenty-five years later, Parker was still in good enough shape to essay her first nude scene in Warners' *An American Dream—*

actually, she wore a G-string. Right after the picture's completion, co-star Barry Sullivan, in a rarely generous digression for an actor having his own interview, announced: "Parker does a nude scene in the picture, but it will be shown only in Europe. They have cut it out of the version to be released here. She is dead on page 30 of the script, but she will get an Academy Award for the performance. I'll place a small bet on it right now." He lost the bet.

TV talk-show host Les Crane, a good-looking unfrocked disk jockey, made his movie debut in *American Dream,* but his part as a hood came out looking like a bit; he cried cut, long and loud.

Yvette Mimieux also started in a Parker film, 1959's *Home from the Hill,* with a cutting experience that only hurt for a little while. Sent down South to join the location company for her one scene, which was to open the picture and had Mimieux flirting at a soda fountain with George Hamilton, she later learned a different beginning had been chosen. Director Vincente Minnelli shipped her footage back to MGM as a "test," where producer-director George Pal saw it. He signed the young lady to co-star with Rod Taylor in the now highly regarded science fiction job, 1960's *The Time Machine,* earning her that practically extinct commodity in post-Golden Age screen days: a long-term contract at the studio.

Evelyn Keyes, an all-around actress who, like Parker, should have been bigger in pictures, had one of the unkindest cuts of all. It has been said that when Miss Keyes fell out of favor with her producer boyfriend Mike Todd, her "cameo"—Todd invented this connotation of the word for this occasion—in his star-filled *Around the World in 80 Days* was snipped to a flash even her mother would have trouble recognizing. Earlier, Keyes had informed an interviewer, "Even Mike's worst enemies can't say he's petty."

7. THE LADY IN A CAGE PROVED HAUNTING FOR 36 HOURS TO THE MAGNIFICENT AMBERSONS

Three more recent victims of the shears in varying degrees were Ann Sothern, Eva Marie Saint, and Claire Bloom.

After several years in TV, Miss Sothern, obviously influenced by the success of Bette Davis and Joan Crawford in their *Baby Jane* bonanza of horror, decided to return to films as a sloppy hooker in Olivia de Havilland's *Lady in a Cage* (1964). So anxious was Miss Sothern to change her image from fluffy comedienne to character actress, as well as to remind Hollywood she was available for films, that when the producers couldn't pay her salary she did the picture for nothing, accepting a deferment and waiving star billing. Miss Sothern has surely made worse decisions than playing Sade in her career, but one of the many things about this picture that disturbed the public and press alike was: what ultimately happened to Ann Sothern, who was locked in a closet by a young hoodlum (James Caan) 20 minutes before the picture's end and never released? Well, in the uncut version Miss Sothern *was* released—from those mortal coils, by the young hoodlum who strangled her. And there are stills to prove it, the actress' tongue lolling, flapping, recoiling in a dramatic fashion that might have meant an Oscar nomination. Perhaps the producers reasoned that there was too much brutality and sadism already in this little shocker; but if so, they reasoned wrong, leaving viewers of the cut film with a sense of dramatic dissatisfaction at not knowing what had happened to their old pal, Maisie. Along with some other hanging items, like what ever happened to Miss de Havilland's suicide-bent son? There are Paramount stills indicating resolution of this matter, too (he returned home)—in the uncut version, that is.

Apparently none of this bothered Miss Sothern who, just before *Cage* opened, told a reporter, "It's the best thing I've ever done." Or maybe she just didn't know her death scene had been cut—that's happened, too—or didn't care. Anyway, even unresolved the part got Miss Sothern noticed again and brought more work. Miss de Havilland, a great actress with a musical voice by which even articles of speech sing, who also has always seemed to have a surprisingly healthy psyche (considering), has been extremely loyal to a movie generally referred to as sick but no joke. "It was ahead of its time," she had said about a film that almost was shelved.

Time was the topic in MGM's *36 Hours* the same year, a far-fetched but diverting melodrama about a man (James Garner) in on the allies' World War II invasion at Normandy who was captured by Germans pretending to be Americans. They tried to convince Garner that it was six years later, thereby freeing him to reveal the date of the still pending invasion. Rod Taylor—who has just the right manly charm, personality and twinkle in a romantic clinch, the only actor yet developed by Hollywood who could possibly inherit the Gable crown—was the Americanized German doctor in charge of the bogus U.S. hospital in which Garner awoke; and Eva Marie Saint, with a German accent that came and vent (mostly went), was the concentration camp refugee forced to feign marriage to the American. Only Taylor gave a performance, though (both Garner and Saint were completely without the Errol Flynn flair needed to carry off this hokum), although Bosley Crowther rapped Taylor as too American—Taylor was born and raised in Australia. One of Eva Marie's big moments, in all fairness, was cut. It was the scene in which she was beaten by two Nazis when it was learned she had aided the American, and she got to writhe in agony, thereby joining an audience that would have been way ahead of her, having been exposed to Saint-ly inertness for well over an hour. All that remained in the film of this business were several close-ups of Miss Saint in sweat, either before or after the thrashing; one can never rely on Miss Saint's face to explain things.

As with *Lady in a Cage,* the brutality may have caused the cut, although it is more likely to have been excessive length or the fact that time had softened our feelings toward the sadistic Nazis of our 1940s movies. Unlike *LiaC,* there was no question of an overabundance of brutality in *36 Hours.* Just the opposite. In fact, most of the Germans were far from menacing, more like comic opera mittel Europeans. If the heroine's beating had been left in, viewers would have had a better reason to hiss those mainly fumbling, funny old Germans.

Miss Saint had another good role a few years earlier in the sensitive *All Fall Down.* (What she did with it was something else.) Nevertheless, the picture suffered from a slight case of *A Star is Born*itis: the ill-starred affair between Miss Saint and the younger n'er-do-well Warren Beatty was never as affecting as it might have been because some of their togetherness had been cut, leaving the audience with, if not exactly the so-what attitude at the suicidal conclusion of the cut *Star,* at least a semi-detached too-bad. (Forget that both Saint and Beatty were at the kitchen sink when charm was passed out.)

Films and Filming had as one of its covers a scene in an amusement park shooting gallery between Saint and Beatty from *All Fall Down* that never appeared in the movie.

As for Claire Bloom, a beautiful and skilled actress who deserves only the best treatment on film but rarely gets it (Claire was the girl who—if anyone—should have done the *Cleopatra* Elizabeth Taylor botched), she had an intriguing role in the ghost story, *The Haunting* (1963), also starring Julie Harris. Miss Bloom played a lesbian artist with extra sensory perception who unfortunately didn't sense that her girlfriend would leave her. The scene which provided these little character insights was cut; and what remained was a shadowy woman with little background explanation who spent most of her role's running time hugging Miss Harris in crises.

By the time Miss Bloom's *The Outrage* rolled around a couple of pictures later, topcasting Paul Newman and directed by Martin Ritt, she was able to say, "After looking at the rushes I could predict what scenes would be cut. They'd be my best ones."

Miss Bloom's next screen appearance was in 1965's *The Spy Who Came in from the Cold* for director Ritt, too, whom you'll recall guided *Hud,* from which Patricia Neal said her best scene had been excised. In a column many months after his review of *Spy,* Andrew Sarris revealed: "Some time ago I was prowling through the Paramount photo files, and discovered a still of Richard Burton and Claire Bloom in *The Spy Who Came in from the Cold,* he obviously ill in bed and she ministering to him tenderly. This sequence was not in the film as it was finally released, and yet it was crucial to an understanding of the girl's emotional commitment to the hero. At the time of my review I had no idea that Ritt had shot this scene, and that it was part of the original conception of the movie. Normally I would not even mention this fact, but it is typical of the additional information that keeps piling up long after a reviewer has rendered his magisterial judgment. This is why no judgments of films can ever be final."

Miss Bloom suffered a similar fate in the film version of Irving Wallace's compendium of copulation, *The Chapman Report* (1962), during this period. Said director George Cukor: "It was my idea to get four rather appetizing girls, to counteract the vulgarity. You had Claire Bloom, for instance, playing a rather high-minded woman who did ignoble things; but in the cutting they removed whatever they thought wasn't lurid, so that the justification for her was cut out, and it became the conventional, sensational thing."

The "they" to whom Cukor referred was Darryl Zanuck, who, after the first preview, was allowed to cut *Chapman Report* (while he was involved with his own production, *The Longest Day*). His son, Richard, was the producer of *Chapman.*

In a later interview, Cukor was franker: "He emasculated it. It was RUINED. When he brought it back to Warners it was absolutely incoherent. Zanuck said, 'I promise you on my word of honor . . . here's my son to bear me out . . . we'll preview it once with the recut version that I did, then we'll preview it your way.' The next thing I knew I was holding a wire in my hands: 'I FIND THERE IS A CLAUSE IN THE CONTRACT. WE DON'T HAVE TIME FOR PREVIEWS. THE PICTURE MUST BE RELEASED IMMEDIATELY SO THE LAST CUT PRINT WILL HAVE TO GO OUT.' I wrote Zanuck a very indignant wire, then he sent me one back, very long and very nasty. He said that some ex-prizefighter friend of his had seen his version and thought it was great.

"Then the censors made us cut hell out of the picture."

One of the scenes Cukor said was tampered with by Zanuck (not the censor) and which was in for the San Francisco preview of the uncut *Chapman Report* was the one where a group of card players raped Miss Bloom.

"The problem was to show all these men raping her," Cukor recalled. "I thought it would be interesting to start it off as a game . . . the men playing around with her, laughing with her and at her, but all the time being terribly disrespectful. It all started out as a joke with the men pushing her from one place to another. Then they did, in fact, rape her. Then the fascinating thing is that she responded to it. A fast series of cuts of pushing, shoving, grabbing, falling, gasping, arms, legs . . . the men holding her down . . . a marvelous scene, cut out by Zanuck. It was a long thing to shoot and we did many, many takes."

In the released version only the beginning of the scene was shown, where Miss Bloom was pushed down. What was omitted certainly sounds censorable to me, hardly the kind of thing noble characters are built on. ". . . they removed whatever they thought wasn't lurid. . . ." What *would* Cukor call lurid?

The *Chapman Report* cutting incidents rather parallel what occurred on 1958's *Touch of Evil,* starring Orson Welles and, not surprisingly, directed by Orson Welles from a screenplay by Orson Welles. Although given carte blanche on direction, the picture was taken away from him on completion and a few scenes he hadn't directed were added and some he had made were cut—as you will discover (or should already know), this appears to be the story of Welles' screen life.

"They kept all the scenes of violence and cut out the moral ones," Welles complained, à la George Cukor on *Chapman Report.*

The elisions: a humorous scene between Welles and Charlton Heston at the beginning, in which their characters were defined and they became enemies; a scene in which Joseph Calleia drove Janet Leigh to the hotel and explained to her how Welles saved his life years ago, thus crippling himself and necessitating the cane which explained the line, "That's the second bullet I've stopped for you, partner"; the scene in which Marlene Dietrich and Welles spent the night together and he saw Heston passing by the window but didn't identify him with certitude, motivating his later line to Calleia, "I thought you were Vargas"; dialogue between Calleia and Heston in which Heston studied the recording machine used at the end and stated his distaste for that part of his job. Also, the credits were to have appeared at the end instead of the beginning where they interfered with the flow of the opening sequence.

Did all this hurt *Touch of Evil?* A study of corruption, the film has acquired its proponents, but I was too busy observing how Welles (and helpers) went about hiding the fact that femme star Janet Leigh had a broken arm through much of the movie—sweaters casually thrown over the arm was one way, I recall.

A more celebrated Welles film whose cuts have passed into folklore is *The Magnificent Ambersons* produced and directed by Welles immediately after his still peak first production, *Citizen Kane.* Joseph Cotten, Anne Baxter, Tim Holt, Dolores Costello, Agnes Moorehead, Ray Collins, and Richard Bennett headed the cast.

Wrote Peter Bogdanovich: "Since he was not allowed to do the final cut . . . and because a few of the scenes were neither written nor directed by him, it becomes difficult to evaluate exactly what Welles wanted the finished film to look like. It is known, for example, that he had shot a lot more footage of the growing, ever-industrializing town than is shown in the movie; clearly it was to have been used as a counterpoint to the Ambersons' decline. Welles was then nearing the end of his tenure at RKO and *Ambersons* is a mutilated work. It is the more amazing that so much of Welles' conception survived the released print."

And Welles has said: "It looks as though somebody had run a lawn-mower through the celluloid." Released in 1942, the running time was 88 minutes.

Robert Wise, director of *West Side Story, The Sound of Music,* and, less creditably, *The Sand Pebbles* and *The Andromeda Strain,* was deeply involved in the filming of *Ambersons* and tells a different story.

After completing *Citizen Kane,* the very young Welles seemed terrified of recording some loops (the insertion of dialogue or other sounds after filming) that were needed and he kept postponing the dubbing session, recalls Wise. When Welles finally did show up he adapted to looping with the greatest of ease and was so fascinated by the whole procedure he decided to take it a step further on *Ambersons* and make a pre-production recording and have the actors work back to it! He assembled the cast, rehearsed them thoroughly, and recorded the entire script. But the day the camera rolled the actors could neither synchronize their lips and movements to the recording nor, with the pressure of it all, act. The innovation, which struck everybody except Welles and the actors as a howl, was not resumed after lunch.

"War was declared in the middle of *Ambersons* production and Nelson Rockefeller approached Welles about making a film in South America (as part of the Good Neighbor Policy)," Wise said. "Welles agreed to report the latter part of February, '42. Although already committed to the Lady Esther radio series, he decided to take on still another project, *Journey into Fear,* so he could clean up his schedule at RKO. He directed *Ambersons* in the day, acted in *Journey* at night (with Norman Foster directing) and on Sundays managed to record 15 shows for Lady Esther."

When he got behind on *Ambersons* he put another camera on it and allowed film editor Wise to direct a couple of scenes. The first sneak preview of *Ambersons* was a fiasco: it was thought to be slow-moving with all the laughs in the wrong places. When Welles was not available for further work on it, Wise made a few cuts which seemed to make the second sneak go better, but the picture still didn't seem right. Wise felt that the war was causing audiences' lack of interest in the theme. He cut some more, also wrote and directed two short scenes to bridge some major eliminations. The third preview's reaction was acceptable, and the picture was released (as was Welles, from his contract, RKO then boasting the slogan: "Showmanship in Place of Genius").

This has been Wise's version. Here is Welles':

"Five, maybe six reels of *Ambersons* are exactly as I cut them before leaving for South America, with the exception of a single cut in the middle of a very long traveling shot. The cut involved a couple of remarks about 'olives'—a novelty in the town. Don't ask me why they wanted it out. The result was a useless jump in an otherwise unbroken scene. I also cut the last part of Ambersons, but it was completely re-done after a preview. About 45 minutes were cut out—the whole heart of the picture, really—for which the first part had been a preparation. The closing sequence in the hospital was written and directed by somebody else. It bears no relation to my script."

Wise feels no guilt about his work on it. "The film I had to work with was tops," he explained. "No cutter can ever take bad film and make it good. He can, though, turn a good picture into a lousy one if he's not in tune with what the picture is all about. We had a picture with major problems, and I feel all of us tried sincerely to keep the best of Welles' concept and still lick the problems. Since *Ambersons* has become something of a classic, I think it's now apparent we didn't 'mutilate' Orson's film."

The significant footage omitted included, besides the industrial documentation, a veranda scene, shot in darkness, with only the Ambersons' voices heard discussing their crumbling fortunes; the silent sequence in which the camera roamed the sheeted, empty rooms of the once lively Ambersons household; and a final duologue between Cotten and Moorehead in the boarding house that was once the Ambersons mansion.

Cotten also had figured in one of the scenes cut from *Citizen Kane,* the thinly disguised life of publisher William Randolph Hearst on which Welles reportedly was autonomous to the controversial end. The scene in point, as seen in a photo still that managed to escape, showed Welles and Cotten to be on the town and dining with a pair of doxies (one of whom was played by Frances Neal, Mrs. Van Heflin for many years, and completely cut from *Kane*) when they were joined by Everett Sloane. More extensive—and meaningful—was the cut courtship of Welles and Ruth Warrick, who became Kane's wife. Miss Warrick has said this omission robbed their relationship of considerable dimension.

Actor-director José Ferrer was initially thought to be almost as promising a "boy wonder" as Welles, but he still does not seem to be heading toward a *Citizen Kane.* Ferrer has had his difficulties, too, unluckily on two of his most important directorial-starring efforts: *The Great Man* (1956), an unflattering portrait of an air personality that couldn't help bring to mind Arthur Godfrey, and *I Accuse!* (1958), based on France's Alfred Dreyfus scandal.

"On *The Great Man,*" Ferrer once said, "I was given complete autonomy and the only place that I ran into any trouble at all was that I felt that the cutting was much too sharp: the producer and the head of the studio took out one or two scenes that I thought were fairly valuable. I don't know that the picture was enormously damaged, but in each case texture had gone. In the case of *I Accuse!* the producer took out something like 20 minutes which I violently disagreed with. I felt that a great deal of quality was taken out, the cutting just hewed to a plot line rather than a character and story line."

Jules Dassin, American-born director and husband of Melina Mercouri, began in Hollywood but made his name in Europe. Two of his last films at home—*Brute Force* in '47 and *The Naked City* in '48—while successful were chopped up by Universal-International, which thoroughly disheartened Dassin, who was soon to be blacklisted there, anyway.

He has said that they threw away about a quarter of *Brute Force,* "cut its very reason for being. For me, it's just a skeleton. All that remains is violence with no reason for it. The character of the warden, you know, was based on a real warden that I knew. While researching for the film I lived for ten days in a prison in California

—not Alcatraz—and there I met this warden. He was a man of enormous charm and considerable cruelty; a very cultivated, educated man. I tried to re-create him on the screen, but it was cut to hell. There was one scene, where he was punishing a prisoner, that I shot like a love scene. For me it was a strange, terrible, erotic love scene. But they cut out the essentials."

Dassin comments on *Naked City:* "I hated the scenario, but I agreed to make the film despite the story because I thought I would be able to make the film I had always dreamed of. I said I would do it if they let me film in the streets of New York, in real interiors, with unknown actors. They agreed, but when it came to the editing the very heart of the film was cut out. I worked myself on the editing for ten weeks, day and night. It was very difficult, demanding work, but they cut it all. When I saw *Naked City* for the first time, I could have wept."

Compared to what happened with director Fritz Lang's first two German movies since *The Testament of Dr. Mabuse* (1933), Dassin's—even Welles' and certainly Ferrer's—troubles never happened. Lang's *The Indian Tomb* and *The Tiger of Eschnapur* were released overseas as a double bill, the running time less than three hours, with Debra Paget and Paul Christian. In 1960 American distributors cut the two films down to a combined running time of 90 minutes, called what was left *Journey to the Lost City,* and gave it the look of just another European drive-in spectacular so popular here at the time.

Nineteen sixty-three's *The Stripper* was the last production of long-time Hollywood producer Jerry Wald, then at 20th Century-Fox, who died before he could complete release details. Starring Joanne Woodward, Richard Beymer, Carol Lynley, and Claire Trevor, the film was first intended as a vehicle for Marilyn Monroe but wound up with Woodward attempting an imitation of The Monroe under the direction of TV's Franklin Schaffner, in his film bow.

Darryl Zanuck was not happy with the original version, titled *A Woman in July* (from the William Inge play, *A Loss of Roses*), and changed the title to the more commercial *The Stripper.* He cut several scenes—including a dance The Woodward did that might have justified the new title—to bring the footage down from just under two hours to 95 minutes. Nothing helped, although audiences *were* spared some of Woodward's Method "allure."

If anything can be said to forget faster than the public, it is the studio.

A week before Fox's *A Guide for the Married Man* opened early in '67, George Jessel plugged his "cameo" appearance in the film on *The Merv Griffin Show.* Jessel did not know that the studio where he had been an important producer in the '40s and '50s (*The Dolly Sisters, Nightmare Alley, When My Baby Smiles at Me, Tonight We Sing,* etc.) had removed his part from the picture.

8. THE LONG SNIPS

Again, not all cutting is criminal—only almost all. Some is legitimate.

In March 1965, George C. Scott (who set precedents when he turned down an Oscar nomination for *The Hustler* and later on the Oscar itself for *Patton,* in favor of the attendant publicity) told an Associated Press reporter that the Dino De Laurentiis production of *The Bible* was running more than 20 hours, and it wasn't even finished. Scott added that his segment (all about Abraham, or Method on the Mount) ran four and a half hours and was only one of six sections. This was all many miles of film before editing, naturally, and when released in September 1966, as a children's-level three-hour feature, the John Huston-directed picture had been reduced (as its title admitted) to merely *The Bible . . . In the Beginning.*

Next, Huston was one of several directors hired to keep the tables turning in Charles K. Feldman's Columbia release, *Casino Royale,* which also had several actors portraying James Bond. Shooting started in late '65 and went on through most of '66, with each expensive day seeming to bring a new, "name" cast addition for a "cameo." When the cameras finally stopped, *Casino Royale* ran about 15 hours. At release it ran an excruciating two hours and 10 minutes.

When his production of *The Longest Day* completed shooting in '62, Darryl Zanuck said: "We have exposed 360,000 feet of film, amounting to 66 hours of footage, and we must reduce this material to something between three and three and a half hours. I don't believe in long pictures unless they have a good reason to be long and can hold an audience's attention. So I will make a decision on the length after I have seen the cut-together sequences." *The Longest Day* ultimately ran about three hours. It only *seemed* to last longer than the D-Day invasion it dramatized.

Take the late Erich von Stroheim, which many a studio couldn't, and whom one producer said had "a fetish for footage." As a director back in the 1920s he turned out three films, *Merry Widow, The Wedding March* and *Greed,* that would probably have run from then till now if they hadn't been severely cut. (They should have happened to some of TV's slice-happy old-movie shows.)

Merry Widow (1925) was Mae Murray's merriest hour as a star (she was Sonia, John Gilbert was Danilo), although she might have had an even better time if the Metro-Goldwyn studio hadn't waltzed off with a barrelful of cut Stroheim footage. Herman G. Weinberg has written: "Much more must have been cut from *Merry Widow.* Existing stills reveal the wedding, wedding feast, nuptial night and sudden death of the Baron Sadoja from an apoplectic stroke; a wild party thrown by the Crown Prince Mirko that degenerates into an orgy; sly sidelights of Prince Danilo's attempted seduction of the dancer, Sally, and of the party thrown by Danilo at Maxim's on the eve of his duel with Mirko; scenes of Sadoja as 'the power behind the throne'; intimate scenes of Queen Milena at bedtime; similar scenes of Danilo being shaved in bed by a lady barber while receiving a feminine visitor; etc."

Wedding March, which started filming in June 1926, and completed the following spring after using up 200,000 feet of film, proved after 12 months of editing attempts to be too much for the director, who gave up and gave Paramount the job. The studio cut it down to conventional feature length, using only the first half, while the mess of leftover film was edited into a second feature called *Honeymoon,* and sometimes *Marriage of the Prince,* but this was released only in a couple of foreign countries and to a few film societies and archives. "Von" had planned his work as the last word on the degeneracy and resulting collapse of Austria-Hungary.

Greed, von Stroheim's most famous film, was made for Metro-Goldwyn and released in 1924—but it was not really the same film he had made. That ran about 40 reels (eight hours) after the first edit and Stroheim suggested M-G show it in two parts. Instead the studio took it away from him and had June Mathis, a staff writer (and with Stroheim, credited with the screenplay), trim it; and the result was a ten-reel *Greed* that Stroheim allegedly refused to look at for years. Nevertheless, the work bore the unusual credit: "Personally directed by Erich von Stroheim."

In his book, *The Liveliest Art,* Arthur Knight wrote: "Perhaps the full measure of the greatness of *Greed* is to be found only by comparing what remains with the original novel [*McTeague*]. So faithful was von Stroheim to the text that his intentions are clear in every scene, even though the structure of the story and the development of its characters were destroyed in the course of re-editing his footage. Such minor characters as the swaggering, cigar-smoking charwoman, for example, seem much too strongly drawn for the insignificant roles they play in the film, unless one remembers that originally they were the principals in an important subplot. . . . Similarly, the strange, symbolic inserts of hands caressing golden cups and fingering sparkling jewels which seem so out of keeping with the rest of the picture were actually salvaged from the avaricious dreams of the old junk dealer. Occasionally in the lengthy subtitles used to supplant eliminated action, abrupt references are made to ideas and incidents for which there is no longer any visual preparation. Worst of all, the McTeagues' descent from middle-class respectability to direst poverty takes place so quickly, so badly as to tax one's credulity. Small wonder that *Greed* remains one of Metro's most expensive flops. It confused and bewildered audiences through what it didn't show—while what it did show is mighty strong meat even for audiences today."

Richard Griffith and Arthur Mayer in *The Movies* went further: "Audiences were not indifferent to it or bored by it—they actively hated it."

In *The Film Till Now* Paul Rotha called *Greed* von Stroheim's greatest picture, "despite its faults: the gold coloration, the too sudden development of the wife's miserly character, the ridiculous makeup of Gibson Gowland as McTeague." (He was referring to Gowland's Harpo Marxist blond coiffure.)

"It is interesting to note," continued Rotha, "that Stroheim's explanation for the length of *Greed* . . . was that he used no more film than was absolutely necessary for the filmic expression of his theme. This is an evasive statement typical of Stroheim, to which there is no answer. Nevertheless, the copy generally shown left much to be desired in editing. The film fell evenly into two halves. It is assumed that the transition period after the wedding was eliminated, an unfortunate act that took weight from the otherwise brilliant performance of ZaSu Pitts as the hoarding wife. Her acting, under the control of Stroheim, had seldom been equalled by any other American screen actress."

Rotha was amazed that the always showmanship-minded Metro-Goldwyn company had allowed *Greed* to be completed, "the essence of sordidness, the depth of depression and the horror of distorted human nature."

A writer to *Films in Review* said it was incorrect to assume that "most of the legendary missing footage" of *Greed* consisted of sequences dealing with the sub-plot involving Dale Fuller (the charwoman) and Cesare Gravina: "Many of Stroheim's original flashback sequences detailing McTeague's early life, his drunken father, his mother's desire for him to become a dentist, etc., were discarded (what was retained from this flashback was used chronologically at the beginning of Metro's 10-reel version). Also discarded were scenes of McTeague in the trolley car conductors' coffee joint; of Trina's family, especially her uncle who held part of Trina's money; of McTeague's wanderings around San Francisco after Trina's murder; of his gradual breakdown on the desert as he realized he couldn't escape (before Marcus finds him).

"The most important discards were scenes showing how McTeague fell in love with Trina, her change in character after winning the lottery and the slow decay of their relationship both before and after the wedding."

Following a 1965 TV showing of the release print of *Greed,* guest William K. Everson revealed that he knew of at least three occasions on which Stroheim had seen his cut film, and he understood the director was not as upset about its treatment as history has it.

Everson said the discarded subplot was impressionistic for the most part and would have clashed with the realistic approach of the main plot line.

Also a guest on the same program, Daniel Talbot, manager of

the New Yorker Theater (specializing in old films), said he felt the film could be even shorter than its approximate one hour and 45 minutes, adding that much more of its "uncompromising realism would have been too much to sit through." He mentioned that there are rumors that MGM has a print of the original eight-hour version in its vaults.

To which Everson replied, with the confident air that every truck driver was as conversant with them as he, "It's that time of the year. *Greed* rumors always begin circulating about now."

Early in '66, producer-director-writer Albert Lewin told me: "I was a script clerk on the old Goldwyn lot while *Greed* was being made—it was filmed during the changeover to Metro-Goldwyn. I may be the only person still alive who has seen the original, uncut *Greed* as von Stroheim, a genius, filmed it. Frank Hull cut the picture, and I was a close friend of Frank's and used to sit in on the film with him. It took me about three days to see it and it ran about 70 reels! But it was all so brilliant, I can't help feeling that the way it was cut is the greatest single tragedy in the history of the film business. Some time after its release, Margaret Booth, eventually head cutter at the studio, searched all the vaults for any remaining footage, but she said there was nothing left, everything had been scrapped."

Nineteen sixteen's surpassingly spectacular *Intolerance,* although directed by an early master (most agree *the* master), D. W. Griffith, set no boxoffice bonfires, either, yet today it likewise is much-esteemed. In its early editing stages, however, the film *really* would have made audiences intolerant: presenting four parallel stories from history, *Intolerance* could have unreeled continuously for about a full day.

According to Eileen Bowser, Assistant Curator of the Museum of Modern Art in New York, Griffith, as was his habit, followed *Intolerance* around the country during first-runs, cutting it right in the theaters in the hopes of improving it. The print shown in New York, therefore, was not necessarily the one shown in Boston.

Three years after its release, Griffith, deeply in debt from its costs, sent out the Babylonian and modern segments of the film as separate features in the hopes of paying off his creditors, but again—nothing.

"Inasmuch as there was no written record," Miss Bowser explained, "it was never possible to restore the *Intolerance* negative to its original state, and any attempt to do so from memory was delayed for many years because the negatives of 'The Fall of Babylon' and 'The Mother and the Law' were still needed to fill print orders. Meanwhile, the original prints of *Intolerance* began to wear out, and portions were cut because of damage or deterioration. The studio records show that Griffith personally tried to reconstruct good prints for the major revivals of *Intolerance* over the years, but they were always short of the original length by at least two reels. Important as *Intolerance* is to film history, to Griffith it was a financial loss, and he did not care to spend more money insuring that there should be good protection material."

In the late 1950s, Griffith discovery and *Intolerance* player Lillian Gish told an English reporter: "*Intolerance* is still one of the greatest pictures ever made. Griffith wanted it to run three-and-a-half or four hours, you know; but he had to cut it to please the exhibitors. That race apart—exhibitors! Of course, he should never have given way. Right at the beginning he could be very firm indeed. Later, though, he couldn't. . . . In the long run, *Intolerance* did a disservice to the industry. It set a fashion for expensive pictures. Everybody wanted his picture to cost more than the next man's.

"Mr. Richard Griffith [no relation] of the Museum of Modern Art wants me to re-edit *Intolerance* some day—to put it back to Griffith's original idea. Of course, it would take a great deal of time."

Another "silent," *The Cabinet of Dr. Caligari,* made near Berlin in 1919 and one of the most famous pictures of all time, was re-made in 1962, minus the *Dr.,* as *The Cabinet of Caligari.* But it got plenty of doctoring.

Produced and directed by Roger Kay, the Robert (*Psycho, Strait-Jacket, The Night Walker,* and *The Deadly Bees*) Bloch screenplay took great liberties with the original, and the newer *Caligari* has nowhere near matched the acclaim of its predecessor. But it was an interestingly devious and exotic approach to the story of a mental patient, done with a maximum of mood-setting photography and effects, and who knows, it may one day be "discovered."

Meanwhile, it can be noted that the film had quite a different ending at first. As the woman patient in question (Glynis Johns) prepared to leave the asylum, cured, the psychiatrist (Dan O'Herlihy) waved goodbye to her—and then put on the wig and beard of

Caligari, the evil villain of the woman's aberration, to indicate that she really was not well yet.

Admitted Robert Lippert, the executive producer of this *Caligari:* "From our screening in New York we found the tempo somewhat on the slow side, especially in the early portion, and by very judicious re-editing we eliminated 11 minutes and achieved what we were looking for. We also eliminated the so-called double ending with which we went back to Caligari. Since we had told the whole thing through the eyes of the woman, this little piece of business was the only untrue part of the film. Therefore, we now end the picture with her leaving with her son and the camera going over the grounds and coming to rest on the kind smile on Paul's face."

It also would appear that slowness prompted some cuts in Greta Garbo's 1935 version of *Anna Karenina.* In the released print and the one that's been revived in theaters and on TV over the years, things still moved pretty lugubriously for a picture that ran only about an hour and a half. It has been suggested that some of the cuts may have taken place soon after Anna and her Count Vronsky (Fredric March) met, for their ill-fated affair was given little build-up. Anyway, one still photo that has been around shows Garbo sitting at a banquet table surrounded by officer comrades of the lover she would eventually give up. Such a scene is not to be found in the final prints of *Anna Karenina.* A younger Garbo got her man in the U. S. version of *The Temptress* (1926) but had to sacrifice the juicier acting opportunities in becoming a prostitute and dying—which was the way the European version ended. (Forty years later, times had changed and Hollywood scribe Mike Connolly noted the following: "Metro revised *The Cincinnati Kid* for its overseas showings. Instead of the downbeat domestic ending, the foreign version shows Tuesday Weld and Steve McQueen riding happily off into the sunset.")

In *The Temptress* H. B. Warner had had a prominent role that was discarded and re-filmed with Lionel Barrymore.

DeWitt Bodeen, biographer of screenwriter Frances Marion, has attributed the following information to Miss Marion, who wrote the 1927 "adaptation" of Garbo's *Love* from Anna Karenina: "Shooting of *Love* began under the direction of Dimitri Buchowetski with Ricardo Cortez and Lionel Barrymore playing opposite Garbo. Halfway along production was halted and $200,000 worth of film was junked. Shooting resumed with Edmund Goulding directing and with Norman Kerry and Marc McDermott in the male leads. Meanwhile, *Flesh and the Devil* had opened to big boxoffice acclaim for the team of Garbo and Gilbert. MGM junked another $100,000 worth of film and began a third time, with Goulding again directing but with Gilbert and Brandon Hurst in the roles of lover and husband." It has been said that Barrymore was replaced because his sardonic villainy had overshadowed Garbo.

Alfred Hitchcock's weirdo *Spellbound* (1945) found its Salvador Dali-designed dream sequences severely cut for general release, for reasons less clear than those offered for the *Caligari* omissions. Producer David O. Selznick did accuse Hitchcock of getting Dali mainly for publicity purposes. But Hitchcock has said, "That wasn't true. I felt that if I was to have dream sequences, they should be vivid. I didn't think that we should resort to the old-fashioned blurry effect that they got by putting vaseline around the lens." Apparently Hitchcock wound up with too much of a good thing, for stills keep popping up of sequences designed by Dali that never appeared in the picture.

There are wonderfully naive stills available, too, showing Lewis Stone being impaled by a huge torture mechanism in 1932's *The Mask of Fu Manchu.* (One kitchen knife would have accomplished the same end, although not in as cinematically thrilling a fashion.) Boris Karloff as Fu watched while Lew got run through. But wait! This scene was cut, and in final form Jean Hersholt, a beefier type, was strapped to the impaling device on the theory that it looked more frightening for a fat man to be stuck.

This kind of executive reasoning hurt *Invasion of the Body Snatchers* (1956), with Kevin McCarthy, Dana Wynter, and Carolyn Jones, according to its director, Don Siegel—but not enough to keep it from becoming a near-model in science fiction-horror filmmaking. Siegel recently said: "Most 'special effects pictures' spend millions on effects (we spent $3,000); have too-wooden characters in front of the effects act badly or strangely and come up with a poor film. My idea, which producer Walter Wanger enthusiastically endorsed, was to face the problem of divulging the idea of 'pods' taking over the world as *normally* as possible. By that I mean that obviously in real life if one were to state 'look out, pods are about to take over' no one would take one seriously and rightly so. So that's what we did.

In the picture the various characters, when first learning about the pods, did not take it seriously, but when they were suddenly face to face with this monstrous horror, their reaction was genuine—as it would be in real life. Allied Artists took Wanger's and my final cut of *Invasion of the Body Snatchers* and cut all the humor because in their hallowed words 'Horror films are horror films and there's no room for humor.'

"In addition they forced me, against Wanger's desire, to shoot a prologue and an epilogue. I resisted shooting this mish-mash as long as I could until they threatened to have one of the janitors shoot it if I refused. In Wanger's and in my version the very last shot of the picture was a close shot of Kevin McCarthy pointing his finger directly at the audience, screaming, "You're next!' At that moment the picture abruptly and very dramatically ended. And what a stir it created when we previewed it this way. When the lights came up everyone looked nervously at his immediate neighbor at either side of him and wondered uneasily if he were surrounded by pods."

Sitting in on a 1965 Columbia University School of Journalism class conducted by film critic Judith Crist, I heard Mrs. Crist sound off to her students on the reviews they had just turned in. She particularly warned them to avoid commenting on areas of filming they knew nothing about, and told them not to believe *anything* the movie companies told them or wrote about their current film releases. She cited the case of Burt Lancaster's *The Train,* which they had reviewed, and one particular passage in a young lady's review: ". . . *The Train* is two hours and 23 minutes of exciting melodrama."

"*Always* look at your watch when the film begins," cautioned Crist. "*The Train* was not two hours and 23 minutes but two hours and 13 minutes. It had been cut since it was first shaped up for release. And, I suspect, cut plenty before *that,* too."

There appear to be no real rules where cutting is concerned. The all-wise director can be wrong on occasion; and the actor, the last person normally to be consulted on the matter of scene cutting (where bloody battles have been fought for one more close-up, reason can reasonably be expected to be at a minimum), can sometimes be right.

In his autobiography, *A Tree is a Tree* (". . . Shoot it in Griffith Park," goes the rest of the quote), King Vidor explained about a near-cut involving the Selznick epic Western, *Duel in the Sun,* for which Vidor got sole director's billing although it has been said the producer ultimately fired him and had William Dieterle finish the picture. (Josef von Sternberg had directed for a week when Vidor was ill.)

"After the preview," Vidor wrote, "I saw that the episode in which Gregory Peck blew up a freight train, killing the engineer and fireman, was distasteful to the audience, destroying what little sympathy they had for the character. I decided to make one last plea.

"I found David shaving himself in the bathroom of his hilltop home. I used every conceivable argument against the scene. Aside from the bad taste, I pointed out that when Mr. Peck sang 'I've Been Working on the Railroad' as he rode away from the scene of destruction, nothing he could do thereafter would restore him to the good graces of the audience. . . . Presently he turned to me and said: 'I want to make Lewt the worst son of a bitch that's ever been on the motion picture screen, and I believe the train wreck scene will help prove my point.' "

Selznick's theory was evidently correct, Vidor conceded. *Variety* soon reported that *Duel in the Sun* was one of the ten biggest box-office grossers of all time. In production from March 1945 until November 1946, *Duel* was one of Selznick's pet films, critics' barbs notwithstanding. Before release, it also had contained a flashily dramatic exercise for Jennifer Jones that probably was shot down because it proved too similar to Scarlett O'Hara's big scene in the producer's *Gone with the Wind*—which Gregory Peck recently said Selznick always strove to equal, no matter what quality the property—wherein Scarlett made her pledge to the ravaged Southern earth, vowing never to go hungry again. Miss Jones, as the part-Indian Pearl Chavez, hit the soil solo on her shapely knees, too, against a typical florid Selznick sunset to pray for divine guidance in the face of temptation from the bunkhouse. She didn't get it, the censors were quick to note, and Selznick had to make some additional cuts to appease them.

Fox's costly *The Sand Pebbles,* filming almost a year in the Far East under Robert Wise's direction, confounded audiences when it opened late in 1966. Its technique and plot were 1930s antique and its production values (while the running time was a contemporary overlong three hours-plus) were less atmospheric than MGM had managed (in half the footage) on the studio backlot in the old Gable-Harlow *China Seas* days. Everyone wondered where all the time and money went. Star Steve McQueen offered one possibility. He admitted he and Wise had disagreed over the way many scenes were to be done, which resulted in their being shot both ways. Asked how many of his versions showed up in the final cut, McQueen said, "None." The actor's ideas *had* to be better than the ones that were used.

Barbara Stanwyck, four-time Oscar nominee and ever the self-effacing pro and friend of the industry, was queried by me on how she felt about her scenes being cut during her 80-some-movies career, and if there were any scenes she particularly regretted had been cut.

"I never think about my cut scenes," Miss Stanwyck quickly replied. "I never say, I would have won the Award if only that scene hadn't been cut. The producers and directors know more about what's good for the picture than I do." Miss Stanwyck, one of Hollywood's all-time super stars, too often has had inferior vehicles for her "forthright," "dependable" (the adjectives most used by critics to describe her at work) presence, has many times been the only redeeming feature of her films. This was discerned by wise producers and directors who were therefore not wont to cut Stanwyck footage, knowing their mishmashes would be the less for it in more than quantity. (Anyway, so thinks an old FOOFF—Friend of Old Film Femmes.)

Certainly Stanwyck should have no real quarrel with 1944's *Double Indemnity,* one of her few really sound film properties, even if her ill-advised long blonde wig did seem to slip a bit once in a while. This tale of an insurance murder was nominated for Best Picture, and Stanwyck and director-co-scenarist (with Raymond Chandler) Billy Wilder went home with certificates, too. Add to all this the fact that following the first preview about 15 minutes were dropped from the end but *after* Stanwyck had died in the story. Omitted were partner-in-crime Fred MacMurray's trial and execution in the gas chamber, the latter watched by insurance investigator Edward G. Robinson.

Feeling pretty much the same as Stanwyck when I got to him was Ray Milland, long one of Hollywood's best and best-looking leading men.

"Cut scenes! I can't even remember how many films I've made, let alone what's been cut out of them," erupted the 1945 Oscar winner for his acting in *The Lost Weekend,* which also brought Oscars finally to Billy Wilder for his direction and screenplay (with Charles Brackett). "Anyway, I've always felt the director and others in charge know best," added the actor as director of several low-budgeters like *Panic in Year Zero* (more effectively dramatizing an atomic attack on the U. S. than the expensive, star-and-sex-heavy *On the Beach* that came just before and ended the world, one reviewer noted, not with a whimper but a bang—"If only I could've had a few more days on *Panic,* I think I could've turned out a good film," Milland has said.)

Coincidentally, the only cut scene of his he could remember took place on a film that co-starred him with Stanwyck in '46, *California.* "I was quite a horseman and trick rider before I went into films," Milland recalled. "And in *California* there was a scene in which I got to do some real riding for the first time in pictures—there was a series of rocks, gaits, rocks, almost like a steeplechase. But the ride was sandwiched between two closely related scenes and was thought to be too long. It was cut. So . . . this one thing I was very proud of and could do well got the axe."

Milland added that all the main film shot for *Lost Weekend* was shown, "Except in Europe, where the scene showing the mouse in the wall being attacked by the bat during the alcoholic's delirium was thought too brutal and was cut."

Gordon MacRae had an experience almost exactly like Milland's on *California* when MacRae took on Rodgers and Hammerstein's *Oklahoma!* (1955). As told to me: "I went on a cowboy kick to prepare for the role. I was broke. I had just bought out my contract with Warner Brothers and did not even know yet whether I had the part of Curly in *Oklahoma!* I wanted so much. But every morning Ben Johnson—who is a real cowboy and has been in many Western films—and I would go out into the field and ride, and I learned to rope."

"When I got *Oklahoma!,*" continued MacRae, "we eventually came to a scene in the script that called for me to ride along in the sunset and rope a steer. Now all my hard work would be put to use. We waited five days to get the sunset just right, and I did the scene with only a minimal assistance—the producers weren't about to entrust the *entire* dangerous operation to their star. Later on, it was cut. Boy, was I mad. To hell with the rest of the thing, I felt; I wanted to show what I could do on a horse!"

The late Dudley Nichols, credited with the screenplay for the 1947 filming of Eugene O'Neill's *Mourning Becomes Electra,* 'fessed-up in the mid-1960s: "Actually I only cut the play and added bridges. I avoided mention of the screenplay or taking credit on the screen. *Electra* was made before our present rage for long films and the studio insisted that I cut an hour out of the rough cut (which ran three and a half hours). I think the loss was very injurious. But they said they could not sell so long a film. Some of the more 'shocking' things were dropped, at studio request or demand, and I think this shock value might have made the difference between commercial loss and success."

The popularity of long films today notwithstanding, O'Neill lost out again—as soon as the smoke had cleared—15 years later with the film of his play, *Long Day's Journey into Night.*

Before production began on this originally slavish transportation of play to film, producer Ely Landau called Katharine Hepburn in Hollywood to play the drug-addicted mother of the Tyrones. "Who's doing the script?", demanded Hepburn. Replied Landau: "O'Neill." There was a long pause, then Hepburn cried: "Marvelous!" and agreed to do it. In fact, she was so taken with the idea of doing O'Neill pure that she accepted with haste the other half of Landau's proposition—to work for $25,000 plus a percentage of the take instead of her usual $250,000.

Much Landau publicity before and after the film's release made over the film's almost complete reverence to the O'Neill original. Only 11 pages of the text were cut to get the movie down to three hours. But—after the initial exhibition around the country, and favorable reviews—Landau and director Sidney Lumet allowed more than a half-hour to be relinquished from their now impure endeavor. There has been no publicity on how Miss Hepburn reacted; nor on the feelings of Carlotta Monterey O'Neill, widow of the playwright and careful guardian of his works who, upon seeing the acclaimed Landau-Lumet TV version of *The Iceman Cometh,* had entrusted to Landau the TV-film rights to all of the O'Neill plays that had reverted to her control.

That sacred camel, *Lawrence of Arabia,* although "Best Picture of 1962," had quite a few cuts made after its early engagements as well, especially in England where, I am told, the opening death of Lawrence in a motorcycle crackup was chucked.

Lawrence was very well received when it opened by the brainwashed reviewers who had been touted for months, years, that coming along at last was the rare combination of intellectual scenario and spectacular production that *Lawrence,* to those who managed to stay really awake for its three-hours-plus running time, proved not at all to be. In recent years intellectual status has become increasingly important on the American scene—in this case, where motion pictures are concerned—but unfortunately intellectual supply out there in the theaters has not kept pace with the demand. The brainwashed rushed to *Lawrence,* squirmed, dozed, waited, hoped, dashed off for the water fountain at intermission, squirmed, dozed, waited, no longer hoped—but left the theater singing the praises of *LoA.*

Director David Lean, a classy-looking, post-middle-aged man with fascinating aquiline features, started out as an editor but is a far more arresting figure than most of the men he has starred in his films. Although he has garnered scads of awards for *The Bridge on the River Kwai, Dr. Zhivago, Ryan's Daughter,* and *Lawrence,* all about equally tedious, inflated drags, Lean wisely calls the more modest and moving *Summertime,* with an inspired Katharine Hepburn, his own favorite.

Lean has admitted, too, that he started *Lawrence* without a completed script. "We had only the first part of the script finished when I began shooting," he said. "I'll never do that again, because it necessitated an interruption midway, and there was an imbalance between the two parts. Right after the film opened, I took it and lopped 20 minutes from its three and three-quarter hours. So many critics talked about its excessive running time, and this began to bother the exhibitors. I did the cutting myself. I'm quite objective about it now." For its 1971 reissue, about 15 minutes more was deleted.

"David Lean's Film of Dr. Zhivago" (as the credits read), examining a couple of uninvolving love stories amid an equally uninvolving Russian Revolution, arrived at a cost of more than $11,000,000 with a bagful of cinematic gaucheries unsurpassed in any single film of its pretentions. To list the worst incidents, as I shall now try to do, is to retrace film history at its least glorious:

(1) At a library musicale in old Moscow, Siobhan McKenna said to a fidgeting Geoffrey Keen: "But Boris, this is genius!" To which he replied, "Really, I thought it was Rachmaninoff."

(2) As Rod Steiger was passionately climbing upon Julie Christie in a sleigh, there was an abrupt cut to dragoon rumps falling into their saddles.

(3) Julie Christie, bent on shooting her seducer, learned from his manservant that he was at a party. As she departed, the manservant called out, "Merry Christmas, Miss Lara!" This precipitated another abrupt cut, to the party, where Omar Sharif said to some guests, "Thank you! Merry Christmas to you!"

(4) About to return from the Russian front, where it appeared she had been the only girl, nurse Christie, ironing, told doctor-poet Sharif "But now that we're going, I feel sad"—she looked behind her out the window—"sad"—and back to her ironing—"really sad." Whereupon he kissed her, distracting her enough so that she burned the bandages or what ever she was ironing.

(5) Christie's husband, razor-lipped Tom Courtenay, was wounded in battle—we knew this not because of anything as mundane as seeing him dropped, but because there was a big close-up of his glasses falling into the snow.

(6) Moving to the country with his young wife, Geraldine Chaplin, Sharif discovered Christie was the town librarian. They had a back street affair. Since this film was about Russia, Sharif's key to Christie's apartment was kept—not under a welcome mat or in a flower pot or even over the door—but behind a loose brick. Christie also left him notes there.

(7) Meanwhile, wife Geraldine was pregnant, and when she ran into husband Sharif on the grounds one day, she asked him playfully to feel her stomach.

About the only cliché *Dr. Zhivago* missed was a finale utterance of "Let's go home" from Rita Tushingham, the illegitimate daughter of Sharif and Christie (chosen because she is homely and could personify the wages of sin?), and her man. Perhaps it was accidentally edited out. Definitely cut out of the film were the small roles of a streetwalker and a father confessor encountered by Christie.

To get *Zhivago* ready for its Christmas 1965 release, Lean had worked day and night for two months to cut more than 31 hours of film to three hours and 15 minutes. MGM put special cutting and projection rooms at the director's disposal on the Hollywood lot, adjacent to a bungalow where he could snooze without leaving the studio. He had tried to do some preliminary cutting on weekends while the picture was in production in Spain. "The results were awful," he said. "When I looked at my work a few months later I disapproved completely of my earlier decisions. I had to tear the picture to pieces once again."

After the opening, it was rumored that Lean would be doing extensive re-editing on the film, which pleased critics the least of Lean's Spectacular Quartet. But he said there would be only a few seconds' worth of cuts, involving just a frame here and there. (A year later, Lean was given a hard time by the Indian Government when, to mollify the Soviet Union, it requested 23 cuts in *Dr. Zhivago* for its New Delhi premiere. Lean finally convinced the Government to settle for seven very brief eliminations.)

While *Zhivago*'s Geraldine Chaplin was picking up more publicity than any ingenue of the day for her work in the film (and because she is Charlie Chaplin's daughter), her brother, Michael, was chalking up more coverage than any young rebel of the day because he wouldn't work (and because he is Charlie Chaplin's son). Then Paramount offered Michael a bit part in *Promise Her Anything,* starring Leslie Caron, which he accepted. His one line of dialogue, however, as a pre-hippie in a delicatessen ultimately was cut from it, although he was still visible, pointlessly.

Shortly afterward, Robert Bolt won an Oscar for *Dr. Zhivago* in the category of "Best Screenplay—Based on Material from Another Medium." Upon learning this, I was—in Bolt's own award-winning words—" . . . sad . . . sad . . . really sad."

Marlon Brando, for an actor who's only been around movies since the '50s, is probably responsible for more wasted film than any living actor, even if one only considers *Mutiny on the Bounty* and *One-Eyed Jacks.* His alleged shenanigans caused the *Saturday Evening*

Post to chronicle the *Mutiny* problems under the title, *$6,000,-000 Down the Drain: The Mutiny of Marlon Brando;* and *Time* magazine to review *Jacks* under the heading *The $6,000,000 Method.*

Bill Davidson wrote in the *Post* that Brando had signed to do the re-make of the Clark Gable-Charles Laughton *Mutiny* movie early in 1960, with shooting to begin early in October. The script was not ready then, however, because of Brando's demands that the closing Pitcairn Island sequence be lengthened, but producer Aaron Rosenberg still had 89 cast and crew members on his hands and salary from Oct. 15, including Brando. This, according to Davidson—and everyone he interviewed for the piece over which Brando later sued—merely set the stage for what was to come once the Bounty had set sail.

Davidson went on to note that the picture, by April 1962, was still not finished, and MGM was considering a new ending proposed by Billy Wilder, the sixth writer to be involved in the script. An entirely different, shorter one from that elongated Pitcairn epilogue shot on the Tahiti location had already been done on the MGM sound stages in Hollywood, minus director Lewis Milestone—Sir Carol Reed quit at the beginning because he hadn't been allowed to make Capt. Bligh the hero—who sat in his dressing room and refused to go near Brando or cameras for the two weeks it took to do the Hollywood scenes.

Milestone, that veteran of the Western Front, minced no words. He told the writer that recalcitrance, pettishness, argumentativeness, and sulking "cost the production at least $6,000,000 and months of extra work. I've been in this business for 40 years, and I've never seen anything like it." Few others associated with the production, Davidson reported, had any kind words for Brando, either, in one of the most vitriolic attacks of a major boxoffice star ever published.

At the home stretch the cost of the movie had soared to nearly $20,000,000, more than MGM's combined expenditure for *Ben-Hur* and *Gone with the Wind.* The studio was almost $30,000,000 in the hole by the time *Mutiny* was released in November 1962. The film proved no *Ben-Hur* or *Gone with the Wind;* it most certainly was no *Mutiny on the Bounty* circa 1935, which (with its own mishaps) had cost $1,700,000 and still plays well.

Obviously, Brando had not learned—although he *did* profit by more than a million dollars in *Mutiny* salary—from his 1958 adventures with *One-Eyed Jacks* at Paramount. This was Brando's first independent picture, planned as a medium-budget ($1,800,000) Western. Brando would produce and star, with Stanley Kubrick directing. The latter exited fast, though, leaving Brando at the reins. Brando walked on the set, tossed his script aside and said, "Let's improvise." Wrote *Time:* "For the next six months, at an average cost of $42,000 a day, Brando improvised. Sometimes he just flicked on the cameras and let them roll while his actors ad-libbed—of 11,000 ft. of film exposed one day, he used only 270 ft. in the finished picture. When an actor accidentally belted him, Brando happily reorganized his story to work the incident in. And the end of the picture is not the end Brando had in mind: the actors, in a democratic ballot, voted for one they liked better. . . . With a cast and crew on full salary, he sat for hours beside the Pacific Ocean and waited for the waves 'to become more dramatic.' For a drunk scene, he chug-a-lugged a pint of vodka, got sincerely stoned and reportedly lost his supper—but kept the footage."

(Brando's leading lady in *Jacks,* Mexican actress Pina Pellicer, committed suicide in 1964, leaving a respectable enough period of time from her *Jacks* stint so that Brando couldn't be blamed for this, at least. He has accepted blame, however, for the fate of his *Mutiny* leading lady, Tahiti's Tarita, a fate that at one time, in dressier climes, might have been termed worse than death: he fathered a son with Tarita sans clergy.)

In his *The Dream and the Dreamers,* Hollis Alpert wrote that Brando had dawdled over the cutting, too, of *Jacks,* which at first ran well over four hours. "Improvised performances," Alpert remarked, "tend to run a good deal longer that the usual kind, and the story development had a tendency to waver. Paramount began to battle with Brando. The executives were emboldened now that they had a relatively finished product. Brando was at last persuaded to leave the cutting job in the hands of professional editors. The film was eventually pared down to two hours and 17 minutes of running time."

One of the cut scenes depicted a rape, indicating that Brando was still shuffling to his own music because: (1) the scene had not been censored; and (2) it came during moviedom's smuttiest period up to then and would have been a fashionable little haydown. Co-star

Karl Malden—who was all for Marlon's original concept of the story which showed both good and bad sides of the major characters but which was changed by the studio to make Malden an out-and-out heavy—has said: "A lot of stuff around the ocean was left out —down there in the Chinese fishing village where he was recuperating. There was a Chinese girl in that sequence whom he fell in love with and had a romance with—that's all out. Oh, *big* segments were cut out of that picture."

Time summed up: "Director Brando comes off better than actor Brando, the Method Cowboy, who incessantly mumbles, scratches, blinks, rubs his nose and sulks. In short, Brando plays the same character he always plays, the only character who seems to interest him: Marlon Brando."

Many members of the still existing but diminishing Brando cult —most of them based in New York—are forever bemoaning their idol's sell-out to Hollywood, "when he should be doing serious things on the stage." But, despite his increasing tendency to treat serious roles humorously (or maybe they just turn out that way), what Marlon Brando has cost Hollywood is no laughing matter.

9. STARTING OFF ON THE WRONG FOOTAGE

Anyway, *Mutiny* and *Jacks* did get finished. Many a major production still exists somewhere only as fetus. Josef von Sternberg is an especially notable example of a director who spent a large part of his career shooting—with the best of intentions—film *and films* that were never seen by the moviegoing public.

In 1924, when von Sternberg was still only a Hollywood cutter-turned-assistant-director named Joe Stern, he teamed up with English-born actor George K. Arthur (who much later became the producer of award-winning short subjects) to make an original story of von Sternberg's titled *Salvation Hunters,* featuring Arthur and a girl who'd never acted before, Georgia Hale. After a troubled three-week shooting period (mostly from lack of funds), the film was previewed at a small, third-run Los Angeles theater. The story of two young derelicts (male and female) living on a mud drudge, it proved tiresomely "arty" for the viewers, and von Sternberg removed about a thousand feet of footage. Then Charlie Chaplin saw it, was snowed, and convinced his partners in United Artists, Mary Pickford and Douglas Fairbanks, that their company should distribute the work that one top critic impulsively called "the first great symbolical picture ever made." The profits proved considerable. Chaplin signed Miss Hale for *The Gold Rush;* Miss Pickford signed von Sternberg to direct her; and MGM signed Arthur to an acting contract.

In '26 von Sternberg made *The Exquisite Sinner* at MGM starring Renée Adorée and Conrad Nagel, a romantic comedy of gypsy life set in France also written by von S. Described as extremely subtle by Robert Florey, Sternberg's assistant on the film, the picture was remade completely by Phil Rosen at the request of the studio. The remake was called *Heaven on Earth* and was not as subtle.

Also in '26 Sternberg started *The Masked Bride* at Metro, starring Mae Murray. Florey says: "He shot only four reels before he became disgusted with his assignment, turned his camera to the ceiling and shot the rafters as his departing gesture to the film. But what four reels they were! No one saw them except L. B. Mayer and his gang, Sam Winston (von Sternberg's cutter), Bill Levanway (MGM's head editor), von Sternberg and myself. Just as in the case of the marvelous first version of *The Exquisite Sinner.* If this one had been finished and kept intact at MGM it would still be showing in the cine-clubs and film societies of today; it was a masterpiece. Von Sternberg never shot a piece of film indifferently." Christy Cabanne directed the released *Masked Bride.*

Nineteen twenty-six proved an incredibly unlucky year for von Sternberg, for his *The Sea Gull* (also known as *A Woman of the Sea*) was never released, either, though it was finished—twice. The picture had been written and directed by von S. for Charlie Chaplin as a dramatic comeback vehicle for Edna Purviance, Charlie's ex-leading lady. This has also received extravagant praise from Florey who said that Chaplin didn't like the first version and requested the second, some of which Chaplin directed, that "for reasons of his own, Chaplin decided not to release." Three possible reasons have been given for Chaplin's lock-up of the picture: (1) It was too sophisticated for him to understand; (2) He was furious with von

Sternberg for previewing the picture without his consent; and (3) Eve Southern stole the acting honors from Miss Purviance, who was said to have been in her cups throughout.

Maybe the number six is unlucky for von Sternberg. Late in 1936 he began filming an adaptation of Robert Graves' book, *I, Claudius,* for Alexander Korda. It starred Merle Oberon (Mrs. Korda), Flora Robson, Robert Newton, Emlyn Williams, and, in the title role, Charles Laughton, who was thought to be the ideal choice for the stuttering, limping, imbecile successor to Caligula, as he recently had scored as Nero in *The Sign of the Cross.* But Laughton proved unmanageable to von S., and the director recalled: "When Merle Oberon had a bad concussion in an auto accident, which meant so much delay that all our preparations and contracts were invalidated, it was decided to halt the film. It might have been my most successful work."

Von Sternberg's autobiography (which a wag once sub-titled, "Film History as Re-shaped by Josef von Sternberg") contains a blistering account of his troubles with an almost unbelievably belligerent Laughton. Von S., not intimidated by Laughton's demise only a few months before his book came out, related: "It was not a nightmare. It was a daymare. There was a rumor that the capers indulged in by Claudius were part of a deliberate plan to wreck Alexander Korda, but I cannot give credence to this, as this was too perfect a performance. . . . Beginning with the first limp, [Laughton] dragged a different foot each time, alternating according to his mood, and sometimes attempted to drag them both." To get in the mood, he filled the stage with the recording of the Duke of Windsor's abdication speech, and he seemed positively to *be* Claudius in his difficulty to remember lines, said von Sternberg.

A quarter of a century before von Sternberg's book appeared, *Hollywood* magazine writer Charles Samuels covered the matter with a wider lens. Laughton, it seemed, had agreed to do *I, Claudius* with his friend, the great art director William Cameron Menzies, directing. But Korda then ran into a financial snag and couldn't pay Marlene Dietrich the last $100,000 due on her $350,000 salary for *Knight without Armour,* which she had just done for Korda. Dietrich said that if he would hire her discoverer, von Sternberg, to direct *I, Claudius* she would forget about the last payment. Korda agreed.

Laughton was furious. Wrote Samuels: "Laughton, playing the rascally Roman emperor, was imitating the Prince of Wales, mimicking his voice and all his mannerisms. That meant the picture could never be released in the British Empire." Called down by Korda, Laughton said he aimed to please and would change his acting technique completely. He then, according to Samuels, began imitating Groucho Marx, explaining: "I've studied the life of Claudius and Groucho Marx is a friend of mine. They seem twin souls to me."

Alan Freeman, the British disk jockey who wrote a column for the trade magazine I edit, *Record World,* was among those to report on the first public viewing of *I, Claudius* scenes.

In an early '66 column for us, Freeman recounted: "On Christmas Eve I viewed *The Epic That Never Was* on British TV. It was narrated by Dirk Bogarde and told how the film *I, Claudius* was abandoned after four weeks of filming way back in 1936. We saw the actual 'rushes' of the film, and it was quite fantastic watching the late Charles Laughton struggling on the set to 'find' the man he was playing. There were interviews with Emlyn Williams, Merle Oberon and Flora Robson, and I think it was my own personal 1965 viewing highlight."

The following is from *An Index to the Films of Josef von Sternberg,* published in 1949: "In October, '38, von Sternberg was contracted by MGM on a one-picture agreement to direct a story entitled *New York Cinderella,* intended as Hedy Lamarr's second American film. After her sensational debut in *Algiers,* made on loan-out to another studio, Lamarr proved to be MGM's greatest headache. They weren't quite sure what to do with her. Von Sternberg was probably chosen to direct her because of his memorable handling of Dietrich, and it is assuredly fascinating to consider how he might have treated the woman generally considered to be the most beautiful and exotic film personality since Dietrich. However, after only 18 days of shooting von Sternberg was removed because of a disagreement with production heads as to the manner in which the film was to be treated. Frank Borzage was hastily called in to replace von Sternberg and shooting continued. The title was changed to *I Take This Woman.* When Borzage completed the film it was shelved. Finally, it was once again re-shot by W. S. Van Dyke, and released Feb. 2nd, 1940."

Meanwhile, stills from the discarded version(s) had been issued and used in some publications, which also in some instances listed the original cast line-up: Spencer Tracy, Lamarr, Ina Claire, Walter Pidgeon, Mona Barrie, Louis Calhern, Jack Carson, Marjorie Main, and, possibly, Fanny Brice, along with Borzage as director. When officially released, *I Take This Woman* offered Tracy, Lamarr, Verree Teasdale, Kent Taylor, Barrie, Paul Cavanagh, Calhern, Laraine Day, and Main and was, of course, directed by Van Dyke.

I talked with an aged Walter Pidgeon recently and asked him about *I Take This Woman,* in which Kent Taylor replaced him. "I don't remember working on a picture called that," he said. I reminded him that it was to be Lamarr's first MGM job. "Noooo. . . .", Pidgeon replied. "I did co-star with Hedy in a film, though, called . . ." *White Cargo,* I suggested. "Yes. That was in 1937." I said yes, although *White Cargo* was a 1942 production.

In the late '40s, early-'50s Sternberg did two films for Howard Hughes at RKO with interesting histories, too: *Macao,* starring Jane Russell and Robert Mitchum, which reportedly was almost entirely re-shot by director Nicholas Ray; and *Jet Pilot,* starring John Wayne and Janet Leigh, which was kept on the shelf almost a decade before finally being released and was re-edited and cut by Hughes.

Orson Welles' *It's All True* also was commissioned by Hughes in 1942 and was to have been a trilogy in color of South America, with sequences shot down there. But Welles was recalled to Hollywood and the project abandoned. The Brazilian episode included the Carnival of Rio, which Robert Florey (one of the few who saw all this footage) described as making the carnival sequences in *Black Orpheus* look amateurish. Welles shot 12 reels of the carnival. "They never did anything with this magnificent film," said Florey. "Hughes never let Orson finish it. Too bad!" Actually, some of its footage has been used for stock shots in various movies and TV shows.

Hughes was responsible for much of the chaos that surrounded the filming of *Vendetta,* which was to launch as a star Hughes' discovery, Faith Domergue. What do you want from the guy who discovered Jane (*The Outlaw*) Russell and Mamie Van Doren, whose first film was Hughes' *Jet Pilot* in which she had one line: "Look!"? When she was barely into her teens, Hughes had signed Domergue to a personal contract but never got around to using her on film until about five years had passed, in a supporting role in Jane Russell's *Young Widow* (1946). Max Ophuls started *Vendetta* (based on an antique melodrama called *Colomba*) in 1946; then Preston Sturges took over and shot about 50,000 feet of film and nearly $1,000,000 when he was stopped by producer Hughes, who phoned him at six one morning and said, "Preston, that bad dream you had last night was me—I just bought out your interest in the picture."

Other directors signed on and off. Even ex-maître d' leading man George Dolenz—who, unfortunately (depending on your point of view, actually), did not live to see his young son Micky achieve success two decades later as one of TV's singing-acting *The Monkees*—found himself guiding Miss Domergue through her scenes. And the shooting went on and on.

When *Vendetta* finally was released in 1950, Mel Ferrer was given director's credit, but the film was a dud, and not even a resounding one. Its leading lady also was predestined to failure. Miss Domergue bore too close a resemblance to another film player of the day: Rudy Vallee.

Hughes had more success with Jean Harlow when he made her a star in his *Hell's Angels* (although it was still poking in the same barrel, really), the aerial epic that started shooting in 1926 and, like *Vendetta,* was not finished and released until four years later. The much-jinxed picture was completed and previewed when sound came in and Hughes, who had rushed sound effects into his production, now felt that audiences would demand an all-talking movie. Greta Nissen had played the silent femme lead, but she was ruled out for the planned talkie "remake" because of her Norwegian accent—she played an English woman. Miss Nissen's agent, Arthur Landau, also represented Hollywood newcomer Jean Harlow, and he convinced Hughes that, with a bit of re-writing, *Hell's Angels* would be a natural for her. When the film opened, the reviews—and audiences—bore out the faith Landau and Hughes had in Harlow. Hughes had shot three million feet of film, only to discard 99 per cent of it for the final version of the movie, and spent almost $4,000,000, a sum far beyond any heretofore spent on a moving picture. A considerably abbreviated version of *Angels* was reissued in 1940.

(If more had been known about dubbing voices in the '20s, Harlow's short but platinum career might never have got off the ground in *Hell's Angels.* Hughes refused to dub another's voice for Nissen, insisting he wouldn't believe the picture if she were given someone else's voice and pronunciation. Today, with "runaway" production to foreign climes and tongues, and ever-dissolving international film barriers, producers do not hesitate to hire actors for leads frequently knowing in advance that their voices will be wanting and have to be dubbed by someone else. Ingrid Thulin, after scoring in Ingmar Bergman's Swedish films, was lured to America in 1962 for the leading female role in the expensive *The Four Horsemen of the Apocalypse,* but her accent was unintelligible and it was Angela Lansbury's crisp English voice we heard coming from Ingrid's mouth throughout the long film. Miss Thulin was no sex symbol—she probably ties France's Anouk Aimée as The Screen's Most Asexual Woman. Five years after the *Apocalypse,* she made her American stage debut in a Broadway flop, *Of Love Remembered,* in which her accent, critics noted, was a problem. Unfortunately, Angela Lansbury was occupied a few blocks away at the time with her own stage role as *Mame* and was unable to help. Just as reasonable was the casting of the dung-scuffling young American actor Michael Parks as Adam in *The Bible . . . In The Beginning.* Once he had been created, with reams of publicity showing him and Ulla "Eve" Bergryd in the buff, there was only one thing director John Huston could do: replace Parks' mumblings with the voice of David Warner, star of *Morgan!* a couple of months earlier and a member of Britain's Royal Shakespeare Company.)

Preston Sturges remained director on comedian Harold Lloyd's ill-chosen comeback try, *Mad Wednesday,* begun in '46 with Hughes producing as *The Sin of Harold Diddlebock* and finally released in '49; but Hughes himself took active part in the six months of shooting, re-takes, and editing.

Several years after George Bernard Shaw's *Androcles and the Lion* (1952) was filmed, *Films in Review* reported: "Producer Gabriel Pascal, director Charles Erskine and RKO began *Androcles* with Harpo Marx as Androcles, Rex Harrison as Caesar, and Dana Andrews as the hero. Pascal felt Harpo was 'the perfect Androcles' and the rushes were said to have been brilliant. But after five weeks of shooting Howard Hughes saw Alan Young on a TV show and insisted he be substituted for Harpo as the henpecked little tailor. By the time shooting got underway again only Jean Simmons and Robert Newton were still available to continue in their original roles, so all the footage that had been shot was scrapped and Maurice Evans, Victor Mature, and Young were used. Hughes' decision helped to make *Androcles* one of Hollywood's costliest failures."

One of Hughes' silliest follies was a film begun in '48 with Jane Russell, Frank Sinatra, and another Marx, Groucho, titled *It's Only Money* which, after mulling its two biggest attributes, Hughes had re-named *Double Dynamite* when it opened in 1951. In the meantime, much of the footage accumulated had been thrown out because Hughes had not liked Russell's clothes and wanted outfits that would leave less doubt as to what the new title meant.

Joan Crawford did a film in the early '30s that was completely remade immediately after it was finished, but Joan stayed on to repeat her top feminine part. It was leading man Johnny Mack Brown who had been relinquished in favor of the rising newcomer, Clark Gable.

Joan and Clark had done a scene together in the previous *Dance, Fools, Dance,* which had gotten considerable attention around Metro. Although Gable had had a relatively small role in *Dance,* he had one scene that demanded he grab Joan and threaten the life of her brother, the impact of his nearness making her knees buckle for real. "If he hadn't held me by both shoulders I'd have dropped," Joan has said.

"My next picture was *Complete Surrender,* with Johnny Mack Brown as the Salvation Army man who restores this cabaret girl's self-confidence. After the preview Mr. Mayer called us back for a total remake. Johnny's performance was excellent, but Mr. Mayer had seen the chemistry between Clark and me and thought he scented boxoffice dynamite. This time the picture was called *Laughing Sinners* and Clark Gable was the Salvation Army man."

One of the most troubled pictures of the 1940s was the Greer Garson vehicle at MGM, *Desire Me,* which many feel clinched her fall from Queen of the Lot. Based on a novel by Leonhard Frank called *Karl and Anna,* which had been filmed in Germany in '28 as *Homecoming,* it had as working titles *A Woman of My Own* and *Sacred and Profane* and gave Garson—who was almost drowned during the shooting—Robert Mitchum and newcomer Richard

Hart as leading men (and for a comparable trio of Frenchmen one had to go back almost a decade to the Ritz Brothers as *The Three Musketeers*). It was directed at various times by Jack Conway, Mervyn LeRoy, and, mostly, George Cukor, but script problems were insurmountable and when the picture opened in 1947 no director was credited on the screen. Even more interesting: actor Hart—who died of a heart attack a few films later—was hired long after the movie's start, and his part originally was played by a bearded Robert Montgomery. The studio's key still books have many photos of Montgomery in them—more than of Hart, actually.

Less well known is the fact that Lana Turner started an MGM film in the early '40s called *The Sun is My Undoing,* which was stopped suddenly early in production. It was about the African slave trade and co-starred an unknown black girl. Tyrone Power was well into the filming of *Solomon and Sheba* (1959) when he died of heart seizure. United Artists put aside the Power material and began again with Yul Brynner. Powell also was involved, indirectly, in the routing given some footage taken on African location by Otto Bower and Mrs. Osa Johnson for the film *Stanley and Livingstone* (1939), which was to star Power. The second unit had used Power's double for the location shooting; but when 20th Century-Fox was able to borrow Spencer Tracy from MGM for the role of Stanley, the scenes with Power's double had to be cut off before he got too close to the camera. Tracy himself filmed a few scenes in the mid-'50s for *Tribute to a Bad Man,* but when he became difficult director Robert Wise had MGM fire Tracy and replace him with James Cagney.

In the early 1930s, MGM's head scenic designer, Cedric Gibbons, pestered the studio to be allowed to direct his own film. The studio acquiesced with *Tarzan and His Mate* (1934), but featured player Neil Hamilton has said: "Cedric did not direct *Tarzan and His Mate.* 'Gibby' had always wanted to direct and they finally gave him that film. He shot 127,000 feet. It was scrapped and re-shot by Jack Conway. Rod La Rocque was in *Tarzan and His Mate* but when 'Gibby' was taken off the picture, La Rocque was replaced by Paul Cavanagh."

But the scissors had not finished with *Tarzan and His Mate* (many believe it to be the best of the Tarzan films). An erotic swimming scene between stars Johnny Weissmuller and Maureen

O'Sullivan—one that was said to "flow across the screen like a poem"—was eliminated either after the previews or during the film's showings. It was edited out of the negative and not usually included in prints shown during later runs, reissues, or on TV (in the United States, anyway). The deletion was the result of complaints from various quarters because O'Sullivan and her double had not taken their brassieres to the lake that day.

The next Tarzan tale, *Tarzan Escapes* (1936), was almost completely re-filmed, according to Ape Man authority Rudy Behlmer: "The entire Karl Brown/John Farrow/Louis Mosher script was re-written by Cyril Hume, and a major character was added to provide comic relief (Herbert Mundin). Also, some high-powered melodrama involving vampire bats was cut after proving in previews to be excessively gruesome for the juvenile trade. Hunt Stromberg's assistant, Sam Zimbalist, replaced Phil Goldstone as producer, and James McKay, who was responsible for the staging of some of the animal sequences in *Tarzan and His Mate,* and who had been given complete directorial reins on the first version of *Tarzan Escapes* (although others contributed—including William Wellman), was replaced on the re-shooting by Richard Thorpe."

Twentieth Century-Fox could waste film with the best. It was said that long-time studio boss Darryl F. Zanuck liked to cut all motivations out of his company's productions. When called on this, he reportedly would reply, "Let the audience think."

Laura, the now classic screen mystery, originally had been completed in 1944 with a couple of endings. One, championed by director Otto Preminger, found Clifton Webb the murderer in the dénouement; the other, filmed against Preminger's wishes, had Webb realize he had imagined the whole thing. The latter was the favorite with Fox brass, until Walter Winchell was invited to a private screening. "Big time," he enthused. "But the ending. I didn't get it. You've got to change it." They did, fortunately, to Preminger's choice.

Webb and Gene Tierney (Laura) also were in 20th's *The Razor's Edge,* which came out in 1946 without an idyllic summer sequence that had been in W. Somerset Maugham's novel and had been shot. Set in the French interior, the footage concerned salvation-seeking Larry Darrell (Tyrone Power) and his unfrocked priest-miner friend (Fritz Kortner) who, as vagabonds, worked on a farm where Darrell became attached to the young daughter (Colleen Townsend). All this was cut, and with it Miss Townsend's entire performance.

In 1945 Fox did *Kitten on the Keys,* starring Maureen O'Hara, Dick Haymes, and Harry James, which was almost completely remade and released in 1946 as *Do You Love Me?*

The eagerly awaited film of the best seller *Forever Amber* was in production for over a month in 1946 at a cost of around $2,000,000, with—following a Scarlett O'Hara-type search—English Peggy Cummins in the sexy title role, when production was suspended. Miss Cummins was showing up too fresh and innocent for such a worldly part, and the script wasn't right yet, either. She soon was replaced by Fox contractee Linda Darnell—who had been right there all along—and Cummins never did make it over here. The baby-faced Briton was not the only one forced to stop on *Amber,* though. Vincent Price was replaced as King Charles II by George Sanders, who earned some of the best notices of his career and ran away with the picture when it was finally released.

During the same year, 1947, director Anthony Mann was just getting started in Hollywood and was assigned the Eagle-Lion film, *Railroaded!,* a B with John Ireland, Sheila Ryan, Hugh Beaumont, Jane Randolph, and Keefe Brasselle. However, Mann was forced to re-shoot extensive sequences (at a cost of $25,000) to eliminate a conflict in subject matter with 20th Century-Fox's A, *Call Northside 777,* starring James Stewart, Richard Conte, and one of the 1940s' most likable but neglected leading ladies, Helen Walker. Both the Fox movie, which was scheduled to start in September, and the Eagle-Lion production, which had been completed in June, were based on the story of Mrs. Tillie Majczek, who scrubbed floors for ten years in Chicago to save $5,000 which she offered as a reward to clear her son of a murder conviction. The Majczek character was omitted from *Railroaded!,* so that the film dealt only with a false conviction for murder.

For unexplained reasons, *Call Northside* 777 had some omissions of its own, mainly—in one of her earliest screen appearances—Thelma Ritter's. She lost about a half-dozen scenes and kept only a brief bit in a police station sequence in which she had some dialogue with James Stewart.

Helen Walker's own true story is a strange one. An extremely able actress who could play both comedy (1945's *Murder, He Says*) and drama (1947's *Nightmare Alley*), the Massachusetts-born stage-trained girl seemed headed for big things. But on New Year's Eve, 1946, while returning from a brief work respite in Palm Springs, she gave a soldier hitchhiker a lift, as was her habit held over from World War II days, and he was killed in the ensuing accident outside Redlands, Calif. Two other men she had picked up in the cold night also were injured—they later repaid the actress' kind intentions with two civil suits. Walker had been working for three weeks on a film called *Heaven Only Knows,* also called *Montana Mike.* It cost producer Seymour Nebenzal close to $100,000 to re-shoot her footage with a replacement, Marjorie Reynolds. Walker herself suffered severe fractures, and while much-publicized investigations vindicated her of any blame, for some reason she never regained her promising position in films. In 1968, out of pictures for over a decade, she died of cancer.

Among the most written about—and mourned—discarded footage of all time was that shot in 1949 of Judy Garland in *Annie Get Your Gun.* Judy had recorded most of the songs for the picture and filming had begun when she had a nervous breakdown and was sent by MGM to a Boston hospital to rest. Betty Hutton replaced Garland and gave her most delightful performance as Irving Berlin's Little Sureshot. And Garland fans have always felt that Annie would have provided Judy—despite her gallery of memorable portraits—with the one really powerhouse personal triumph her screen career always lacked. Some of her Annie recordings turned up later on MGM Records albums—in fact, they are still being reissued.

Simone Signoret went to Germany in '54 to star in a film of Brecht's *Mother Courage* that was abandoned when only half-finished. Signoret also started *Zorba the Greek* (1964), but she and director Michael Cacoyannis both agreed that Signoret's stasis of the chassis was working against the part of the lively old whore and the little known Lila Kedrova replaced her and won 1964's Best Supporting Actress Oscar. Some time earlier, Signoret's young daughter, Catherine Allegret, made her cinema debut in something called *L'Envers,* which was never completed because of director Henri-Georges Clouzot's illness.

Gloria Swanson's famous 1928 venture as producer and star,

Queen Kelly, directed by Erich von Stroheim, was stopped by RKO-Pathé chief Joseph P. Kennedy well past the halfway point because, says the record, Stroheim's interpretation of the script was turning out to be highly censorable, as well as costly. Talkies were coming in, and it was decided not to throw good money after bad morals.

The film never had a theatrical release in the United States (except, in various conditions, to museums and film societies), but it was shown in Europe and South America and early in '66 had a television outing, with a discreet to the point of vague commentary by Swanson. Having tried to finish it no less than four times, she finally managed to shoot a death-scene ending for her character that had not been in the script and "which they cut off in France because von Stroheim was still alive and wanted it that way." Her director once said that while they were making *Kelly* Miss Swanson left the set one day to make a phone call and simply never came back. Some brief film from the picture was used in Swanson's great *Sunset Boulevard* comeback for Billy Wilder.

When columnist Florabel Muir learned that *Kelly* would have its first public showing at a 1966 Rochester, N. Y., "Gloria Swanson Week" festival of her films, Muir wrote: "If *Queen Kelly* is exhibited as I saw it back around 1930, it's going to be a bombshell! Kennedy was absent from the Culver City lot at the time. When he came back and saw what von Stroheim and Gloria had done, he blew his cool. Gloria is shown in a bawdyhouse and one of its patrons is depicted as a Catholic priest. Joe told me he was shocked, horrified and stunned. Realizing the irreparable harm it could do him as a leading Catholic layman, he ordered the entire 800,000 feet of film hidden away in a vault. Truthfully, I thought it had been destroyed. Would John F. Kennedy have enjoyed a political career that took him to the White House if *Queen Kelly* had got into the nation's theaters? Would Joe have become an ambassador? Would the course of history have been changed?"

The TV print of *Queen Kelly* contained no bawdyhouse scenes. Indeed, Swanson led viewers to believe they had not yet been filmed when production stopped.

As 1966 was ending, I learned positively that bordello scenes had been shot for *Queen Kelly.* Raymond Rohauer, Film Curator and Program Director for New York's Gallery of Modern Art (Including the Huntington Hartford Collection), had acquired the rarely viewed film in question (which he opined was all of this troublesome plot turn that had been shot), and was kind enough to help me dispel some of the myths that have sprung up around Herself in cinema circles over the years. He screened for me the footage to which Swanson had alluded only covertly on TV. The brothel part included a few posey hookers but no overtly sexual passages. What it had mostly was a still virtuous, convent-raised Patricia Kelly (Swanson) apparently forced to marry a decrepit old lecher (Tully Marshall, who had played a similar role, Baron Sadoja, in Stroheim's earlier *Merry Widow*) at the bedside of her dying old aunt-madam, with a black priest officiating, as it were, in two hats. The setting was South Africa, where, had the picture continued shooting, Patricia would have become queen of a chain of brothels. For the 20-minute running time, there was a continuous series of close-ups of Marshall salivating and Swanson suffering, but that was about it.

Outwardly, *Queen Kelly's* resistance to being born appeared to be based on the realization by parties involved that it just wasn't turning out to be a good movie; although after seeing the bordello material there can be little doubt that Himself saw the picture as a threat not only to his Catholic standing but to the political aspirations of the entire Kennedy clan. All of the film was little edited and extremely slow-moving—with most of the scenes seeming to go on at least 10 minutes longer than necessary—and silly even by '28 standards. The most memorable moments (and they were more bizarre than artful) came in the feature-length telecast version when the mad queen (Seena Owen) found heroine Kelly with the queen's fiancé, the prince, and went after the girl with a whip. With great flamboyance, Owen put the whip between her teeth while she ripped off Swanson's coat, then proceeded to beat her through corridors, down steps, and out of the palace. Owen, incidentally, spectacularly dressed and tressed, seemed to have a bigger and better part than star Swanson in the latter's authorized television print.

Swanson never had a better part than the mad movie queen Norma Desmond in 1950's *Sunset Boulevard,* but the Academy's Best Actress that year was Judy Holliday for *Born Yesterday.* And *Sunset* director-co-writer Billy Wilder says: "We originally had a weird kind of framing sequence containing some of the best material I've ever shot, but when we previewed the picture in Chicago and in the suburbs of New York people just screamed with laughter, so we cut it. We showed the corpse of a man being brought to the morgue in downtown Los Angeles, where we actually did much of the shooting. And in that section of the morgue when he arrives there are eight bodies—a woman, an elderly man, a young boy and so on. And the corpses tell each other events leading up to their deaths. The boy drowned, the old man had retired and had a little avocado grove in Tarzana here, and had a heart attack. And so on. And now William Holden tells the story, but by the time the corpse has been labelled and the tag tied to the big toe the audience is helpless in the aisles. A pity. The opening as we finally shot it wasn't logical but it was riveting, and as long as something is riveting, they will swallow it."

Another film about films, United Artists' 1937 release, *Stand-In,* had a pertinent plot twist. The climax found Humphrey Bogart, as a boozing producer, the victim of a scheme by leading lady Maria Shelton to fold his studio by making his last-chance picture, a jungle epic called *Sex and Satan,* a flop. At the last minute, the Bogie character rallied and re-edited *SaS,* cutting out most of Shelton's scenes and making the gorilla the star.

10. CELLULOID GUILLOTINING

On Easter Sunday, 1965, columnist Leonard Lyons hatched the following egg laid by MGM: "Paul Henreid, the Austrian-born actor-director, went to England for three months to play the role of a German general in *Operation Crossbow.* The movie sequence was filmed in German. MGM invited Henreid to come to N. Y. for the premiere, give interviews, see the plays, etc. He flew to N. Y., saw *Operation Crossbow*—and discovered that his entire sequence had been cut from the movie."

Henreid was still in the film, and with a number of scenes.

The movie companies themselves do not always know what is going on behind their own flats. In his *Films in Review* critique of Richard Burton's pre-Liz life of Edwin Booth ('55), Robert Downing remarked: "The advance Fox publicity for *Prince of Players* listed Mae Marsh as the second witch in *Macbeth,* but there is no Macbeth sequence in the final film. The old-time theatrical superstition about *Macbeth* being a hard-luck play must be true." (When I attended a critics' screening of *What Ever Happened to Baby Jane?,* the synopsis handed out by Warner Brothers' publicity department described a scene in which Bette Davis ran over and killed her leading man, Victor Buono. This scene never appeared in the picture—whether or not it was filmed, I can't say—and Buono was still alive at the fadeout.) Also cut were Eva Le Gallienne's scenes as Queen Elizabeth in the *Richard III* excerpts in *Prince of Players.*

Many other actors rather well known at the time have found their entire performances missing from their released movies. Including Rita Johnson as the warden's wife in Warners' *Unchained* (1955); at Fox, Joan Chandler as Mark Stevens' girlfriend in *The Street with No Name* (1948); and Patricia Morison, whose role as Victor Mature's suicidal first wife in *Kiss of Death* (1947)—well covered in magazine photo spreads and looking like Supporting Actress Oscar material—was cut but who got herself a far more important *Kiss* a few months later as star of Broadway's *Kiss Me, Kate,* Cole Porter's musical masterwork.

One of the best known names ever to be cut completely from a released feature is Agnes Moorehead, who, in 1947, made a semi-documentary film for MGM about our development of the atomic bomb called *The Beginning or the End.* A two-time Supporting Actress Oscar nominee at the time (there have been a couple of more nominations since), Miss Moorehead played a German scientist who escaped into Sweden. When a legal release from the real-life scientist could not be obtained, the actress' footage was taken out of the movie. The following year, Audrey Totter, one of the leads in *Beginning or the End,* had her whole appearance dropped from the same studio's Margaret O'Brien vehicle, *Tenth Avenue Angel.*

Award-winning Broadway actress Marian Seldes remembers her role of a mother who brought her son to a police station in her first Hollywood-made film, Universal's *The Young Stranger,* in 1957. Apparently doomed from the start, Seldes says director John Frankenheimer told her as they were shooting that hers was just the kind of part that could be cut out without paining the picture. They both laughed. Later, the director was proved right. *Fiorello!* star Tom Bosley got no little publicity for his co-starring spot in 1967's

The Flim-Flam Man (especially in a New York *Times* interview done at the film's southern location), yet was cut from this Fox product.

E. G. Marshall, fresh from his multi-awarded TV series *The Defenders* (well, perhaps spoiled a *little* on the way by such flops as—on screen—*The Chase* and—on stage—*This Winter's Hobby*), was delighted to accept a "cameo" along with many other stars in Paramount's *Is Paris Burning?* (1966). Described in the "final production notes and synopsis" as the American Intelligence officer who questioned the French resistant (Pierre Vaneck) sent to the American lines to ask for aid, Marshall was not in the picture premiered. Paris did not burn, but the edited Marshall did.

In 1959 comedienne Ann B. Davis, the secretary called "Schultzy" on Bob Cummings' most successful TV series, was one of the principal speakers at the Hollywood Cinema Editors' annual banquet. She said: "Thanks for asking me to speak, even though one of you edited every inch of me out of my first movie, *Strategic Air Command*, and left me on the cutting room floor!"

About the same time as Miss Davis was trying to get started in pictures, Nancy Kulp, another talented cut-up who would eventually click on the same Cummings show (she was magnificent as the bird-legged bird-watcher Pamela Livingstone) and as Jane Hathaway on TV's *Beverly Hillbillies*, was being cut from an early film credit of her own: Judy Garland's *A Star is Born*, a production doomed to a state of perpetual labor.

S. Z. Sakall's meaty little bit as a patriotic butcher was improvised for director Clarence Brown and *The Human Comedy* but cut from the 1943 film when released.

As the late, loveable and extremely adept scene-stealer told it in his book, *The Story of Cuddles—My Life Under the Emperor Francis Joseph, Adolf Hitler and the Warner Brothers* (probably the best title a Hollywood personality ever had for his biography, although Louella Parsons' *The Gay Illiterate* nudges it): "I had devised a little business. It was in the morning and the butcher was cutting up meat in his shop. In the meantime he noticed the newsboy who hurried past with the papers. He rushed out, bought a paper and brought it back to the shop. He placed the paper on the slab and went on reading, still slicing the meat. He read the headlines greedily while he waved his huge cleaver about. The war news was bad. The butcher stabbed the side of beef angrily. Then he pulled the knife out and stabbed the meat again and again. In his anger he maltreated the poor side of beef cruelly, as if it represented the enemies of America. Finally, he used his knife as a skewer, spitting the lump of meat on it and lifted it high, looking around triumphantly. He had won the desperate battle!"

The Young Lions, starring Marlon Brando, Montgomery Clift, and Dean Martin, was under three hours when released in 1958, but it originally had run considerably longer. Yiddish- and English-speaking theater star Jacob Ben-Ami, in a rare celluloid performance, had his entire role as Clift's father cut, including a death scene that director Edward Dmytryk thought excellent. Two other major Dmytryk pictures suffered in the cutting room. *So Well Remembered* (1947), with John Mills and Martha Scott, was held up several years and when finally released attracted little attention, largely, Dmytryk feels, because RKO boss Howard Hughes cut it to senselessness. Shot in 54 days, Columbia's *The Caine Mutiny* (1954) originally ran three hours but was reduced to just more than two, and Dmytryk thinks it was better before the scissoring began.

William Wyler, too, hated to cut *The Collector* (1965) and omit Kenneth More's entire co-starring role. Wyler said: "Some of the finest footage I ever shot wound up on the cutting room floor, including Kenneth's part. Something had to go—the first version ran four hours!" From England's Kenneth at the time: "Of course I'm bitterly disappointed. It was my first film in Hollywood. Seems too bad to start out—missing." More, with Alec Guinness and some others, had been vital to the Popularization of British Films in America movement that got up steam in the 1950s, appearing in such as *Genevieve* (which brought stardom to the marvelously soignée comedienne Kay Kendall, whose death in '59 left a void the movies are yet to fill), and *Doctor in the House* (which helped Dirk Bogarde's name mean something on the international market).

Great Britain also sent us the witty character actor Peter Bull for 1938's *Marie Antoinette* at MGM, although we didn't have sense enough to keep him, not even in the movie he'd come to do—he was cut *in toto.*

Marie, of course, under the direction of W. S. Van Dyke (who took over from Sidney Franklin the night before production began), was to be a collossal vehicle for Norma Shearer. Bull and his pal, the incomparable Robert Morley, had been imported to play, respectively, Gamin, the French blacksmith, and the much more important role of Louis XVI. Upon Bull's arrival, producer Hunt Stromberg told him there were great things being planned for Bull, but the immediate concern was to teach him the American language so he could play the Frenchman. Bull had an hour every day to this end "with a nice lady who turned out to be of Swedish extraction, but she made me promise not to tell," he recalls.

Most of Bull's scenes were with Morley (who pulled down a Supporting Actor Oscar nomination that year for this job, although we somehow let him go right back home, too) and were not directed by Van Dyke, who was off directing Shearer personally (she then owned 51 per cent of MGM), but by Julien Duvivier, who was called in to direct crowd and odd scenes. Bull did two days work in the first two months of shooting.

Then came the big revolutionary scenes in Versailles, the violence of which all the actors were dreading. When Bull arrived on the massive set, he became apprehensive when he noticed someone among the mob of extras dressed exactly as he was. He asked the fellow about this, learned that the man was to do "the dangerous bits" for Bull, that he specialized in this kind of work and only recently was seen as an ape in a *Tarzan.* After the brawl was over, and Bull was suffering from abrasions and a minor fracture or two, he wondered what the double looked like.

There also was a scene in which Barry Fitzgerald (another good French type) had to stab Bull in the back, which proved slightly traumatic. "I was given small bags of chocolate sauce to bite on at the crucial moment, so that it spurted attractively out of my trap," he has remembered. While all this was going on, someone was parading by a nearby window with a replica of Anita Louise's head on a stick. Bull said it was some time before he could look chocolate in the pan again.

Bull got to sight-see the West Coast during his six months on *Marie and Toilette,* as Morley came to call the production, which was fortunate because Stromberg's big plans for him never materialized. And Bull, as mentioned, was the victim of celluloid guillotining on *Marie.*

Also from overseas, actor Jacques Charrier got a setback when his importantly billed role in *Les Créatures,* directed and written by

France's "New Wave" pioneeress, Agnes Varda, was dropped for the premiere at the Fourth New York Film Festival in the fall of 1966—and never picked up again. However, Charrier's name had figured prominently in the exploitation preceding the Franco-Swedish picture's unveiling.

Neil Hamilton played Claudette Colbert's serviceman husband in the long, affecting drama of World War II family life, *Since You Went Away* (1944), but his whole performance was cut—except for photos of him scattered around the house. Another old-timer, funnyman Allen Jenkins, was cut from *It's A Mad, Mad, Mad, Mad World* (1963), although his photo remained prominent in the lush souvenir book. Ernest Gold, composer of the *Mad World* score, told me that producer-director Stanley Kramer "vastly overshot. The picture was originally about five hours and 26 minutes long. Then it was three hours and 40 minutes—this was the version I loved. But United Artists kept after Kramer to cut it some more, and he did. . . . Most of Spencer Tracy's motivation for turning crooked cop disappeared." Kramer originally had thought of showing *Mad World* with *two* intermissions.

Earlier, Mrs. Richard Nixon, a student at the University of Southern California, was doing bits in pictures and had one line of dialogue in *Becky Sharp* (1935)—that was cut.

One of the most important persons yet cut from a feature film for theaters is . . . well, let director Richard Brooks tell it:

"*Something of Value.* A best-seller, and when I got to Africa, they got hysterical laughing at me. They were laughing at the novelist and at me for even coming near Kenya with the book. It was trash. Eventually, I got what I thought was rather a good script, but this was a subject that I don't think anyone in the world wanted to know about. At the time, they didn't care about it. Of course, it's all come true now, it is just as we talked about it: unless black and white were going to be partners, the white man would have to get out. I liked Sidney Poitier in it, and Rock Hudson was fine.

"I had done a lot of research. One of the things I read in 1907 predicted the problems they would have in Kenya if they were not careful. That book was written by Winston Churchill, and here we were around 1956, when I made the film. So I wrote a letter to Mr. Churchill and asked if he could do a foreword, quote his own words in relation to today. Finally he said, miracle of miracles, 'Very well.' And he wrote something down on a page. We sent cameramen to his home to photograph him. We took it up to the preview. At that time at MGM, they had 14 guys sitting around a table, and one guy would say, 'I didn't like the music in the sixth reel.' And another would say, 'My dentist hates it.' And someone said, 'What's this crap with the Churchill thing? Who in hell knows who Winston Churchill is? It kills the picture dead. Some goddam Englishman there talking.' So they took the thing and cut it right out. I think he swore never to appear in another movie as long as he lived; I don't think he ever did."

Shortly after Pierre Salinger had run for—and lost—the post of junior U. S. senator from California, he was given a "cameo" role as the American Consul in Doris Day's comedy, *Do Not Disturb.* As release time approached, producers Marty Melcher (Doris' husband) and Aaron Rosenberg found ten minutes had to be cut from the picture's running time, and Salinger's entire part just fit these measurements. He lost again. *Do Not Disturb* opened sans Salinger, once press secretary to U. S. president John F. Kennedy.

A California winner, Gov. Ronald Reagan, was dropped from the second of his dozens of features, Warners' *Submarine D-1,* in 1937. Reagan had provided a surprise ending by winning Doris Weston after she had led three others—Pat O'Brien, George Brent, and Wayne Morris—a merry chase. At the last minute, Reagan's footage was submerged permanently and Morris was given the girl. Because the studio had done much promotion on this Reagan appearance, the acting governor says he received mail from fans who told him they loved him in *Submarine D-1.*

At least these cut actors did not have to suffer the added indignity of being replaced after they had filmed. New York actor Paul E. Richards was not so lucky. In June 1965 (after scenes from his footage had been reproduced in various publications), still several months before the film would be released, *Variety* reported: "Gene Saks has replaced Paul Richards in the key role of the kookie TV star in the film version of *A Thousand Clowns*—almost a year after production of the film was completed." Saks, who had originated the role on Broadway, had fallen ill just before initial filming, and the part fell to Richards, who had done it in the national company.

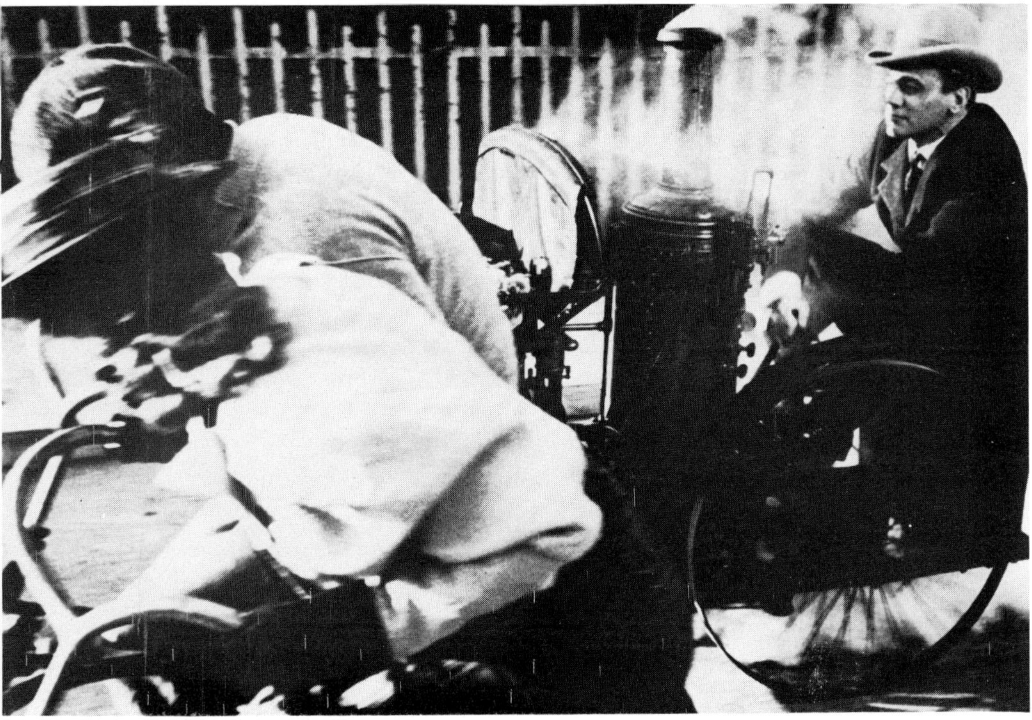

Joseph Cotten is pictured above at the right on the steam auto in a race with a double cycle that was among several sequences cut from Orson Welles' The Magnificent Ambersons.

Ruth Gordon's entire movie comeback part in The Loved One*—including this bit with Robert Morse—was excised from the released production.*

Edward G. Robinson (fifth from left) watched Fred MacMurray die in the gas chamber in the original ending to Double Indemnity. *This was all cut by the time the picture went into general release.*

The above desert dream sequence with Susan Hayward and Rex Harrison —although extensively publicized—was missing when The Honey Pot *premiered.*

Ronald Reagan appeared in Viveca Lindfors' first American film, Night unto Night*—but this scene didn't.*

In this scene from The Keys of the Kingdom, *Mary Anderson responds to Gregory Peck as if he's just told her she has been cut from the flick and replaced by Jane Ball—which she was.*

Margaret Dumont and W. C. Fields in Fields' segment of the all-star Tales of Manhattan *which was cut from the film as released.*

Victor Mature, Marilee Grassini, Iris Mann, Coleen Gray, and Patricia Morison in Kiss of Death, *the film that made Richard Widmark a star. Miss Morison's part as Mature's wife, however, was completely cut.*

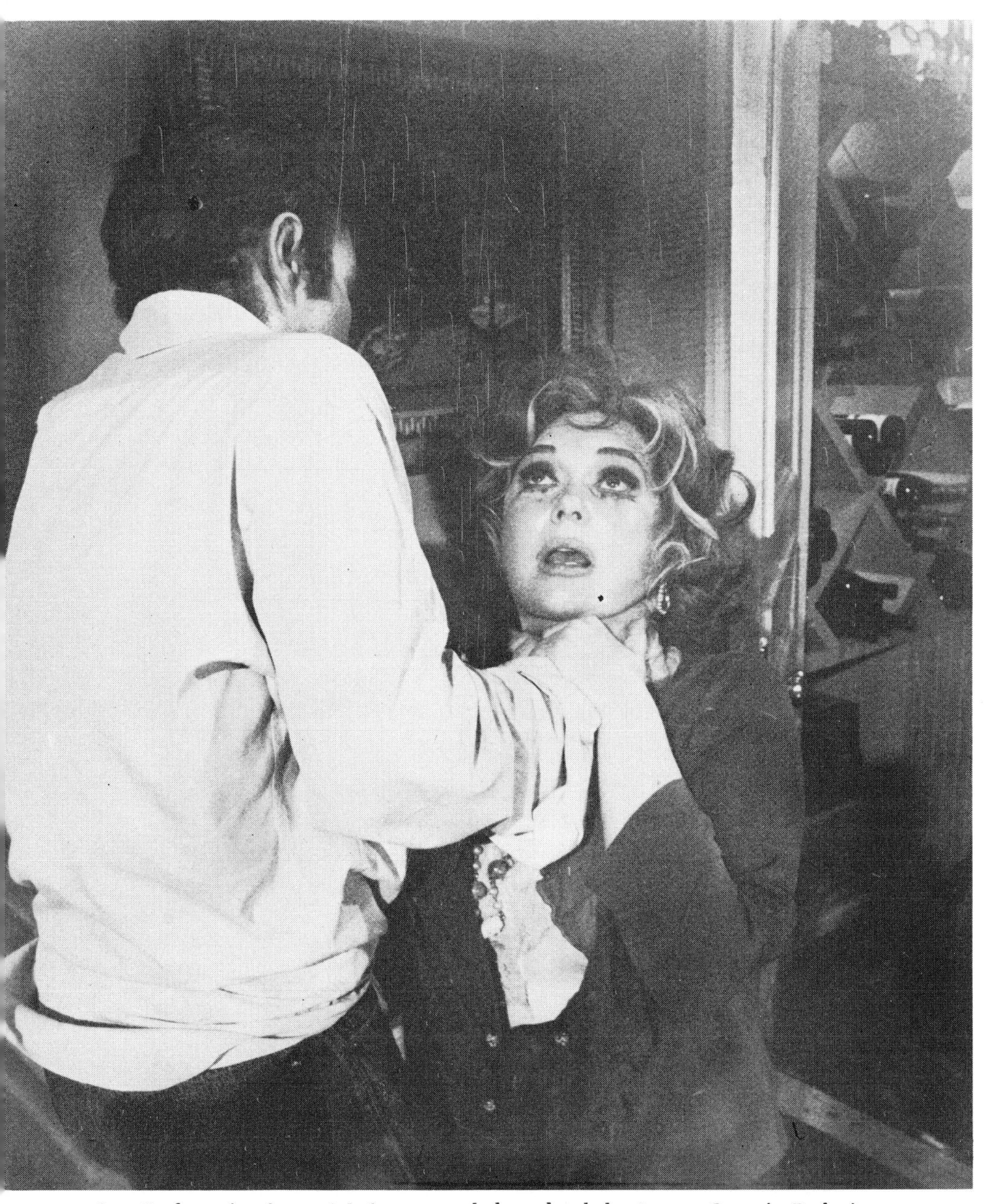

Ann Sothern is pictured being strangled to death by James Caan in Lady in a Cage. *Unfamiliar? That's because it was cut out of the finished film.*

Cesare Gravina and Dale Fuller in a scene cut from a subplot that was almost entirely removed from Greed, *one of the most notoriously scissored motion pictures of all time.*

A deleted Citizen Kane *scene featuring, from left: Everett Sloane, Frances Neal, Joseph Cotten, unknown actress, and Orson Welles.*

Pierre Vaneck and E. G. Marshall emote in a scene that was cut from Is Paris Burning? *Marshall's entire role, in fact, wound up on the cutting room floor.*

Patricia Neal is visited by Brandon de Wilde in her favorite bit in the Oscar-winning Hud. *The scene, however, was cut.*

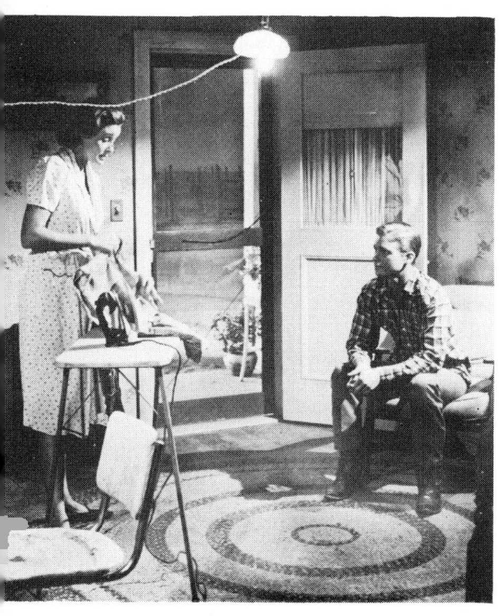

Above, the stylish Epilogue That Never Was from Deborah Kerr's fine The Innocents—*the whole sequence was lopped off.*

Claire Bloom was a lady with unnatural desires in The Haunting, *and this sequence, which set the stage for her problems, was omitted from the final print of the movie.*

Richard Burton is administered to by Deborah Kerr in this officially released scene still from The Night of the Iguana. *One thing: Miss Kerr did not wear this dress in the movie!*

Betty Grable and Dan Dailey in the "Rolling Down Bowling Green" number from their most popular picture together, Mother Wore Tights. *The entire segment was cut.*

Producer-director Fred Coe, not wanting to reflect upon Richards' ability, said it was just a question of the right actor for the right part and had shot the new (but a bit too feverish) Saks footage in three days.

Another Manhattan player, Elia Kazan protégée Barbara Loden, snared a good role in Burt Lancaster's *The Swimmer* (1966), but a few months afterward she was replaced by Janice Rule.

When MGM's *Twelve Miles Out* (1927) was withdrawn after previews because it was "too downbeat" and fourth-billed Betty Compson's part excised, it was something of a consolation for Miss Compson to know that it took *two* actresses (Paulette Duval and Dorothy Sebastian) to replace her in the now re-written for comedy relief role(s).

This kind of total annihilation almost happened to Viveca Lindfors' portrayal of the spinster librarian in *Sylvia* (1965), which also starred George Maharis and Carroll Baker, with several movie "names" in "cameos." Funny thing is, if her smallish part (Maharis told me it already had been shortened before filming began) in this film *had* been cut, no one would have been surprised, least of all Viveca.

For this handsome, stylish, and interesting Swedish actress, brought to the United States by Warner Brothers in 1946, was wasted by Hollywood and later ignored on the art house circuit. She could have—should have—been as big as Ingrid Bergman or Garbo. (Someone who knows her today says she suffers from "a Garbo complex," whatever that is, exactly; it certainly can't mean that she won't work, for Lindfors is constantly working regardless of the size or value of a part "so when the right thing comes along I'm ready—I'm not stale.") Her first film here seems almost an omen: *Night unto Night* (1949), the downbeat but intelligently (if unsuccessfully) made and acted Philip Wylie love story of an epileptic scientist (Ronald Reagan) and a young woman (Lindfors) who practically believed in ghosts because her naval officer husband, killed in action, had been washed up on the beach near their Florida home. *Night* was not released, though, until *after* her second and third American films, *To the Victor* (1948) and *Adventures of Don Juan* (1948), were in theaters. Lindfors said the hold-up was because "Warners hoped my second one would be 'the great picture.'"

In his book, *Where's the Rest of Me?,* Reagan offered another possible reason for the *Night unto Night* delay.

"If you are thinking this was a hard story to bring to life on the screen," Reagan put it, mildly, "you are right. We were doing pretty well, however, except for a key scene, where for the first time I learn the reason for her disturbance—namely, the finding of her husband's body. We photographed this scene four times, and rejected it each time when it was shown in the rushes. The producer had fallen in love with a pictorial shot of two riders on horseback far in the distance at sundown on the lonely beach. His justification was that seeing them triggered Viveca into telling me that her husband had been asleep on the beach, waiting for her (she was late), when two riders had stepped on him and killed him. It seemed the producer had decided that, Wylie or no Wylie, we weren't going to mention war or the Navy. We did this scene the fifth time, and I knew—as we all did—it was no better than the other four. Thus happened my first foray into script doctoring. I asked Don Siegel, the director, if he'd shoot one more version with a slight change of lines and keep it on hand. I'd figured a way to keep the producer's sunset horse shot in.

"I told Don that, number one, a horse wouldn't step on a man if he could possibly avoid it and, number two, even if a man was killed that way, it sounded funny. The scene as I rewrote it had the horseback riders asking her for directions to a phone to call the Coast Guard: they had come upon bodies and wreckage on the beach. Going back with them, she had discovered her husband. Her traumatic condition was explained in the line (somewhat poetic), 'It was almost as if in death he had tried to come back to me.' Frankly, I was kind of proud of it. After all, it was a basis for believing in ghosts when you stop to think he could have drifted in on any part of four thousand miles of coastline." Reagan's scene was kept, but other scenes were cut after filming, among them probably some of Reagan's frothings. In those pre-TV medico days, epilepsy was still a touchy subject.

The highlight of Lindfors' career (which includes innumerable TV appearances) is *Anastasia,* originated by her in '54 on Broadway in the title role that brought Ingrid Bergman an Academy Award in the film. So her Broadway musical comedy debut in *Something More!* in the fall of '64 was eagerly awaited by Vivecaphiles. There was only one hitch: a few days before the opening in New York, Lindfors withdrew because of cuts that were being made in her part and was replaced by Joan Copeland, playwright Arthur Miller's sister, who proceeded to give an imitation of Viveca's casually elegant style.

Now *Sylvia.* Heralded as Miss Lindfors' first Hollywood-made picture in many years, her role in it was completed just before *Something More!* (a flop, by the way) rehearsals began. And a few days after she quit *More!,* word leaked out of Paramount Pictures that her role in *Sylvia* was being discarded and had been (or would be) re-filmed with another actress! Even the slightly jaded Miss Lindfors would have found this double deal rough, but it finally was decided that her part in *Sylvia* would appear intact. Paramount did not divulge the name of the actress who had filmed the alternate scenes, nor why, nor if.

What ever the case, Paramount was wise to include Lindfors' intelligent turn in a film studded with "cameos"; for, next to Ann Sothern's bravura camping as a fat bimbo, Lindfors' bit was the best performance in *Sylvia,* her high point being her single eloquent expression when investigator George Maharis asked if she has known the enigmatic Sylvia (Carroll Baker). With this one protracted look, Lindfors somehow managed to convey the required surprise at the question as well as this woman's probable perverse yearnings, lifetime of loneliness, and her once deep affection for a knowledge-hungry, poor, adolescent Sylvia.

Her bad—or, at best, left-handed—luck, however, continued with a film she made in England in 1961 called *The Damned,* directed by American expatriate Joseph Losey and awarded the 1964 Critics Prize at the Second International Science Fiction Film Festival at Trieste, Italy. Early in '64 British critic Raymond Durgnat enthused: "Viveca Lindfors triumphantly displays the warmth and attack worthy of Losey at his best. This is undoubtedly one of the most important British films of the year, even, perhaps, of the '60s." So far so good. But, *The Damned* was not released in the United States until the summer of 1965, when it had been retitled *These Are the Damned,* cut from its original 100 minutes to 87 and brushed off on the bottom half of light-topped double bills. Only the *Times* reviewed it the day after opening in New York—a rave—where it has been playing at one theater or another almost continuously since.

Much worse off, though, was Losey's *Eva* of the same period, his own personal favorite film. The director has said: "It was so mutilated by cuts made without my approval that Jeanne Moreau, Stanley Baker and I drew up a petition to have our names taken off it."

Another English-made film, one that did nothing for its star, Jennifer Jones, was *The Wild Heart,* co-produced by her husband, David O. Selznick, and London Films (Alexander Korda) in 1950. Filmed on the Welsh border and dealing with fox hunts, it gave its Oklahoma-raised leading lady, who already had a slight speech impediment, a real hurdle in a Welsh Gypsy accent. The beautiful color photography dominated when it was ready, and the picture was withdrawn, partially re-shot, and drastically re-edited—its 110 minutes were reduced to 82. Michael Powell and Emeric Pressburger had directed the original *Heart,* but Rouben Mamoulian helmed the revised edition, without billing.

All that is a matter of record, as is the shambles that was *Indiscretion of an American Wife* (1954), which Miss Jones made in Italy under producer-director Vittorio De Sica and the overall supervision of Selznick. The latter—who, because of De Sica's trouble with English, co-directed but took no credit—also worked on the script with Cesare Zavatini, Carson McCullers, Paul Jarrico, Truman Capote, and Alberto Moravia. It was all made in Rome's new railroad station with Montgomery Clift as Jones' Italian-American lover. The thing turned out such an audience ordeal that a third had to be cut for American release, including hundreds of feet of film in which De Sica lingered his cameras over the new station's architectural features.

In late 1966 I talked briefly with Miss Jones. When I asked if she would discuss her cutting room experiences, she said, with a blinding, fixed smile, "Oh, it all seems so long ago. I can't remember." I tried to prime the reputedly erratic, elusive actress by mentioning my own favorite of her pictures, *Portrait of Jennie,* Robert Nathan's very original tale of metaphysical love and an unforgettable experience for me in 1948. I'd heard considerable footage had been cut from this unique Selznick Studio production, four years in preparation and over a year shooting but its fragile story running under 90 minutes. The widely publicized climactic storm sequence, I knew, had been filmed several times.

"I never saw the picture," she giggled. When I told her it was on TV all the time and she really ought to, Miss Jones laughed, "Then I guess I don't have any excuse." Remarkably cordial, nevertheless, for the Jennifer Jones of column renown, she sobered to tell that "the nature of the story [*Jennie*] made it very difficult to transfer to the screen, I know. What ever success it realized was my husband's work." William Dieterle got director's credit on this one.

11. TODAY, THERE ARE MORE STARS IN HEAVEN

Few Hollywood actors have looked more like a leading man than the late Alan Marshal, tall, dark and suavely handsome, slightly British-sounding with a thin mustache, in the best tradition of the '30s, which was when he arrived from Australia by way of Broadway. He was boyfriend to Ginger Rogers in *Tom, Dick and Harry,* lover to Merle Oberon in *Lydia,* and husband to Irene Dunne in *The White Cliffs of Dover,* among many uphill assignments. But he was never really a star. The ladies always had all the lines—the scripts and scissors saw to that.

In a 1944 article he by-lined titled *I Can Take It,* Marshal wrote: "I began to feel like an outcast; to wonder if I were the little man who wasn't there. The studios collaborated in promoting that wonder. For instance, my wife Mary and I would go to a picture I had worked in. (I always wait to see them with her.) So we sit there and I say, 'Mary, there's a big scene—my big moment comes pretty soon!' She glows with anticipation; she squeezes my hand excitedly. The moment arrives, there is a fast flash, a black streak across the screen, my mustache going by. 'They must have cut it,' I explain patiently, not even disappointed any longer. But Mary never fails to be disappointed, no matter how often it happens."

In Hollywood's '30s–'40s salad days, glamour was the key word and the stars—particularly the ladies—always looked their best, on screen and off. The cameraman was mighty important to the gals (Garbo owes much of her claim to legend to the magnificent lensing she got from—mostly—William Daniels), and one of the best of that era is still around: versatile James Wong Howe, probably the only cinematographer whose name is known to a scattered industry non-pro or two.

In his very amusing and readable (but overall hardly fair) book, *The 50-Year Decline and Fall of Hollywood,* Ezra Goodman said that when Wong photographed *Whipsaw* in '36, "one scene required Myrna Loy to wake up in the morning looking tired after a late night out. Howe suggested that she be filmed with her hair a little mussed and not looking as if she had just emerged from a beauty salon. This was a rather revolutionary idea in that period at MGM, but Miss Loy went along with it. Howe shot the scene that way and after the film was developed and shown with the day's rushes, he was called into the office of one of the studio high command, Eddie Mannix. Mannix was irate. 'What do you mean by shooting that kind of stuff of Loy? Here we've spent a couple of million bucks building her up as a glamour girl and you knock the whole thing for a loop with this one shot!'

"Howe tried to explain that this was what the script called for and that Loy and the director had agreed to her being photographed that way. But Mannix would have none of it, and so Howe re-shot the scene with the actress looking immaculately groomed, flawlessly made up and thoroughly glamorous after her all-night toot."

At least in those early days Howe had a choice, of sorts. Today, he would be—and has been—hard put to glamorize a field that features the mono-mannered "kitchen sink" actress of New York, the Cockney "mods," the whore house-blowsy European contingent, and the beach-blanket-bingo blondeness of Hollywood's paper-doll parade. Mr. Wells, the time machine, please.

Most of today's most distinctive film performances are given on TV film, despite the television medium's deserved bad reputation for B movie standards in material. Whatever else is true of TV and its producers, they are providing work and exposure for many potential great stars, some of whom have achieved fame, some of whom will, and some of whom won't—but they won't fail because they lack the talent or looks or personality; rather, aside from bad luck and/or their various personal needs, or "hang-ups," because they are strongly individual in a shaky movie age that is afraid of taking a chance on them, actors of presence such as provided the very foundation of the motion picture industry.

TV-bred actresses like Joan Hackett, Gail Kobe, Lois Nettleton, Beverly Garland, Sally Kellerman, Kathryn Hays, Diana van der Vlis, Brenda Benet, Barbara McNair, and Diane Baker have as much to offer as any of the screen greats of old, and certainly of new. And they do this without being painstakingly, lovingly photographed, and despite rushed shooting schedules of a few days—but with even more celluloid hours of experience to their credit already than many of the long-established queens of the cinema. George Maharis, in the "Eternal Outsider" John Garfield mold, had to come along via video's *Route 66* series; and Rod Taylor, a hero star in the great tradition, struggled for years until his *Hong Kong* TV show made him known.

The much-maligned "Hollywood Rajah" did indeed have his quirks, as anyone who knew him during his almost 30 years tenure at the helm of Metro-Goldwyn-Mayer will admit and does, at the drop of a check for a book, article, air interview or—as late, even, as 1967—play (Norman Mailer's *The Deer Park*) on L. B. Mayer. About the best any ex-MGMite could do for Mayer was the following recent quote from Mickey Rooney: "Mayer had his impossible moments, but he was, after all, the man who kept the store going." Under his guidance, the studio produced—as its slogan once boasted —"More Stars Than There Are in Heaven," strong personalities who could act and who had individualistic faces audiences could recognize a second time, which is more than can be said for the faceless inbreeds or gargoyle-featured ciphers of today's entertainment galaxy.

Under Mayer, there also were some of the greatest pictures ever made, like *The Good Earth, Grand Hotel, The Wizard of Oz, Pride and Prejudice, Mrs. Miniver, National Velvet, The Green Years, The Yearling*—but why go on; the list only gets longer. Whatever Mayer was personally (and it has been said that the turn-out for his funeral in 1957 was large because everyone wanted to make sure he was really dead), he *produced* as no other Hollywood rajah before or since has. Only Jack Warner crowds Mayer's record of achievement, and maybe Darryl Zanuck. (Warner could still have the edge on Mayer in one department: Warner's cutting room continued to be one of the busiest places in town long after Mayer's demise.) During the '30s and even into the '40s the lion's roar was synonymous with glamour—actresses such as

Warners' Bette Davis longed for the lavish "Metro mounting." Warners was the last "doity woid" in the hard-times dramas of the day and Fox the home of the blondes: Shirley Temple, Alice Faye, Betty Grable, June Haver, Carole Landis, Charlotte Greenwood, etc.

Most assuredly, Mayer had his lapses, but they are not always the familiar or popular anecdotes. . . .

Good looks, as I've indicated, have become a stumbling block for quite a few actors and actresses nowadays—not the lack, but the presence. Plainness, homeliness, or even in some cases downright ugliness is "in" with many of our leading men and women. Once, a lithe, pretty girl was ushered right into a producer's office; now she watches some drab literally trip in before her and get the part. A presentable appearance today is thought to mean no talent.

One of Mayer's fixations, in spite of his studio's glamorous image, was the Average American Family. With fierce fatherly fervor, Mayer guarded in his films what he thought was the essence of this worthy institution. (The anti-mom movement of recent years would probably have brought L. B. to an earlier passing.) He felt especially close to the Andy Hardy series. At a preview of one of the Hardy films, Mayer was furious to see Andy (Mickey Rooney), blue over rejection by his teen-age sweetheart Polly Benedict (Ann Rutherford), disregard his mother's (Fay Holden) concern and turn down her dinner. Mayer screamed at producer Carey Wilson, "I thought you told me you were brought up in your mother's kitchen! You lied to me! So you've insulted the American home and mother! Anybody who has been brought up in the kitchen knows that the average American boy at 16 is hungry *all* the time!"

In spite of the series' low budget, Mayer insisted that the scene be re-done so that Andy could thank his mother for her interest and *assure* her that her cooking was hunky dorry, but he was out of sorts.

Was Mayer right? Well, in 1942 the Academy gave the Hardy Family series a special Oscar for "furthering the American way of life."

Just about this time, a celebrated friendship was blossoming at MGM on the set of *Woman of the Year,* the smash comedy romance that first exhibited as a team the unique star magnetism of Spencer Tracy and Katharine Hepburn, indeed together at last. The preview audience laughed right up to the closing scene, where the film sank. Director George Stevens realized a new ending was in order, and he explained his idea to Hepburn who thought he was crazy at first but ultimately gave in.

Said Stevens: "By now Tracy was married to Kate, the woman who'd conquered everything. So I slipped in the kitchen scene. The audience said to itself, 'Now she's going to prove what a smart wife she is, too.' Then, just when the nausea set in, the customers got fooled. Everything came unstuck. The coffee pot exploded, the waffles expanded like helium gas bags. And the patrons howled because they'd been victimized by people they thought they'd out-guessed."

Five years and two Tracy-Hepburn vehicles later, Elia Kazan directed them in *The Sea of Grass* at Metro. Still new to directing, Kazan approached the project with some apprehension: for one thing, Hepburn was known then as a rather cold actress and there was one scene that called for the character to tear herself to emotional shreds. "Don't worry," Hepburn told Kazan, "I'll weep buckets." And she did. Both director and star were thoroughly pleased with the way the difficult scene had come off. Then, there was silence around the lot for a day or two—"Beware of silence around movie studios," Kazan has warned. Finally, Mayer sent for him.

Mayer had seen the rushes of Hepburn's crying jag and thought it terrible. "Some people cry with their eyes, some people with their nose, some people with their throat," Mayer advised, "but Hepburn had all of them going at once! And, besides, her channel of tears was all wrong."

Kazan said, "What does *that* mean?"

Mayer explained: "Her tears come down alongside and under her nose, and they look like something else."

Kazan re-did the scene.

They really *cared* in those days.

12. SAVE MY BABY!

There are times when previews can be dangerously misleading, as distinguished French director Jean Renoir learned with one of his American films, *The Woman on the Beach,* released in 1947.

"I was wholly responsible, and I've never shot a film with less script and more improvisation," Renoir said. "I took the opportunity of attempting something I had long wanted to do: a film based on sexual attraction into which sentiment did not enter. I made it, and was pleased with it. Perhaps it was a little slow, but the scenes were well balanced and excellently played by Robert Ryan and Joan Bennett.

"RKO, the actors, and I were all pleased with this film, but we had some doubts about the public reaction, so we agreed to have several previews. I remember one in particular, at Santa Barbara, before an audience of college kids. They didn't like the film, and I had an impression that my method of showing emotional scenes devoid of emotion shocked them—or perhaps it wasn't what they were used to. I was so discouraged that I was the first to suggest cuts and alterations. The film had been expensive to make, for to arrive at the style I wanted I had to work slowly. Joan had succeeded in completely altering her personality for the part—I even asked her to lower her voice, which was rather sharp. The studio authorities were most considerate, and said: 'All right, we shall have to make changes, but you must do it.'

"I carefully re-shot about a third of the film, mostly the scenes between Ryan and Joan. I produced a film which was, I think, neither one thing nor the other, and which had certainly lost its *raison d'être.* I had allowed myself to be too greatly influenced by the Santa Barbara preview, and, at the thought of losing contact with the public, I had flinched."

Taking the blame for the failure of *Woman on the Beach* proved Renoir was a stranger in town. Hollywood veterans—like William Wellman, whose serious Western starring Clark Gable, *Across the Wide Missouri* (1951), was cut to ribbons—know enough to blame everyone else in sight for their much-cut bombs (and probably rightly so).

Hollywood (or Howard Hughes) was taking no chances with Bette Davis' *Payment on Demand* (1951)—the story of a divorce—which was shot at RKO with three different endings: happy, unhappy, and middle-road. The picture was sneaked with all three endings, and audiences were asked to indicate which they liked best. The ending that see-sawed a bit won hands down and was used. The late Montgomery Clift's swan song, *The Defector* (1967), also was lensed with three different endings. The producers used the one that best fit the current scene at time of release.

Meet John Doe (1940), starring Gary Cooper and Barbara Stanwyck, which already had had four different endings, was playing in a number of cities when the still dissatisfied director Frank Capra received the following letter signed "John Doe": "I have seen your film with many different endings . . . all bad, I thought. . . . The only thing that can keep John Doe from jumping to his death is the Joe Does themselves . . . if they ask him." Capra pulled back his picture, re-assembled his large cast, and made the fifth and final finish suggested in the letter.

In 1924 while filming Thomas Hardy's *Tess of the D'Urbervilles*, with Blanche Sweet, director Marshall Neilan was forced by Metro-Goldwyn to shoot two endings, one unhappy and one happy—the latter completely negating the author's intention. The film was released with both endings and exhibitors were allowed to choose whichever finish they liked.

The late French director Max Ophuls, having completed in Hollywood his exquisitely evocative Valentine to Old Vienna, *Letter from an Unknown Woman*, and gone on vacation, returned to find 20 minutes had been cut "to speed things up." While the plot basics remained intact, relieved of its even more vital ambiance the production now seemed to move more slowly. It took all the persuasive powers of Ophuls, scenarist Howard Koch, executive producer William Dozier, producer John Houseman and star Joan Fontaine (never better as the heroine) to convince Universal to restore *Woman* to its original form for release in 1948.

Ophuls was less fortunate with his last film, *Lola Montes* (1955), which was cut by panicky producers from 143 minutes running time to 110, then 93, and finally, for the U. S., 72 minutes, with its unorthodox narrative technique "simplified" of its recurrent flashbacks so that what was left of the story was told chronologically, robbing the picture of its whole point. *Lola* was one of the most expensive films ever produced by European filmmakers; but in its cut condition, it opened in the states as an associate feature.

When the World War II-set *The Victors* was premiered on television in late 1966, the *Thursday Night at the Movies* prime time program had slashed almost an hour from the film's length. The next day the network received countless complaints from viewers. One angry gentleman wrote to *TV Guide:* "When released in its original form for theaters, *The Victors* presented a strong argument against war. When released in its edited form for the CBS movies, it presented an equally strong case against television."

Of course, the cutting up of movies by TV stations has been going on for years, with worthier films than *The Victors* desecrated. But by '66, the public (grown wiser with two decades of assistance from the one-eyed culprit itself) had become increasingly aware of the practice. Movies are all over television now, almost every evening being somebody's night at the movies. As the spectacularly high ratings of the late-'66 aired *The Bridge on the River Kwai* proved once but (being TV) only *perhaps* for all, feature films on television are audience grabbers. Thus the studios to refill the diminishing libraries of old pictures are turning out features expressly for television release. And since the movies being shown at these early, non-*Late Show* hours are recent vintage, frequently talked-about features with talked-about contemporary stars, and which some viewers already have seen in theaters, the audiences at home are likely to be more hip to any scissoring than they were when the MGM backlog of old features was released to television a decade and a half ago.

One television critic said that these "snippets shouldn't be palmed off as movies. They should be labeled *Bits of Hits.*" The same reviewer had a friend who carried a pad and pencil around while televiewing films, noting the sponsors and, if cutting ensued, taking further note not to purchase any of the products involved.

Early in '66, while Otto Preminger, George Stevens, Billy Wilder, and Alfred Hitchcock were making headlines attacking TV for the cutting of their films, Carl Lerner, the New York editor who edited *Requiem for a Heavyweight,* was complaining because CBS-TV, planning to air the picture, had put *back* ten minutes Lerner had taken out for its release in 1962. Director Ralph Nelson tried in vain to have his name removed from the credits because of this late tampering.

Originally clocked at 85 minutes, *Requiem* ran 95 minutes on its premiere telecast because "an 85 minute movie was too short to provide the requisite intervals of entertainment between commercials," Lerner explained.

"When you live with a film four or five months in the cutting room and give it careful, dogged consideration," said Lerner, "you don't like to see someone later put something back in. I'm disturbed by some cuts television makes in movies, but it's even worse to add something. It's as if you go out and buy a painting but it's two inches short at the top and bottom to fit the frame you had. So you call a house painter to add to the picture at the top and bottom, so it will fit the frame."

Lerner said there was nothing he could do to stop CBS from adding to *Requiem.* This control had rested with producer David Susskind, who gave approval to revive—from about 40 minutes of leftover footage—a saloon scene between Anthony Quinn, Jackie Gleason, and Mickey Rooney.

Commenting on the addition of out-takes (film shot but never used) inserted by people who had nothing to do with the creation of the film (his first feature directing job), Nelson, unencumbered by beginner's modesty, declared: "It's like adding a mustache to the Mona Lisa."

Nelson revealed that during the shooting of the picture, "Susskind had a 'thing' with Jackie Gleason, so he removed all scenes with motivation for Gleason's character. The lines were drawn between Jackie and myself on the one hand, and Tony Quinn and Susskind on the other."

(At year's end, Nelson was given the go-ahead from CBS to make the necessary—in the network's opinion—trims in his 1963 film, *Lilies of the Field,* which CBS was planning to telecast in the spring of 1967. "The development is something of a breakthrough for Hollywood movie-makers amid their distress over the TV chop-jobs on their work," a television columnist reported. "More presumably will be asking for similar privileges.")

Susskind, as producer again, also was responsible for what featured player John Cullum told me was the "ruination" of *All the Way Home* (1963), from James Agee's prize-winning novel and Tad Mosel's play. "The screenplay by Philip Reisman Jr. was really beautiful, it made you cry, even the *directions,"* Cullum recalled. "But the picture never really came off. We were over budget and overlong, and Susskind wanted to cut it down to a more conventionally showable length. Our director, Alex Segal, already had cut it beyond what he believed right, and refused to cut it any further. So Susskind went to work on it."

"Robert Preston lost about 45 minutes' footage alone—Preston's drinking and religious problems with his wife, Jean Simmons, which were very important to the development of the story, were cut. Alex tried to have his name removed from the credits, but it was kept on," related the actor.

"Sometimes it takes fully as long to edit extensive footage of a film epic as it took to write the script or shoot it," *Daily Variety* announced in March of '65. "A case in point is duration of John W. McCafferty's assignment on 20th-Fox's *The Agony and the Ecstasy,* which lensed over a four-month period last summer. First as an assistant cutter, then working on his own, McCafferty put in over four months on the Carol Reed production. . . . Film will run a little over two hours."

Oddly, when *Agony and the Ecstasy* opened Samuel E. Beetley was credited as editor. And right after its initial reserved-seat run, the film was shorn of its beautiful 15-minute prologue on Michelangelo's sculptures written by an expert on Vatican history, Vincenzo Labella, and narrated by TV's *The Millionaire,* Marvin Miller. Many felt this section was the best part of the picture.

Hollywood cutter Herbert G. Luft had a job that was almost a career: he spent two years working on a vehicle for the difficult Maria Montez, first called *Atlantis,* finally *Siren of Atlantis.* It was produced by Seymour Nebenzal, who also produced an earlier version of the tale in 1931.

Luft recalls: "Nebenzal began the Maria Montez remake in the summer of '47 at the Goldwyn Studio with the late Arthur Ripley directing. Neither Montez nor her husband [Jean Pierre Aumont] had anything to do with dialogue or direction [as had been rumored], and Nebenzal raised all the money for it from banks and finance companies. He did, however, give Montez a personal note when she agreed to defer some of her wages, approximately $50,000. When the picture did not succeed at the boxoffice, Montez sued Nebenzal over this obligation.

"United Artists refused to accept the version of Ripley's *Atlantis* that was completed in '47 on the ground that it was 'too artistic.' Incidentally, Ripley had had two writers with him all the time and no one but he changed any dialogue. Moreover, Nebenzal was very proud of the 'philosophical' treatment. Anyway, after the UA turndown the film was re-cut and location-shot desert footage from the earlier picture was incorporated. Douglas Sirk then attempted a rewrite, but dropped out to direct a Charles Boyer film. John Brahm directed the watered-down scenes added in '48, but was so displeased with the result he refused screen credit, which went to Gregg G. Tallas, the very capable head editor who hadn't directed one scene but who had been able to eliminate the worst of Montez' heavily accented dialogue."

A similar, though less harmful fate had befallen an earlier Arthur Ripley-directed film, *Voice in the Wind*, a 1944 United Artists release shot in 13 days for $50,000 (and still a money-loser), with Francis Lederer, J. Carrol Naish, and Miss Sigrid Gurie, Samuel Goldwyn's Scandinavian discovery from the fjords of Flatbush. (Born in Brooklyn, Miss Gurie hoodwinked Goldwyn with an accent, she claimed when her real birthplace leaked out, she "always had," and he gave her a big build-up. But, like an earlier Goldwyn discovery legitimately from across the seas, Anna Sten, Miss Gurie flopped.) Individualist Ripley was an editor, writer, and director in films, and was head of the Motion Picture Division of the University of California when he died in the early '60s.

An excerpt from *Cue* magazine's review of *Wind* stated: "As originally edited, this film was one of the most remarkable pictures of the decade—an almost surrealistic combination of sight and sound, of realism and imagery, of instantaneous photo-montages and compressions that at times became almost overpowering. . . . Since your reviewer saw this picture in the projection room some three months ago it has been re-edited into a more orthodox pattern. Lacking the greatness of its original form, it is still a stirring drama." The story examined the tragedy of a mentally shattered refugee pianist who found his lost love on a tropical isle.

Director Robert Siodmak has claimed that his Gregory Peck–Ava Gardner vehicle, *The Great Sinner* (1949), like *Siren of Atlantis*, was practically re-made after the first filming because MGM thought it was "too artistic," although he had liked it. Another director re-shot most of the story and turned out a film *no one* liked. In a mid-'50s article on studios re-using old footage, William K. Everson evinced surprise "that Metro re-used *familiar* sequences (in some new releases), for this studio must have had sufficient unused out-takes to pad several features, due to its habit of wholesale re-shooting before release (in the '20s the MGM lot was referred to as Re-take Valley)." A film company executive once explained the difference between an added scene and a re-take this way: "When the director makes a mistake, it's an added scene. When anyone else makes a mistake, it's a re-take."

But let's get back to Judy Garland, whose long career made her familiar with—far from immune to—scene cutting. The classic example of a near-cataclysmic single cut took place when the wonderful *Wizard of Oz* was screened back in '39, and studio executives felt her "Over the Rainbow" song slowed up the action and should be cut! It played a few sneak previews minus "Rainbow," but Judy's signature number was, of course, put back in for general release.

One song, though, stayed permanently out: "The Jitterbug," which Judy later reprised with some guests on her early 1960s TV series. According to Margaret Hamilton, the memorable witch of Oz, no one dreamed the film would be the classic it has become. "We thought it would be very good," she recollected, "but we had no idea television would come along and make the showing of it an annual event. I remember right after we finished it they cut one of the numbers, 'The Jitterbug.' It was a lovely number, and I asked why it wasn't going to be used. They said because it would date the picture in ten years."

Eddie Bracken, who starred in a couple of 1940s Preston Sturges written-and-directed comedy classics, *The Miracle of Morgan's Creek* and *Hail the Conquering Hero,* told me that he didn't see how a Sturges film could have any scenes excised.

"His scripts were always so tight," Bracken said. "There were certainly no scenes of any consequence cut from the films I did for him. Sturges never did as some did, and still do: take the picture to a preview theater, get the reaction and then take the film back for doctoring up. He didn't have to."

Strictly speaking, this was not all true.

In 1944 Sturges made a failure called *The Great Moment,* the story of the discovery of ether by a Boston dentist, Dr. W. A. Morton, with Joel McCrea and Betty Field. As originally conceived, it was a drama, but Paramount officials were uneasy about a serious Sturges and had him cut almost three reels. What remained was mostly a series of even more uneasy comedy episodes in a context of physical misery. Sturges should have taken a look at his own 1941 gem, *Sullivan's Travels,* which told of a Hollywood director (also McCrea) who wanted to do heavy drama until he mingled with the downtrodden and learned they wanted to forget their troubles, not be reminded of them.

Getting back to Bracken: "I did several films with Betty Hutton—Paramount saw us as a team for a while—and there were times when I was disturbed by things that were *added,* not cut out of these. Our roles were supposed to be equal, but when I went to the preview I found out that two or three Hutton numbers had been added after what I thought had been the picture's completion."

Bracken could remember only one cut scene that was seriously damaging to one of his performances, but it was extraordinary. In his first big movie (he had done *Our Gang* comedies), the RKO filming of the George Abbott–Rodgers and Hart Broadway success, *Too Many Girls* (1940), Bracken had re-done for the cameras his show-stopping stage number, "Recognize the Tune," aided by film collegians Lucille Ball, Desi Arnaz, and Richard Carlson. But it was taken out of the release print. Why?

Swore Bracken, just 25 years later and looking ready and able to reprise the tune: "The movie was only so-so, and they told us the number was too good, it threw the rest of the picture off balance."

The cutting (or editing, splicing, etc.) of a film also can provide unintentional—if mood-jarring—fun. In George Stevens' *A Place in the Sun*, Shelley Winters started a walk down the street in saddle oxfords and finished it in loafers—or was it the other way around? (I am unaccountable when Winters walks.) This kind of cutting-continuity error is especially notable when associated with Stevens, a man almost *notorious* for the painstaking care—sometimes many months—he takes cutting his pictures. He raised all kinds of hell just before *A Place in the Sun* was to have its first NBC TVcast, trying to get the work—which, when it was originally released, already had seen Anne Revere's mother role cut to a shirt-tail relative—shown uncut and without any commercial interruptions. Superior Court Judge Ralph H. Nutter ruled that the film could not be televised if its artistic qualities were harmed, and it was aired whole—including Shelley Winters' extraordinary constitutional quick-change—but with plenty of commercial breaks. It was a precedent-setting ruckus, however.

The fun in Burt Lancaster's *The Crimson Pirate* (1952), talk had it, was mostly unintentional as well. Produced with sets and costumes left over from Errol Flynn's heyday at Warners (and from Lancaster's own 1950 *The Flame and the Arrow* there), the picture's success in some of the unlikeliest critical quarters provoked the following from Hollis Alpert: "The story goes that it was made quite seriously, but proved such a hopeless muddle that the film editor put it together with his tongue in his cheek. The result was that some film critics saw it as a satire on pirate epics, and hailed its cleverness. [The producing team of Harold] Hecht and Lancaster suddenly discovered the value of 'prestige' in Hollywood."

Britain's *Tom Jones,* 1963's Academy Award Best Picture, might have had a different outcome. Supporting player Peter Bull has confessed, "After the film was completed, rumors went whizzing around about the product. The air was rife with reports that it was uncuttable, dull, a mess, had no chance of general distribution, etc., etc. That United Artists, who had largely backed it, was alarmed. Director Tony Richardson went quietly about cutting it with Tony Gibbs, and engaged Michael MacLiammoir as commentator, speeded up some of the film to a Keystone Cop pace, took out masses of extraneous dialogue, and the rest is cinema history."

In her MGM-minded book, *This Was Hollywood,* Beth Day said that the celebrated "Thalberg touch" of Irving Thalberg, that studio's fair-haired executive producer of the '30s, belonged primarily to a skilled cutting hand.

"Any producer on the lot with a 'sick' picture brought it to Thalberg," she wrote. "He had an uncanny ability to determine the precise changes which could alter a production from possible failure to assured success. When they had completed *Laugh, Clown, Laugh,* with Lon Chaney and Norma Shearer, and feared they had a flop on their hands, Thalberg disappeared into the cutting room and didn't come out for two days and a night. But when he had finished, they had a successful picture. It is indicative that in today's film parlance the 'cutter' has graduated to the title of 'film editor,' and a number of able directors and producers have come up through the cutting rooms." (Thalberg, of course, married Miss Shearer and guided her career to its peak.)

Albert Lewin, who produced *The Good Earth* and *Mutiny on the Bounty* under Thalberg, and then quit the studio when he died in the late 1930s, said Thalberg was "the opposite of producers who indiscriminately cut up pictures. Irving *built* them up. He did that with *The Big Parade,* for one, in 1925. After it was completed, he felt it needed more and saw to it that it got it. The picture was a great success. He was creative and saw possibilities all the time." (When *Parade* was reissued in '31 with further additions—sound effects and a musical background—it didn't do too well; and in 1967 Janus Films edited the feature from its original 130 minutes to 52 for release to collegiate film groups.)

Alfred Hitchcock expounded in *Sight and Sound:* "In those days it was a producer's cinema, absolutely. I remember what surprised me when I went to work for Selznick on *Rebecca* was that he always spoke with admiration about Thalberg as 'a genius with finished film.' But I soon got to understand that this was just what all the great producers were. They couldn't begin to visualize what a film would look like: they had to have it tangibly there, in front of them, to work on.

"In the great days at Metro they would have a script drafted, and then get W. H. Van Dyke or someone of the sort to direct it in about three weeks. They would put a roughcut together, and the producer would come in to look at it. Then they'd preview it somewhere out in the wilds, check the cards and make notes. And then they'd reshoot and re-edit all over the place for another three weeks or more. And finally they would have a film. They got a lot of successes that way, but when you think of the number of films they were making altogether I doubt whether the proportion of successes was any better then than it is now.

"All this still went on when I arrived in Hollywood. Do you know, they wouldn't allow a director to do any retakes during shooting even for some purely technical reason, like that there wasn't any film in the camera? What was the point? The sequence might not be in the final film anyhow. This was all very strange and worrying to me on *Rebecca,* as I had never worked this way in England. But even worse was when Selznick came up to me on the day I finished shooting and told me they were previewing it in a fortnight.

"And so they did: we threw a roughcut together, put on some temporary music and carted it off to a preview in some one-horse Western town. Then Selznick brooded over the audience reactions, and we began another three weeks or so of reshooting, combining two sequences into one, shot in a different location, adding and eliminating characters, rewriting dialogue. Of course you could do that then: stars were on contract and just around the corner anyway. When it took five days to get from Hollywood to New York, instead of just a few hours, it stood to reason that they would be.

"But I did get my own way more than most, right from the start. Not being used to this way of shooting, I shot only what I knew I was going to need for the way I intended to edit the scene. I never bothered about 'cover,' mastershots and all the rest. So when Selznick came to re-edit, he found that all he had to play with was what was actually in the edited film. 'You and your damned jigsaw shooting methods,' he said to me one day. 'How do you expect me to get a film out of *this!*' "

Rebecca won the 1940 Best Picture Oscar, plus the black-and-white cinematography statuette and nominations for director Hitchcock and actors Laurence Olivier, Joan Fontaine (starring), and Judith Anderson (supporting).

In 1965 20th Century-Fox European production chief Elmo Williams reflected that graduation to editor was not yet over for the cutter: "The cutter is trained at the mechanical end and often is not an editor."

Williams, who came up in the industry as an editor, also discussed the different standards in editing between U. S. and European filmmakers.

"The American, trained in a major studio, is inclined to lean to the view that the director, having completed his job, can, and should, leave the editing to a qualified craftsman operating independently. The European director, on the other hand, has always assumed responsibility of putting his own film together, and thus being totally responsible for it." Williams attributed the latter to his belief that many European directors work with cutters who never became editors, in part explaining their insistence on cutting their own films.

Williams also asserted that the wise director always will avail himself of the services of a good editor, although he felt that directors who started their careers in the cutting room should have charge of their work to the end.

Orson Welles says: "No one can pretend to be a film director unless he does his own editing."

Shakespeare, on stage and screen, always has been fair game for scissor parties. Upon completion of his British-made film of *Hamlet,* Laurence Olivier—after much heart-searching—decided that the "How all occasions do inform against me" soliloquy, important in showing the development of Hamlet's character, should be cut. Olivier hated to do it, but the scene ran almost five minutes at a time in the continuity when it did not seem wise to be loquacious, and Olivier wanted to hold his movie audience. He did, and won 1948's Best Picture of the Year Oscar from Hollywood, along with the Best Actor trophy, among others. Olivier's *Hamlet* marked the first time a foreign-made film had ever won the Best Picture honor.

Charles Laughton, also a gifted classical actor, appeared in the episodic, all-star *On Our Merry Way* (1948)—up through the sneak previews only. First called *A Miracle Can Happen,* the United Artists production presented Laughton as a Protestant minister who read from the Bible (the kind of thing the actor himself is said to have enjoyed doing most, in concerts and on recordings) in the second of the three stories Burgess Meredith told. But Laughton was excised before the picture went into general release.

Meredith has said it was "one of the most beautiful sequences I've seen," but "the United Artists people said it was too serious and that Charles Laughton was boxoffice poison. David Selznick looked at it, and he thought the only *good* sequence was the Laughton sequence. He offered them a million dollars to sell him the picture as it was, which would give them a slight profit, I think, and a percentage, if they would allow him to re-do the rest of the film and keep the sequence in that they were going to throw out. They thought they were going to make a fortune . . . it had all these big names, and refused it." The film was a bust.

It took two stars to replace Laughton in the continuity: Dorothy Lamour and Victor Moore. (Laughton is dead now, and of course he is irreplaceable.)

Another deceased irreplaceable, W. C. Fields, played in a 1942 film similar to the aforementioned Laughton one titled *Tales of Manhattan* (with Laughton again in a guest star bit, but one that got in this time), a five-part potpourri with Fields in the sixth and concluding episode, which never made it to theaters. The film, about a tailcoat's travels to different stations of life, was overlength, and this 20-minute segment seemed the easiest to drop. Also cut in this section were Phil Silvers and perennial Marx Brothers foil, the regal Margaret Dumont. There was talk it would be sent out as a short subject, but it never was. With the cult still growing today for the irascible comedian who, in his waning years, is said to have driven around in a huge car threatening pedestrians, there is still a chance this Julien Duvivier-directed footage may show up. *Tales* was a 20th Century-Fox release.

So was *O. Henry's Full House* (1952), yet another omnibus picture with Laughton, in five parts plus a Fred Allen–Oscar Levant segment, "The Ransom of Red Chief," that was cut in some parts of the U. S. and Europe. Director Howard Hawks said: "I imagine it was cut because it wasn't really O. Henry. I started out just to make a comedy and got a long way from O. Henry. They probably didn't think it fit with the other episodes that had been made for the picture."

Universal had its problems, too, on the all-star route back in the early '40s. Duvivier's *Flesh and Fantasy* opened without a lengthy sequence dealing with a blind girl (Gloria Jean) and an escaped prisoner (Alan Curtis), which nevertheless eventually did reach theaters as a one-hour feature film known as *Destiny.* Furthermore, only about half of the Edward G. Robinson footage filmed for his *Flesh and Fantasy* vignette was used.

A couple of years before, in 1941, soprano Gloria Jean faced a destiny of an even more hazardous sort when she teamed with W. C. Fields on the same Universal lot where Fields had been seen to sit at his window with a rifle he'd sworn to use on Deanna Durbin. Their vehicle was *Never Give a Sucker an Even Break,* and things were even chancier for Gloria because she also was an adolescent (Fields' regard for children was lower than his opinion of sopranos). The picture went well enough, though, for a Fields vehicle. In the last reel Fields even was heard to tell little Gloria that he'd promised her mother he'd look out for her. However, the audience really had no idea what he was talking about because Gloria's mother was shown only briefly in the beginning, and no such vow had been made then.

Raymond Rohauer told me: "Once when I was doing research on Fields, I came across a still from *Sucker* showing Fields with Universal contract player Anne Nagel as an aerialist who was obviously dying in the scene which was not in the film I saw. From this still I deduced that her dialogue was undoubtedly something like 'Will you take care of my daughter?' The producers may have found this section too serious for the thoroughly wacky movie that ensued. I knew the director, Eddie Cline, but I didn't come across the still until after he died." Corroborating Rohauer, the still later popped up in William K. Everson's book, *The Art of W. C. Fields,* as a deleted scene.

The official studio synopsis read: "Gloria's mother, Madame Gorgeous, is killed in a trapeze fall while working in a circus picture." The elimination of this Nagel footage obviously was a last-minute decision, and may even have been in for initial engagements and cut later on for reissue.

Repeat, *nothing, no one* is exempt from the shears, not even lovable old character actresses like Beulah Bondi. Miss Bondi played Frau Koerber in Garbo's *The Painted Veil,* was in the version previewed at New York's Capitol Theater in December, 1934, and got reviewed by several publications. She is also seen in most of the key still books of that picture, as well as in some of the histories of Garbo's career that pop up to this day (including *The Films of Greta Garbo* by Michael Conway, Dion McGregor, and Mark Ricci), and was billed sixth in the credits originally. Later her scenes were re-shot with Bodil Rosing, although there remains a glimpse of Miss Bondi in one party scene.

Peter Bull has told the *Painted Veil*-like story of the prophetically titled *The Lost People,* which he did at England's Elstree Studios some years ago with Mai Zetterling, Dennis Price, Richard Attenborough, and Herbert Lom. As first filmed, the cast had contained an internationally known temperamental star actress who, due to unintelligibility, was cut out of the picture. This was decided months later and only one cast member was still available for re-shooting with the replacement, posing no small problems. The first lady ultimately sued the film company, not because she had been cut out, but because one long shot had been left of her and (she claimed) this made her look like an extra.

Early silents star Lillian Gish, who still works hard and regularly, had been off the screen for almost a decade doing theater when she returned in '42 for Paul Muni's *The Commandos Strike at Dawn.* Although she got third billing, Miss Gish was reduced in the release print to minor support as the wife of a Norwegian (Ray Collins, the fine actor who died in 1965, best known as Lt. Tragg in the *Perry Mason* TV series) tortured by Nazi invaders.

Dame Flora Robson had her role as the poverty-stricken mother of the young Sean O'Casey in *Young Cassidy* (1965) slightly snipped. In this brawling, sentimental look at Irish life at the time of the Trouble, Miss Robson died half-way through and was seen in bed only when her son (Rod Taylor) discovered her there, dead. There is a still showing her sitting up in bed, hardly ready for a jig but very much able to enjoy a kiss on the forehead from her doting son, a scene cut from the release print.

At a Manhattan cocktail party in 1967 celebrating character actress Blanche Yurka's 60th year in show business, the guest of honor told me the story of perhaps *the* disappointment of her career. It had happened 27 years before in Hollywood, but her still riveting eyes blazed when she recalled her experience.

"It was a film that could've done for me what *Little Caesar* did for Eddie Robinson," Miss Yurka, as grand a figure as ever, believed. "When finally released—there were several title changes—it was called *Queen of the Mob.* A friend at Paramount asked if I would consider playing a perfectly horrible woman who, it turned out, was based on the real-life mob leader, Ma Barker. (Our 'Queen' was named Ma Webster.) I said sure, if it was a good part. He sent me the script and I saw that I would play this woman in four completely different phases of her life, from housewife and mother to cold-blooded murderess to her 'dear' little-lady-who-made-cookies masquerade to the real, suffering woman. I jumped at this fantastic acting opportunity.

"There was one remarkable long section that was like a stage scene: it built gradually to a peak of excitement. We worked all day on it, and I was so pleased I went to the director and said, 'Take my name off the credits, do anything you like with the picture, but *please* don't do anything to this scene.' I felt it would make all the difference in the quality of the picture. In the scene J. [Carrol] Naish, a fine actor, had his big moment when he told Ma he wanted to get out of the gang, adding 'I want what's coming to me.' Then I had a wonderful line: 'You'll get what's coming to you.' With that, I signaled one of my sons to kill J., which he did.

"A long time went by before I was allowed to see the finished picture. When I did, I saw that, among other things, they had cut out all of this last business with Naish, which was the whole first half of the long scene that was so vital. His disappearance from the story was now unexplained. He just went up in smoke. Studio politics had quite a bit to do with it all. The producer was on his way out, and the incoming fellow wanted to show that the outgoing one was no good. They finally released *Queen of the Mob* as a B movie."

Miss Yurka, perhaps best known to moviegoers as Madame DeFarge in Ronald Colman's *A Tale of Two Cities* (made in 1935), continued—as Ethel Griffies once put it—"yurking" in films, and beautifully, but in subordinate roles that offered little glory.

Not even death is sacred. The last picture in which Steve Cochran appeared, *Tell Me in the Sunlight,* also directed by Cochran, was released in 1967 (three years after it had been made and many months after Cochran's death) cut from its original more than two hours length to 82 minutes.

Social position won't save you. Dina Merrill, the daughter of cereal queen Mrs. Merriweather Post May and New York stockbroker E. P. Hutton and cousin of Barbara Hutton, has said that her best scene was cut from the John Frankenheimer-directed *The Young Savages,* starring Burt Lancaster.

Early in her career (which was pretty early), Shirley Temple landed an unbilled role as a sharecropper's child in Janet Gaynor's *Carolina*, but much of Shirley's footage was edited out. Nevertheless, it acquainted the Fox Films casting department with her and she was soon the sensation of the movie world. Shirley's own favorite part came in 1937 with *Wee Willie Winkie.* This was released as a roadshow attraction running 105 minutes, but when it went into general release some months later it was 12 minutes shorter.

With the exception of his Cowardly Lion in *The Wizard of Oz,* a deathless performance and film, Bert Lahr, the master clown with numerous top roles on Broadway, had few worthwhile picture parts. In *Zaza* (1939), a film adapted from a moth-eaten play, Lahr had a prominent role in what the producers hoped would be a recreation of Paris in the '90s. New Italian import Isa Miranda was given the title lead first, but her accent proved too heavy and Claudette Colbert played the can-can dancer. The plot was too hoary to be overcome, though; and director George Cukor has said that the film would have been better if several of Lahr's comedy scenes hadn't been cut.

Ann Sheridan was at her dry funniest in RKO's *Good Sam* in 1948, directed by the improvising-prone Leo McCarey with Gary Cooper in the title role of the hapless Good Samaritan. Sheridan's infectious laughing jag when she saw another of her husband's good deeds backfire is a comedy gem, but she has said the film was much funnier before cutting. "It was a huge, elongated picture and I worked for 11 weeks on it," Sheridan reminisced. "It was an amusing script and it was a delight to work with Leo and Gary. I think the main thing wrong was that Cooper and I did not have that spark together. Cutting may have had something to do with it, because they stuck really to the family thing. There was a lot of comedy, but so much was cut out, you cannot believe it."

Not even Vera Ralston gets away, the "actress" wife of the late Republic Pictures' late chief, Herbert J. Yates. She was "about 30" and he was over 70 when they married.

Vera, who came to the states in 1939 as Vera Hruba Ralston, was an ice-skating Czech cow whom Yates tried to turn into a silk puss, giving her his studio's most important dramatic properties and, obviously, the blind devotion only a man insanely in love could summon. For Miss Ralston, surprisingly graceless (for a skater) and burdened by a cumbersome peasant's frame, was one thing on ice but *another* on her own. Acting and personality were beyond refugee Ralston's rink.

Still, Yates, at the time of their merger the grandfather of 12, whom Miss Ralston called "Baby," quickly stashed her skates and starred her in his films for about 15 years, perhaps only coincidentally the same years in which the studio where Roy Rogers had risen to fame began to lose ground and eventually went out of existence. Yates might have done better to promote Trigger—for films, I mean—who, when he died not long ago, Rogers thought enough of to have stuffed.

Not that Miss Ralston's properties ever amounted to much. Republic studios had established a niche with low-budget, fast-action crime or Western pictures, features, and serials. Having a First Lady on the lot was something Republic never really got used to, and the scripts Ralston got showed it. A particular beaut was *Surrender,* formerly *That Barton Woman,* and made, incredibly, as late as 1950. A still has fallen into my hands showing the two heavily accented femme leads, that Slav Ralston and that Teuton Maria Palmer, playing their big confrontation scene in an early West town, Miss Palmer in bed, Miss Ralston hulking over her in yards and yards of period finery. The only thing is, in the released print the scene was played with both ladies on their feet.

I have long toyed with the idea of collaborating with a gifted music man on a Broadway musical based on the life of this Baby-sans-Bogie called, naturally, *Hruba!* And if we could get Carol Channing on ice skates. . . .

13. CROCODILE SHEARS

Some actors, finding their careers sinking, have been known to blame the shears for insignificant parts they have grabbed at.

Anne Baxter is an Oscar winner for her support in 1946's *The Razor's Edge,* but she was less and less in demand when a fancy-lady role came along in the sudsy 1960 Maria Schell–Glenn Ford remake of *Cimarron* at MGM. Miss Baxter accepted it, but, according to a reporter who attended the Oklahoma premiere of the epic, she left the theater almost in tears because her part had been so terribly cut. I have it on good authority that Baxter's performance on screen appeared just about as filmed, so it would look as if this excellent actress—who shouldn't have to—was doing a bit of face-saving.

Claire Trevor, a Best Supporting Actress Oscar winner (*Key Largo* in 1948) like Baxter, claims a similar problem with *Honky Tonk,* a Clark Gable–Lana Turner vehicle of 1941, in which Trevor, too, played an easy-virtued ladyfriend of the hero's, also on the MGM lot. But Trevor's story had confirmation from MGM, begrudgingly—the studios aren't anxious to spread the word that their product is incomplete. (Frequently actors don't want to talk about studios cutting them, either: they feel it might lessen their chances of working that particular lot again. Furthermore, it is really somewhat unnatural for the occupationally self-absorbed actor to admit that any film on him might be expendable, and the actor who tells anyone his work was junkable can be expected—like the woman who would tell her age—to tell anything.)

"I had some great scenes in *Honky Tonk,*" says Trevor. "At least I *thought* I had them until I went to the press preview of it. My scenes had been scissored. 'Where am I?' I kept asking myself as I watched it on the screen. 'What happened to me?' I cried all the way home and swore I'd never make another picture. There were a lot of nights when I felt like that."

Even a great trouper like Joan Crawford, after almost half a century in pictures and a Best Actress Academy Award (1945's *Mildred Pierce*), is not above suspicion. Not long ago when her career was in a brief slump she made a horrible film called *The Caretakers* (1965) in which she played the subordinate, faintly unsympathetic asylum head nurse bucking change. As written, you couldn't even hate this woman, and were only anxious for her departure from a scene to get on with it—a rare emotion to feel in the presence of the dynamic Joan Crawford. She later said it originally had been a very good part—the nurse had been bitchy because doctor Robert Stack didn't return her feelings—but it had been cut. Another player in the picture has informed me that this is not really true, but was said to excuse Crawford's taking the only work available at the time in the medium she loves. And Crawford, *certainly,* is a Star who shouldn't have to do this kind of thing, a lady who, over a longer period of time than any lady still leading (with the possible exceptions of Lillian Gish and Gloria Swanson, neither of whom had been as consistently active in films as Crawford), has done enough for the screen to deserve only the best of all possible roles.

The only cuts in *Caretakers* that I have record of took place when the film opened in England a couple of years later under the title of *Borderlines.* The running time—listed for U. S. showings as either 97 or 95 minutes—was now 88 minutes. Critic Allen Eyles related: "It once carried a closing message from President Kennedy, and besides this at least two other scenes have vanished, one in which shock treatment is applied to Polly Bergen . . . and another in which she wandered into a men's ward and was almost violated."

Better documented Crawford cuts were those on *The Best of Everything* earlier. Biographer Lawrence J. Quirk on the matter: "Several of her best scenes, including what was reportedly a superbly acted drunk episode, wound up on the cutting room floor, due to the producer's decision that the film was too long."

Phyllis Newman, the New York TV and stage giddyguts (that

way, perhaps, at realizing her extreme good fortune in marrying Adolph Green, of the songwriting-performing team of Betty Comden and—), has said that her role in 1955's *Picnic* was shorn of her scenes with William Holden, making it look like little more than a bit. An informant at Columbia Pictures tells a different story: Phyllis' film debut in *Picnic* (and practically her farewell film appearance) was a minor role to begin with, and suffered no significant scissoring in the final negative.

There is more substantiation to Phyllis' story about her experiences on *The Vagabond King,* a Technicolor-VistaVisioning, 1956 style, of the oft-done Friml operetta starring Kathryn Grayson and the Maltese import, Oreste, Paramount's answer to MGM's Mario [Lanza] who had, among several things fellow tenor Oreste didn't, a last name. (Actually, Oreste did have a surname: Kirkop—it rhymed with ker-plop—which he discarded over here to give him more of an aura. But *Vagabond* was such a gobbler that it provided Oreste with both a much-touted introduction and an immediate stateside swan song, and also just about finished La Grayson's decade-and-a-half as a leading tinseltown soprano.)

Miss Newman has said the film originally was almost twice as long (it ran 88 minutes when finally released many months after completion), and in the cutting her part as Lulu became hardly that—little more than a quick flash and about one line. This came as a shock to Miss Newman, who had proudly gathered her family around for her first viewing of it.

14. MGMUSICAL CHAIRS

What happens to the cut film?

As we've learned, the answer varies. Some is saved, some put back later (sometimes for television), some used again in other films, some discarded. Pat O'Brien, whose most famous role is probably *Knute Rockne—All American* (1940) for Warners, had this to say in his autobiography, *The Wind at My Back:* "The research and stories I heard about 'Rock' helped me see the man clearer and closer, and I tried to evolve the full figure. It was not easy in a fast-moving, action-packed picture. The actor in any Hollywood film is up against the problem of telling a story that brings in and holds the customers. The directors, cutters, editors, producers are all at work trying to move the picture faster, cutting, trimming, pacing it so that the actor is often aware that if every inch of film isn't vital, it is going to end up on the cutting room floor. And some very marvelous footage has ended up in the discard cans that went out to the refineries, which burned them to recover the metal in the silver nitrate the films were coated with." The latter was especially true during the metal-precious days of World War II.

As for MGM's Judy Garland (Hollywood's Most Cut Star?), songs of hers that were deleted from her 1941 *Ziegfeld Girl* were used in a 1942 industrial short called *We Shall Have Music.*

The same thing happened to Ethel Merman in her '34 *We're Not Dressing,* which also starred Bing Crosby and Carole Lombard. Merman's big number, which took weeks to film and used 40 elephants trained to circle her in Busby Berkeley-like unison while she belted out a tune called "The Animal in Me," was cut. Merman was told: "It distracted the audience from the story"! Incongruously, when everyone reprised his songs at the end, there was Ethel with a snatch of "Animal in Me"—leaving the audience to wonder where *that* tune had come from! The production number reappeared in *The Big Broadcast of 1936,* and LeRoy Prinz earned an Oscar nomination for his direction of it, along with his Viennese waltz number from *All the King's Horses.* Merman is rather bitter about the treatment she got in her early pictures. In *Alexander's Ragtime Band* (1938) Merman footage again was cut, this time to boost Alice Faye's on-screen time.

Miss Garland was less fortunate than Merman with *her* big production number from *Meet Me in St. Louis.* It was a ditty by Rodgers and Hammerstein originally written for *Oklahoma!* called "Boys and Girls Like You and Me," and when author Sally Benson saw it on film she decided it was inappropriate to the folksy, intimate feel of the movie as a whole, so it was cut—*never* to be seen. Still, the picture was probably Judy's most popular, next to *Wizard of Oz,* and was said to be the highest-grossing filmusical up to that time (1944). Interestingly, the rest of the score was by Hugh Martin and Ralph Blane.

The tune "Last Night When We Were Young," called by Judy

"one of the great love songs of all time" and reputedly the favorite of its composer, Harold Arlen, was written for Lawrence Tibbett to sing in *Metropolitan* (1935), but was cut during the final editing. Judy got it into her *In the Good Old Summertime* but again it was cut. (Years later, it was included in an MGM Records long-playing package of Garland tunes—and listed as a number from *Summertime.*) Then Frank Sinatra heard the discarded piece of soundtrack and sang it in *Take Me Out to the Ball Game*—and again, cut. It is yet to be heard on the screen.

MGM has always played a wicked game of musical chairs. Howard Keel's entire "cameo" singing appearance in *I Love Melvin* (1953) was cut. The now highly regarded Rouben Mamoulian-directed Americana musical, *Summer Holiday* (1948), had its most exotic scene zapped—perhaps for just that reason: an Arabian nights dream sequence with Mickey Rooney and Gloria De Haven. John Kobal, in his superbly illustrated book, *Gotta Sing Gotta Dance,* revealed: "This scene, designed by Walter Plunkett with inspiration from Persian miniature prints, was cut from the final print of the film." In *Broadway Melody of 1938* (released in 1937) Eleanor Powell sang an Arthur Freed piece titled "Got a New Pair of Shoes" that got the old heave-ho. It was quickly picked up by Judy Garland in *Thoroughbreds Don't Cry* (1937).

Universal's queen of song, Deanna Durbin, had her troubles, too —aside from having to look out for W. C. Fields. In *Up in Central Park* (1948), Deanna's next-to-last movie, only two numbers from the original Mike Todd Broadway production were heard. Most of the Sigmund Romberg–Herbert and Dorothy Fields songs were filmed but later cut.

If patrons had known what—and how much—film they were not getting to see that had been shot for *Ziegfeld Follies of 1946,* a theater manager or three just might not have been around to see 1947. For this multi-star extravaganza that was three years in preparation and two years in the making (best part: a breathtaking "Limehouse Blues" number danced with hands as well as feet by Fred Astaire and Lucille Bremer) probably had the costliest, most extensive scene discards in filmusical history.

Several years ago, Bob Osborne of Hollywood revealed in a letter to a film magazine: "On a recent data collecting visit to MGM's still department at Culver City I came across some scene-shots from completed sequences for *Ziegfeld Follies of 1946* which were cut from the final print. Among them: (1) Lena Horne, in a showboat setting and backed by Avon Long and nine colored dancing girls, singing 'Liza'; (2) Fred Astaire, in white shirt, white slacks and white shoes, and backed by 23 male dancers, singing and dancing 'If Swing Goes I Go, Too,' which he wrote and choreographed; (3) Fanny Brice and Hanley Stafford in a 'Baby Snooks' skit; (4) Jimmy Durante singing 'Start the Day with a Song' and also participating in a sketch with Edward Arnold, Kay Williams [the last Mrs. Clark Gable] and Stephen McNally that satirized the income tax; (5) James Melton, in black Western togs and a Western setting, singing 'Cowboy's Lament'; (6) the spectacular bubble finale, so cut in the final print that it made a strangely abrupt ending to the film—all that remained were a few bubbles and a few models and Kathryn Grayson singing 'Beauty is Everywhere,' and nothing of Astaire and Bremer in evening clothes, dancing amid thousands of bubbles cascading down black rhinestone cliffs, Cyd Charisse and chorus boys dancing on the rocks, on which were spotted girls wearing elaborate Ziegfeld headdress and gowns."

The first of many pictures at Metro for Lena Horne was *Panama Hattie* (1942), with Ann Sothern, Red Skelton, Dan Dailey, Ben Blue, Virginia O'Brien, and Marsha Hunt. "But I never worked with them," Lena recalled. "I did a musical number that was not integrated into the script. The idea was that it could be cut out of the film, without spoiling it, by local distributors if they thought their audiences would object to seeing a Negro. It was ridiculous, but that's how show business—and especially the movies—docilely bowed to prejudice 20 years ago. The number I did was a Latin thing, in which I danced with the Berry Brothers. I was beautifully gowned, I thought, and the number was directed by Vincente Minnelli. I felt that it came off rather well. But, of course, it occasioned more criticism. A number of white people wrote the studio to inquire about their new Latin-American discovery and some Negroes charged that I was trying to pass. That, in particular, hurt. At no point in my career had I ever pretended to be anything but what I was and so naturally I thought this criticism unjustified."

Gwen Verdon's experience on Fox's *David and Bathsheba* (1951) was like Horne's on *Panama Hattie.* Verdon, raised in Hollywood and dancing coach for many of the town's top musical stars, had several small parts in films before becoming one of Broadway's first ladies of musical comedy. Including *Bathsheba,* from which her specialty number was cut in the South because she was an Egyptian Negress dancing for a white man—"It was the Bible, what could I do?", she shrugged.

By 1966, the South had become sufficiently enlightened to allow *A Patch of Blue,* the love story of a blind white girl and a Negro office worker, to be a big boxoffice hit in southern playdates as well as up North. Nevertheless, MGM cut the brief kissing scene between Elizabeth Hartman and Sidney Poitier for the southern market.

Musical numbers in films are probably the easiest to cut, being fundamentally extraneous, usually, and God knows how many have been omitted over the years, particularly in foreign countries. According to producer Ross Hunter: "Europeans don't have the musical comedy tradition that we have in this country. The Italians have been schooled in opera, the Germans in the whipped-cream operetta.

"In the old days, Hollywood could afford to make musicals for the American market, which provided the major profit for films; anything from foreign distribution was pure gravy. Nowadays we count on the foreign take for 50 per cent of our income. We can't afford to make musicals if the foreigners aren't going for them."

In a *Life* article early in '65, Thomas Thompson noted: "Hollywood believes a musical film must have two basic ingredients to succeed abroad: (1) spectacular dancing, as in *West Side Story,* and (2) a story of universal appeal (i.e., not something strictly American like *The Music Man*)."

Thompson also related: "When the movie version of Rodgers and Hammerstein's *The King and I* opened in the U. S., it was a financial hit. But when Fox booked it into a first-run cinema in Paris, the French saw a different film. Since the Parisians did not like musical numbers, Fox went through each print with a pair of scissors. When Yul Brynner or Deborah Kerr opened a mouth to sing, the number was snipped out. The picture thus was a hit, although considerably shortened and more than a little jerky. Four years later, with *Can-Can,* Fox scissors men did the same sort of snipping for its French release. *Carousel* suffered the same indignity for its Italian showings."

The just-released *The Sound of Music,* opined Thompson, was the ideal filmusical for overseas consumption because "it has spectacular musical numbers, is set in Austria, has the ugly threat of war throughout and has no Americana whatsoever."

How wrong Thompson was. Several months later, after *Sound of Music* had proved one of the great film successes of all time, it opened in Munich, Germany, with about a third of its running time eliminated. In the city where Naziism grew, the picture ended right after the wedding of Baron von Trapp and Maria, with their Nazi-predicated flight from Austria completely omitted. Thus, German villainy was virtually unnoticeable in the cut print. The U. S. home office of 20th Century-Fox soon announced they had had no knowledge of the cutting and that the picture had been restored to its original full-length form.

Around the same time, a Miss M. E. Buckles wrote to *Films and Filming* to inquire about the Peggy Wood song, "Climb Ev'ry Mountain," which had been cut from the Rotterdam showing of *The Sound of Music.* "I can't think the time factor entered into it at all as the program was a leisurely one," she related, "including news, the trailer of a forthcoming film and advertisements; there was, too, the usual interval of about 15 minutes during the main feature. The Dutch friend who was with me suggested that there may have been some religious significance about the cutting of this song, but this surely could not be so. Perhaps you can tell me the reason for what seems to me a pointless cut in this delightful film."

In another letter to the same magazine, Londoner A. C. Sharman wrote: "What happened to the Apache scene from *Can-Can* which *Films and Filming* praises in the review of this film (May, 1960)? I saw *Can-Can* at a local cinema with *The Third Secret* and did not see this scene, which had obviously been cut out. I realise I am not the first to complain about this type of thing, and am very much against it, but surely if a scene has to be removed to make room for a double-bill why take out the reputedly best scene?"

United Artists' film of the Broadway smash, *How to Succeed in Business Without Really Trying* (1967), was shot two ways by director David Swift to thwart overseas operations. One version featured Robert Morse, Michele Lee, Rudy Vallee, and the others singing the Frank Loesser songs. The other had the actors speak "dialogue bridges" that would allow the numbers to be eliminated if continental audiences didn't like them. Meanwhile, cut from *How To* prints everywhere by opening time at Radio City Music Hall was the

"Coffee Break" number rendered by Anthony Teague, Kay Reynolds, and the office girls.

In *Steps in Time,* his autobiography, Fred Astaire (how many others can you think of who are the undisputed top in their fields?) explained about the cuts that had taken place with MGM's *The Band Wagon* (1953): "Funny, with all that hoofing I did in that picture, I remember at the big Hollywood premiere a kindly old lady shouted to me as we were filing out of the theater, 'You didn't dance enough!' I had to laugh. Actually, four dance numbers were cut out because we had too much. That film was a bit unwieldy to get down to reasonable running time and we had shot too much stuff."

Carefree (1938), an Astaire–Rogers vehicle, lost a couple of Astaire vocals of Berlin tunes. "The Night is Filled with Music," a ballad, and a song the composer intended for Astaire's golf dance were used as background music but excised as vocals by release time. Regarding the following year's *The Story of Vernon and Irene Castle,* the last teaming of Astaire and Rogers for a decade, featured player Frances Mercer told *Film Fan Monthly:* "I played Claire Ford, the actress Vernon was in love with before he met Irene. So they shot an awful lot of me in the theater and scenes with him. But Irene Castle had complete say-so on the film, and she decided that she didn't want anyone to know he'd been in love with anybody before her. So I go to the opening, after shooting for months on it, and my part was cut down to the basics."

Ginger Rogers, never known for her singing in spite of her many musical roles, has lost many a vocal chord to cutting room forceps. Her singing of "I've Got to Sing a Torch Song" was removed from *Gold Diggers of 1933,* as were her vocals of "Suddenly It's Spring" and the beautiful "My Ship" from *Lady in the Dark* (1944). Mitchell Leisen, director of *Lady,* recently divulged the reason for the "Ship" scuttling: "The head of the studio, Buddy De Sylva, hated Kurt Weill, the composer, with an undying hate—loathed the song, and he got it out of the picture. It was the best thing Ginger did in it . . . it *was* filmed. She sang 'Ship' a cappella against a foxtrot from a gymnasium, sitting all alone outside the gym. We blended it together so the foxtrot made a background accompaniment. And he couldn't stand it, he said 'Take it out.' I said, 'Over my dead body—

it's the basis of the whole plot. When she suddenly remembers that song, her problems are all finished'; but it didn't mean a thing to him. Then he discovered that her lover was supposed to be a father image. Well, he said, 'I am not going to have incest in any picture made by Paramount,' and I said, 'Then why did you buy this story? That's the whole plot!' " In *Stage Door* the vocal of "Put Your Heart into Your Feet and Dance" was cut, but the tune was danced to by Rogers and Ann Miller.

When Rogers' "Suddenly It's Spring" number went, incidentally, so did the whole appearance of Macdonald Carey, who had had a main role in the Gertrude Lawrence Broadway original. Three years later, however, the song turned up in, and as the title of, the Paramount comedy *Suddenly It's Spring,* with Paulette Goddard, Fred MacMurray, and, in his first post-war part, Carey.

At MGM studios in '51, Ava Gardner was assigned the old Helen Morgan role in their musical spectacular, *Show Boat* (a role originally intended for Judy Garland). Anxious to do her own vocals, Ava studied with a coach and sang "Bill" and "Can't Help Lovin' Dat Man" well enough, giving one of her most adroit performances as the tragic mulatto, Julie. But it was decided to dub her singing in the movie with Eileen Wilson's voice, although the soundtrack album was released on MGM Records using Ava's vocal renditions. She still receives royalties on the LP that only serve as a reminder.

Joan Crawford has had it a lot easier since she departed her "dancing lady" quasi-musical roles for dramatic assignments. In her book, *A Portrait of Joan,* the star recalled her experience in *The Ice Follies of 1939.* Said Joan: "This was trash. MGM had hired the entire International Ice Follies, they tossed in an old stage play they had sitting on the shelf, *Excess Baggage,* and Jimmy Stewart, Lew Ayres and I kept trying to figure out where we came in. Advertising art showed me on skates but I was no skater. And though I was supposed to be a singer in the picture, my three much-touted songs hit the cutting room floor because they slowed up the skating numbers."

A couple of years after Ava Gardner's unusual experience with her *Show Boat* recordings, Miss Crawford, long ensconced as a first lady of film drama, limbered up leg and vocal chords for another try at musical comedy in MGM's *Torch Song.* Crawford, too, recorded all the required tunes but at the last minute it was decided that

India Adams' voice better suited the role and her singing was dubbed in. However, while MGM did issue an album of *Torch* songs, Miss Crawford's vocals did not show up. Miss Adams served again.

More recently, Jaye P. Morgan, a singer who also happened to be a likable comedienne but who hadn't been overworked at either then, was signed to sing the title song of *John Goldfarb, Please Come Home* over the credits of the Fox film and again at the end. She did, through the trade showings. But then the film ran into trouble with Notre Dame University, which sued to keep the picture's comedy portrayal of its football team as boozing chasers from ever reaching the public. The film's release, scheduled for Christmas '64, was held up, and for a while it looked as if the million-dollar-plus production might be shelved permanently. Notre Dame lost, however, and *John Goldfarb* tackled theaters in March '65.

While the ads read "Original Uncut Version!", this was not so. In the interim star Shirley MacLaine (whose husband, Steve Parker, also happened to be the producer) became enamoured of the title song, recorded it on a single record for 20th Century-Fox Records, and replaced Miss Morgan's off-screen rendition and on-screen credit with her own.

A bad break of a like if more visible—or nearly visible—nature occurred when country music recording star Molly Bee signed to do a song in a nightclub sequence of Howard Hawks' *Man's Favorite Sport?* (1964). Molly had played leads in several teen-age musical quickies but, she told me, this Hawks film would be a prestige job that could get her more—and bigger—roles in major pictures. Hawks, she added, had even liked her enough to request her for other pictures of his.

"Making *Man's Favorite Sport?* was such a lot of fun," Molly said afterward. "There was no script to speak of, and everybody winged it much of the time." It's a good thing Molly enjoyed the filming—the finished product was shorn of her entire appearance. The film had run too long. And, poor girl, Howard Hawks is not one of Hollywood's most prolific filmmakers.

Another budding film career that may have been nipped by a snip was that of Barbara Ruick, the daughter of actors Melville Ruick and Lurene Tuttle. Barbara knocked around MGM in small roles during the early '50s, and in '56 snagged her best part: Carrie Pipperidge in Fox' *Carousel,* with Gordon MacRae and Shirley

Jones, the lavish filmusical in the heralded CinemaScope 55, one of the surfeit of wide-screen processes (or sucker lures) of the day, this one disappearing by the end of '56. *Carousel* presented Barbara in a pleasing light, but she would have shone brighter if Fox hadn't cut one of her big numbers, "You're a Queer One, Julie Jordan." Barbara never again got as important a movie role as Mr. Snow's featherbrained Carrie. P. S.—the song turned up on the Capitol Records soundtrack LP.

Baritone Allan Jones was already an established filmusical star—*A Night at the Opera, Showboat* (1936 version), *The Firefly,* and, with his lovely wife, Irene Hervey, *Boys from Syracuse*—when he did Universal's *One Night in the Tropics* in '40. But what happened on this may have been one of the reasons he was soon doing Bs, and why by 1966, when we talked after a performance at New York's Living Room (where his son had started in The City), Allan was known to many simply as recording and club star Jack Jones' father. (It was almost gratifying to overhear a young woman seated near me ask her date "Who's he?", learn he was Jack Jones' old man, and then hear her reply, "Who's Jack Jones?")

Allan—traveling by trailer decorated with stills from his movies—had no difficulty recalling: "I had a contract at the studio with story, cast and director approval. One day they came to me with a good story they'd had around for a while called *Love Insurance,* and suggested I do it with Nancy Kelly, Bob Cummings and Peggy Moran, to the music of Jerome Kern, Eddie Sutherland as director. I said fine. A little later the producer said, 'I've got two comics, Bud Abbott and Lou Costello, and I'd like to fit them in the picture.' I had seen the boys in New York and, frankly, I couldn't imagine how they would fit into the picture. The producer said we'll just spot a couple of their routines here and there. I said all right, if you think it'll help the picture.

"After we'd completed the film, the director asked me if I had cutting approval. I said—no. He told me I was in for a shock when I saw what they were doing to the picture. And I was. Many of my scenes were cut, scenes that meant so much to the continuity. *One Night in the Tropics,* as it was finally called, now made no sense, had become a vehicle for Abbott and Costello's antics. It made them Universal's biggest stars."

More disastrous was Mel Tormé's experience on 1950's *Duchess of Idaho,* an Esther Williams aquacade at MGM that might have launched Mel—a jazz-oriented singer known as "the musician's musician" but an all-around performer—as a major movie personality. Twenty years later the diminutive Tormé could still taste his disenchantment on *Duchess* and told me so.

"The producer of the picture, Joe Pasternak, saw me at, oh, the Casbah in Los Angeles, I think it was," Mel explained. "Pasternak had pushed many a musical personality to stardom, people like Deanna Durbin, so I really broke my back that night to impress him. The audience backed me up, too. He told me about the Esther Williams musical he was starting and my part as a bellboy and I said yes. (I already had a picture-to-picture contract at Metro—which meant I did two pictures a year and was free to do other things instead of going to school there and like that.) Next thing I knew Esther Williams was pregnant. When they asked me for a six-month extension of my contract to give her a chance to have the baby and get back into shape, I said okay.

"I got my script and we began shooting. They gave me my song, 'Cold Hands, Warm Heart,' a butterscotchy, mock beguine tune I really didn't dig"—he sang a few bars—"but what the hell, I did it and the picture was eventually wrapped up.

"When you're doing a movie the producer and director *must* believe in you. Pasternak never really believed in me. (He had the hots for another male singer at the time.) And MGM never knew how to use me. Once I begged an executive to let me have one of the parts in the dramatic *Battleground* they were preparing—I'd been acting since I was a child. But he said nothing doing, Mel, we're planning great things for you in musicals.

"Well, when *Duchess of Idaho* premiered I found that not only had my song been cut, but my part had been shredded to about nine lines. It was brutal. It was not concomitant with my career: there I was, starring in a big New York club when the picture opened in which I had only a bit. Connie Haines, a fine little singer but who wasn't *that* big a name, had several songs in it; and her manager, Bullets Durgom, was even in a number, while I, who got $30,000 for the job, carried people's bags and not much else. I was terribly upset and depressed over it at the time. It was my last film at MGM for many years."

Mel has appeared in a couple of dozen pictures such as *Higher and Higher, Good News, Junior Miss* and *Words and Music,* but mostly in small roles. He has never been able to get a foothold in movies. A press agent once told me this was because The Velvet Fog, also known at one time as Testy Tormé, had offended producer Pasternak somewhere on the way to *Idaho.* Mel says they now speak cordially enough. Still, I don't think Pasternak is likely to request "Cold Hands, Warm Heart" at a Tormé performance.

The Revuers, comprised of Judy Holliday, Betty Comden, Adolph Green, Alvin Hammer, and John Frank, was a chic satirical fivesome that got its start in Greenwich Village back in the late '30s and eventually moved up to posher showcases. In 1943 they headed for Hollywood where, just as in the Betty Grable movies the studio was whipping up then, Fox executives saw them but wanted to sign only blonde Judy, who told them she wouldn't leave the other kids. After some urging, she accepted the Fox offer with an agreement that provided for the Revuers to have a part in the first film she did. Appropriately, the picture was *Greenwich Village* (1944), which made "Cherry Blonde" Vivian Blaine (replacing a pregnant Grable) a star but did nothing for Miss Holliday—and the Revuers' act as such was cut from the film. The group got very good collective billing as "The Revuers," yet they never got to do any of their turns and were seen only in stock bits as Village characters.

Janis Paige and Edie Adams had a couple of roles once that showed promise, among other things. In *Please Don't Eat the Daisies* (1960) Janis played a musical comedy star and got to do an elaborate number dressed in cellophane. But the piece never made the release print of the film that opened at New York's Radio City Music Hall. Miss Paige, albeit dandy, was really supporting Doris Day and David Niven and could have used the footage. Edie signed up at Hollywood's Pink Pussycat Club College of Stripping to study with "pro" Sally Marr (the late comedian Lenny Bruce's mother) for her role as ecdysiast Barbara of Seville in *Love with the Proper Stranger* (1963). And although her puny part could have used a pound of flesh, the routine Edie did was ultimately dropped from the movie. Edie sighed: "Elmer Bernstein had composed some *crazy* music for the number, too."

Lola Albright (runner up to Martha Hyer as The Screen's Longest Running Starlet) struggled along in bits and Bs for a decade until fleeting success as the torch singing girl on TV's *Peter Gunn* series. After that, she co-starred with Elvis Presley in a musical remake of the old Wayne Morris film, *Kid Galahad* (1962), but her only number wound up cut.

The first true screen musical, *Broadway Melody,* with an original score by Nacio Herb Brown and Arthur Freed, also was MGM's first all-talking picture. Furthermore, it used color for the big chorus production number, "The Wedding of the Painted Dolls," which, when Irving Thalberg saw its inhibited, stage-bound camera work, he ordered completely re-shot—although the film had been produced under great pressure to forestall Universal's imminent *Broadway.* The 1928–9 Best Picture Oscar went to *Broadway Melody.*

Melody is historically important, too, because it is the first example of pre-recording musical numbers. When the initial "Painted Dolls" sequence was scrapped, studio sound engineer Douglas Shearer (Norma's brother) explained to Thalberg that it would be a waste to discard the perfectly good recording of the number as well, and expensive to call back an orchestra to re-do it all. He convinced Thalberg they should shoot the scene to an amplified playback of the recording and then match the footage and the recording in the cutting room. Before too long, singers were recording their songs before the numbers were filmed and synchronizing their lip movements to the playback while the scene was being photographed.

One of the most aggravated cases of filmusical cutting was United Artists' *Reaching for the Moon* (1931), with Bing Crosby in a specialty role. In a 1964 career article on Bebe Daniels, DeWitt Bodeen wrote: "Everybody was sure it would be a smash, for Douglas Fairbanks was still an athletic hero and Bebe was a perfect feminine counterpart. But it proved a big disappointment, probably because it had been devised originally as a flimsy plot upon which to hang an Irving Berlin score, and then, because screen musicals were temporarily on the wane, all the numbers save one were cut . . . excepting a few choruses of 'Lower than Lowdown' sung by Bebe, June MacCloy and Crosby (in his first real part), all the musical numbers landed on the cutting room floor, leaving a thin succession of well-dressed gags about a playboy-stockbroker and playgirl-aviatrix' romance."

A Laurel and Hardy vehicle, 1934's *Babes in Toyland,* was reissued for years as *March of the Wooden Soldiers* with two of its most charming sequences missing: the Mother Goose prologue and the Slumber Scene. Since the latter led into the climactic fight between the hero, Tom-Tom, and the villain, Barnaby, the picture's continuity was a mess. William K. Everson included a whole section called "Deleted Scenes" in his book, *The Films of Laurel and Hardy,* "A roundup of some of the many intriguing and frustrating stills that exist of sequences shot for Laurel & Hardy films and deleted prior to release."

In the fall of 1966, when United Artists' film of the long-run Broadway musical comedy *A Funny Thing Happened on the Way to the Forum* was screened for the trade, under Beatles pictures director Richard Lester it had become more comedy than musical. Star Zero Mostel spotted New York University cinema professor Robert Gessner laughing a lot, and later told him: "There were just as many funny shots left on the cutting room floor."

Proposed Gessner: "Why not use them in a sequel and call it *On the Way Back*?"

Although not a musical, Jackie Gleason's *Gigot* was directed by Gene Kelly, who complained that 20th Century-Fox had taken it out of his (and Gleason's) hands and cut it beyond redemption. It flopped. Eddie Fisher's entire non-musical stint as an assistant director in the same studio's *All About Eve* got snipped out, too. *Eve* survived.

Another star who got her twinkle toes stepped on when she stepped out of her musical element was Ann-Margret. Early in '65 Mike Connolly wrote: "Universal is in an uproar over two Ann-Margret movies, both made in too much of a hurry. *Kitten with a Whip* isn't drawing as many customers as expected, and they're afraid to release Annie's new one, *Bus Riley's Back in Town.* As a result they're recalling playwright William Inge and the entire cast and crew for retakes." At the same time, with characteristic accuracy, Louella Parsons noted in her column: "Secretly, many changes are being made on the sexy Swede's recently completed *Bus Riley's Back in Town.* It's too violent and downbeat, particularly following on the heels of the equally brutal *Kitten with a Whip.* Although *Riley* is cut and ready for release, a rewrite job on certain parts is underway to give it a lighter touch, and another director, Brian Hutton, has been called in to direct the new scenes with Ann-Margret."

Obviously, the *Bus Riley* changes were not meant to be kept secret.

The studio must have felt that any publicity on these two B-budgeted dogs was better than none.

The early ads run in trade publications by Universal read "Screenplay by William Inge"; but when the film opened, the much-awarded Broadway dramatist, unhappy because of the picture's "damaged integrity and loss of satiric thrust," insisted that the credit read: "Screenplay by Walter Gage," who did not exist. Several writers had had a hand in the revised *Bus,* even though the Long Beach, Calif., preview of the original version was supposed to have gone well enough. "The studio had decided, for one thing, to enhance the role of Ann-Margret who had become a more important star since the start of the picture," said Inge. According to the reviewers after the film had opened, abetting this cause was unwise. In *Cue,* William Wolf hissed for most of his colleagues when he wrote: "Ann-Margret, playing a sex-starved wife, is about the worst actress imaginable . . . Bus Riley should leave again."

Veteran comedienne Natalie Schafer—whose portrayals of downy domed matrons are equaled only by Billie Burke's—*did* leave the picture. Although *Bus Riley* opened while Miss Schafer was co-starring as Jim Backus' wife, "Lovey," on the TV series *Gilligan's Island,* her entire *Riley* role was cut from the film. She had appeared with several pet dogs in a scene in which Michael Parks (Bus), just out of the Navy, tried to sell her a new cleaning device called (appropriately, in view of Parks' style of acting) "The Atomic Method."

A 1963 Susan Hayward picture, *Stolen Hours,* while also not a musical, had an interesting musical XXXing, of sorts. Twist King Chubby Checker was brought to London where this underrated remake of Bette Davis' favorite Davis film, *Dark Victory,* was being shot, to teach star Hayward to Twist for a party sequence. In the completed picture, the beginning of the dance sequence was left in, but the middle—the Twist part, it would seem—was cut. Consequently, when Hayward finished the now brief dance interlude, out of breath and the recipient of the observation "What a work-out!", the audience wondered just what kind of work-out the onlooker had in mind. The producers probably figured the Twist would be passé by the time the film was played off, which it was.

Other stills from this picture show Hayward—who gave a fine

performance as a dying playgirl (they don't stoke Hayward's kind of fire anymore), in some ways better than Davis' classic but today rather overdone-looking characterization—partying on top of a hotel ledge, and this was cut, too, although it figured in much of the advertising. Another still circulated for Hayward's *The Marriage-Go-Round* (1960) showed her watching while Julie Newmar stood on her head, apparently practicing Yogi. This amusing-looking scene was not in the movie I saw, which could have used it.

So, for that matter, could *The Honey Pot,* a Joseph Mankiewicz written-and-directed comedy begun late in 1965 but not released until 1967 and probably the most sliced up work ever to bear Oscar-winner Susan (*I Want to Live!*) Hayward's name.

Trouble beset from the start (Hayward's husband was dying, and she flew back and forth to the states from the Italian locations to be with him; and cinematographer Gianni di Venanzo died long before shooting was completed), the film had lost much expensive footage by opening time. Hayward, taking second billing (to Rex Harrison) for the first time in over a decade, and badly photographed, nevertheless vivified the picture as the coarse, wealthy Mrs. "Lone Star" Crockett Sheridan. She might have turned it into a minor personal triumph if some of her best moments had not been excised, notably a much-publicized dream sequence in which Harrison, as her *bon vivant* common law husband Cecil Fox, was a prospector dying in her arms in the desert—"Be ya daid, Ceece?"

Others suffered, too. Co-stars Edie Adams and Capucine, as well, both lost dream interludes that might have broken up the conversational monotony; but worst off of all was Herschel Bernardi who played movie star Adams' agent. Starring in *Fiddler on the Roof* on Broadway when *Honey Pot* premiered, Bernardi discovered his entire appearance in the still plotty and too-long movie—of which Harrison was said to own more than United Artists—had been cut.

There was at least one more time in her long and distinguished career when scissoring seriously damaged, or minimized, a Hayward portrayal. It was in *The Snows of Kilimanjaro* during the actress' early-'50s heyday at 20th Century-Fox. And while Hayward as a rich huntress did manage a rafter-rattling closing sequence as she labored over husband Gregory Peck's gangrenous leg in African wilds, her personal relationship with Peck was sketchy because a couple of their scenes together had been cut in favor of his more romantic, audience-pleasing liaison with Ava Gardner. One of Hayward's missing scenes did turn up in the trailer for the film that author Hemingway re-titled *The Snows of Zanuck.*

15. GOING FAMILY PLAN, OR RADIO CITY MUSIC HALL WILL GET YOU IF YOU DON'T WATCH OUT

When they had had time to get the sand out of their shoes, Ingrid Bergman and, much later, her daughter, Pia Lindstrom, found that islands were unlucky for both of them.

First there was Stromboli, the famous—or infamous—Italian island on which Bergman and her paramour, director Roberto Rossellini, acted out a clandestine drama of passion before and behind the cameras back in the late '40s. Saint Joan's voices not yet stilled in her ears (from her then recent stage and film characterizations of the Maid), Bergman had forsaken husband, home, and hearth and, even worse, Hollywood for the balding, rotund Roberto. She had found herself on an ugly, primitive island impregnated and, worst of all, acting out a film drama sans script, with only Roberto to lead the way. The proof of where he could lead a girl was becoming more and more visible every day.

Robert Daggy of the Yale University Library sniffed out for me some of the once molten poop on *Stromboli,* the mish-mash, [broken] home movie that resulted from Bergman's eagerness to work with the flash-in-the-pan Italian "master" whom, of course, she eventually married—and divorced.

"There was quite a controversy between RKO and Rossellini about the film," Daggy wrote me. "The first item of interest was in July, 1949, when the Motion Picture Sales Corp. filed protests claiming prior rights to the title, *After the Storm*—other early titles for *Stromboli* were *Against the Storm* and *God's Earth.* The controversy began when Rossellini refused to abide by his contract to come to Hollywood to cut and edit the film. He preferred to stay in Italy and cut (doubtless the refusal of Bergman to return to the United States had something to do with his decision). RKO's office in Rome, fearing some such thing, had already appropriated the prints of both the Italian and the English versions as completed up to then. They had rights only to the English—the Italian belonging to a production company formed by Rossellini and Bergman. Rossellini refused to deliver the last three days' rushes unless he was allowed to cut the film in Italy. RKO refused to give him back the Italian version unless the film was cut in Hollywood. RKO for a time considered releasing the film without the benefits of the last three days of shooting, but the scenes must have been crucial, for they finally acquiesced. Rossellini was to be allowed to cut the film in Italy.

"However, RKO, because of the scandal, wanted to cut all scenes referring to Karin's, i.e., Bergman's, approaching motherhood, feeling that, under the circumstances, a pregnant Bergman scrambling up Italian volcanoes would only appear ridiculous to American audiences. Also, to play a pregnant woman was one thing, but Bergman herself was illicitly pregnant and there seemed no reason to play up this fact by emphasizing motherhood in the film. Rossellini did not want to tamper with his film's artistic integrity. He felt that to cut any of these scenes was to destroy the crux of the film, since through the expected child Karin finds herself and God. RKO apparently went ahead and cut as much of this out of the film as they could without completely destroying continuity. Rossellini said, of course, that this was done without his sanction or approval."

Just before the picture was seen here, Rossellini further flashed that he had heard the American distributors had clipped out the sections that were intended to describe the heroine as "a typical post-war rationalist who gradually succumbed to a belief in God." The rest of the film, describing the life of a woman who had been almost a prostitute, would make him an imbecile if used without the religious part, Rossellini believed.

The New York *Times* called the film "banal" when it opened in New York in 1950. Said *Cue*: "In the original story . . . there were more cogent reasons in [Karin's] personal and professional background for the islanders' resentment of her—for her boredom with her husband—for the casualness with which the lighthouse keeper gives, and she accepts, money—and for the hint of suicide at the volcano's crater when she knows she is pregnant. All these, however, were removed—either before shooting, during editing or since the original negative was brought to Hollywood.

"Prudently—as though they recognized the great gaping holes in the mutilated drama—the picture's distributors inserted several interludes of bridging narration: at the film's beginning, to explain what is about to happen; at the end, to explain what did happen; and at intervals in between, to cover up when nothing happens at all."

Rossellini claimed no responsibility for the American version, saying that its artistry had been sacrificed to commercial ends (although *Stromboli* ended up being anything but a commercial success, either). Later, he and Bergman tried to impede the foreign distribution of the film and were sued by RKO for their trouble.

Ingrid's discarded husband, Dr. Peter Lindstrom, and daughter, Pia, then a child, were understandably aghast and embittered by everything, and so was America, where the good sister of *The Bells of St. Mary's* was ostracized. One movie company, planning a documentary comprised of historical moments clipped from films, took out the Bergman-Joan of Arc scene they had planned to use before the scandal. Pia even changed the name her mother had given her to Jenny. Some years later, however, after Rossellini had worked his familiar "magic" on a married Indian actress and he and Bergman had split up, and Ingrid had scored a comeback in *Anastasia,* Jenny became Pia again and decided she wanted to act.

In *Marriage—Italian Style,* voted the Best Foreign Film of 1964 by Hollywood's Academy, Pia had what must have been one of the most frustrating roles ever played, not only to the actress but to the audience that had been alerted via publicity to Pia's "supporting" part in the popular film. Why director Vittorio De Sica allowed her to be presented the way she was is a mystery, but this is what happened: Pia played a cashier, a brief interlude in the skirt-chasing career of shop owner Marcello Mastroianni, appearing only in two shots, the first with her face hidden by a kiss from Mastroianni, the second showing only her back as she returned to her job.

And early in '65 Sheilah Graham said Pia had told her that she was "still wondering what had happened to most of her scenes in *Zorba the Greek.* The way it came out of the cutting room, Pia has an itty bitty part." An interesting film shot on the island of Crete, the *Zorba* I saw contained *no* discernible Pia Lindstrom footage.

Just one week before the Graham squib appeared, Louella Parsons carried a similar wail from Pia. "Heartache for Pia Lindstrom, Ingrid Bergman's daughter," began Louella—the same Louella who broke the story of Bergman's pregnancy on Stromboli. "The dramatic sequence she did in a film in London has been cut because of the over-length. While the role was brief, Pia had counted on her good performance to help launch her as a screen actress other than in Italian films.

"Now she's back in Rome where she has one of the leads in the Italian movie, *La Dame au Lac,* which Franco Rossellini will produce. Franco is the nephew of Pia's former stepfather, Roberto Rossellini. At one time there was talk of a serious romance between Franco and Pia. But I hear it has simmered down to just 'family' affection these days."

Pia obviously is not a girl to hold a grudge. Shortly after this, it was learned that Pia was living in Rome with her half-brother and two half-sisters, Rossellinis all. And Louella, well, only she could prosaically call Roberto Rossellini the "stepfather" of Pia Lindstrom and in the same sputter forget to name the movie around which the newspaper item revolved. Lolly said the film was made in London, so perhaps it was not the *Zorba* from which Miss Lindstrom also had been cut. Although you never can tell.

The third femme in Hollywood's then first-string press corps of three, Hedda Hopper, detailed the all-around emotionalism that followed the filming of a dance scene in *The Pirate,* a Judy Garland-Gene Kelly vehicle directed by Miss Garland's husband, Vincente Minnelli. In her book, *The Whole Truth and Nothing But,* Hedda praised Louis B. Mayer's long-time secretary, Ida Koverman, "who stood behind King Louis' throne . . . the behind-the-scenes arbiter of good taste," and mentioned the time Mrs. Koverman broke up Mayer's meeting with New York investment bankers to get him to look at the "haircurling" rushes of the Kelly-Garland dance of the day before. Mayer crabbed but went to the projection room.

"Gene and Judy had flung themselves too eagerly into the spirit of things. It looked like a torrid romance," wrote Hedda. Mayer cried, "Burn the negative! If that exhibition got on any screen, we'd be raided by the police." The next morning he gave Kelly quite a chewing-out for nearly shattering the Garland-Kelly screen image. Ironically, years later when Judy had her own television series, one of the major faults critics found with it was that she was "too physical" with her guests, kissing, hugging, fondling them with tasteless frequency.

Several years earlier (1942), another important Garland scene was scrapped before it ever made a preview. It was the finale to *Presenting Lily Mars,* the second film Joe Pasternak produced at MGM following his successful tenure at Universal. Some friends of Judy's had obtained admittance to a rough-cut screening of the modest story that had been modestly told, and wailed to the star that she was not getting the plush vehicle treatment befitting a luminary of her brilliance. Still in her teens and relying heavily on the opinions of others even then, Judy believed her "advisers," feeling that the new producer from a lot that specialized in inexpensive pictures had let her down. Mayer called Pasternak into his office and said, "You are no longer at a studio where expense counts—re-do the finale." Against his better judgment, Pasternak had the closing number re-done at great cost, which pleased most of the principals involved but which Pasternak felt threw the simple story out of kilter.

In her book, *Elizabeth Taylor,* Ruth Waterbury recorded that Miss Taylor could not sleep for anxiety the night before Eddie Fisher, then still her husband and only a *film* flunkout, was to do his big scene with her in *Butterfield 8.* She called Daniel Mann, the director, at two o'clock in the morning and said that although she felt ill, for Eddie's sake she wanted the scene to be good more than anything in the world and would be there in the morning. That night Eddie called her mother and said he'd never realized how great Taylor was until he'd acted with her—"Why, she even made me look good!", he exclaimed.

Miss Waterbury went on to relate that "One evening Liz and Eddie, together with her agent and his wife, were the only audience at a very private preview of *Butterfield 8* in a studio projection room. Her first shock was to see that the big scene she had made with Eddie had been cut out entirely. This made her angry, and she began yelling at the screen. Later it was whispered around MGM that she had kicked both her slippers at the screen."

Dan Dailey, one of the screen's most versatile performers, once told me that during his big years of stardom at 20th Century-Fox (late '40s, early '50s) his biggest problem was convincing studio head Darryl Zanuck that he was able to handle more in musicals than the old soft-shoe. Although eminently successful opposite Betty Grable in such as 1947's *Mother Wore Tights,* which made him a star, and *When My Baby Smiles at Me,* which got him an Oscar nomination as Best Actor of 1948, Dailey longed to perform some routines more complex than his and Grable's charming but basically prosaic "Kokomo, Indiana" norm.

"There was a dance number I loved in *You're My Everything* that was cut when the picture was released," Dailey said. "It was all in blue and was done to 'Serenade in Blue' and I did it with a young lady partner—not Anne Baxter, my co-star in the film. (Anne could do the Charleston called for in the picture, but she was an actress, not a professional dancer.) Zanuck didn't think it was my kind of dancing unless it was 'Tea for Two' and the whole thing was cut. Once they got you into a mold of any kind, it was almost impossible to get out.

"I remember I worked for four months on Stravinsky's 'Firebird' but was forced ultimately to do 'Birth of the Blues.' But I shouldn't complain. It could've been worse: Warner Brothers. I hear that was a real hell-hole."

Dailey said it was different when he went over to Metro to work (after Mayer's reign had ended). Referring to *It's Always Fair Weather* (1955), he went on: "Gene Kelly, Michael Kidd and I had the freedom to do some really crazy things in that one." For all the good it did him; by then, of course, the filmusical was on the wane as a Hollywood production staple.

In the main, the easygoing Dailey said he had suffered little under the knife—"Oh, maybe a line here or there." What ever operations did take place on him in the Fox cutting room were relatively painless, perhaps because, as Dailey opined to another interviewer, "Zanuck is a great film editor." He did mention that a number he and Grable did for *Mother Wore Tights* called "Rolling Down Bowling Green"—"It was a thing we did on bikes"—had been omitted and kept in only "as off-stage music, I think." The song, however, was reprised with the rest by the two stars in the finale.

Dailey also cited some minor cuts in his "cameo" role in Fox's *Hemingway's Adventures of a Young Man,* which came about 15 years after *Tights.* "It was at the beginning of my part," he recalled. "I was to put up some posters for a traveling burlesque show and the script said simply, 'Ad lib for 15 minutes,' so I did. A lot of what I did was cut out, but I expected that. The big cuts in *Young Man,* though, were made in the early part of the picture." Dailey's performance in the kind of Pagliacci role at which he is unsurpassed provided the only moving moments in a stiff of a film; and shame to the Academy for not recognizing this with at least a Best Supporting Actor nomination for Dailey's Billy Campbell.

Betty Grable had a fancier turn than the one cut from *Mother Wore Tights* omitted from her 1953 Harold Arlen–Dorothy Fields musical, *The Farmer Takes a Wife.* It was a dream number utilizing the talents not only of The Legs, gotten up like a goddess of the crop, but also of her co-stars, Thelma Ritter, Dale Robertson, and John Carroll, along with a horse and a corralful of chorines wielding sprigs of wheat. Zanuck axed the routine; but chances are, if he had known then what he should know now, he wouldn't have. For clearly present among the dancing girls were two Misses who would later become stars: Gwyneth (Gwen) Verdon and Julie Newmeyer (Newmar). A few years later, in fact, Verdon and Ritter were teamed in the successful Broadway musical, *New Girl in Town*—with Verdon top-billed.

"It's very tough when you're not the star," comic Frank Fontaine feels. A decade before he hit it big on television and recordings, Fontaine was providing bright but inconspicuous support in pictures such as 1951's *Call Me Mister,* starring Grable and Dailey. "I had a couple of very funny scenes with Dale Robertson in it that were cut out, to my embarrassment," Fontaine told me recently. "I remember I took a couple of my kids to see it, and I whispered to them, 'Now wait till you see this next scene in the barracks . . .' Christ, the next thing I knew everybody was in Tokyo!"

Zanuck must have been a hard man to convince. Also in the early '50s, Richard Brooks relates, he wrote and directed a Humphrey Bogart starrer for Zanuck at Fox titled *Deadline—U.S.A.* It was forgettable Bogie, but that was not Brooks' point.

"It had to do with the power of the press and the monopoly of the press," Brooks said. "Zanuck got nervous about the picture. He particularly objected to one impassioned speech that Bogie, as the editor of a dying paper, made about a newspaper not being just desks and typewriters, but something personal. Zanuck wanted to cut that out. There had been some touchy goings-on in Los Angeles around that time with consolidation of newspapers and cries of monopoly. Bogie was very unhappy about this. He was a man of convictions. We tried to keep the material in the picture, but Zanuck overruled us."

Joseph Mankiewicz recently admitted that Zanuck, "unhappily," has always had the privilege of cutting Mankiewicz's films. The director mentioned, particularly, his multi-honored *All About Eve* of 1950, whose style Zanuck altered quite a bit. In the script and the picture, as first shot by Mankiewicz, were flashback scenes that were shown over and over, in several different lights, as they were diversely remembered by the various participants. Mankiewicz, who in his work has always been especially interested in the dependency of past and present upon one another, said this device in *Eve* bored Zanuck and he obliterated it in the cutting room.

After years in film chorus jobs, George Chakiris landed the colorful role of Bernardo in *West Side Story* in '61 and won the Best Supporting Actor Award for this much-awarded filmusical. But George couldn't forget the bad times—1956—when he called himself George Kerris.

"The studio was Metro, the picture was *Meet Me in Las Vegas* and the part they gave me would absolutely, positively put me up there in that Big Movie Star League I had dreamed about," George related, Oscar still hot in his hands. "Producer Joe Pasternak assigned Betty Lynn and myself as young honeymoon couple who danced around the tables of the Sands Hotel lounge in Las Vegas while we sang a song called 'It's Fun to Be in Love.' The stars were Cyd Charisse and Dan Dailey.

"We finished our big 'star-making' routine, after 10 weeks, but I kept coming back to the studio to see Cyd Charisse do her big solo number in the Sleeping Beauty Ballet. One day Mr. Pasternak's assistant spotted me while Cyd was dancing, called me over and whispered, 'Gee, kid, I hate to tell you this but the picture's so long they might have to cut that number you and Betty did in the lounge.'

"I knew right away they were breaking the news to me gently. Our number *was* cut, because the picture was too long. That's what they said. I hope it wasn't because I was so lousy!"

Shortly after a bloody but unbowed Larry Parks became the sensation of Hollywood in '46 in Columbia's *The Jolson Story* (only three films before it made more money, *The Birth of a Nation, Gone with the Wind,* and *This is the Army*—coincidentally Evelyn Keyes was featured in both *Wind* and *Jolson*), a *Modern Screen* writer told of Larry's long apprenticeship at the studio in every conceivable kind of minor role. "When he did see a little light," the story said, "as in *Counter-Attack,* it got snuffed out.

"Larry struggled through that picture for weeks, with high hopes. He was Paul Muni's friend in a war story, and he had a hero's part. Most of his role was played in a swamp—a studio water tank—and if you've ever seen one of those torture tubs, you'll know it was no picnic. It was cold and dirty and Larry stayed there, sopping wet, day in and out, giving everything he had."

Parks attended a preview of the production in '45 and thrilled to his billing right up there with Muni and Marguerite Chapman. But he soon found his part had been severely cut; and "what few feet remained saw him wandering around in dim light between the swamp and a bombed out cellar and you couldn't tell whether that hazy character was Larry Parks or the Shadow."

The Jolson story was six months in the cutting room. The first preview—in Santa Barbara—was a success, and Columbia chief Harry Cohn only found one fault: although Parks' rendering of the Jolson standard "Sonny Boy" was effective dramatically as well as musically, Cohn thought the number slowed things down. When the film opened at Radio City Music Hall, "Sonny Boy" had been cut out.

Radio City Music Hall, big but benign-looking and plop in the heart of Manhattan, is actually a more formidable influence on the cutting of films than any of the families lined up outside would dream (or perhaps care, since most of them are standing in that holiday blizzard mainly to warm to the military drills of the "dancing" Rockettes).

The Music Hall is one of the most important bookings a motion picture can get. Over the years the theater has established a reputation for showing quality films by, on a good average, showing quality films. This, coupled with elaborately dreadful stage shows like *Alice in Easterland, Tuliptime in Holland,* etc., make a trip to the Hall a bargain and a must for tourists, nearby out-of-towners, and frequently New York sophisticates themselves, when no one is looking.

To get a much-sought, lucrative Music Hall booking, a film company will do practically anything—even slash its own product to suit the theater's demands in running time and/or snip scenes that might be objectionable (in management's opinion) to family audiences (that never seem to mind the fleshy line of fannies that parades out of the wings with—and pun intended—no end in sight).

Two Paramount productions of recent years cut to satisfy Music Hall demands were *Breakfast at Tiffany's* and *Come Blow Your Horn.* Both instances involved dances ignored by the censors but which the Hall felt were too suggestive for their audiences, and, like most of the cuts made to please this theater, they remained out for all subsequent engagements.

In *Breakfast* the cut occurred with a dance Audrey Hepburn watched while in a cheap bar. In the released version, the young lady's gyrations—apart from her fully clothed introduction—were fleetingly reflected only in Audrey's dark glasses; but in the original print the camera cut back and forth to show the actual turn. By the time television got into the act, only her introduction remained. In *Blow* the clipped tripping happened at a party tossed by juvenile lead Tony Bill: one young lady's twisting torso was deemed too extreme for a flock weaned on Elvis Presley.

One of the most drastic examples of cutting to placate the Music Hall took place in 1964 with United Artists' charming, funny *The World of Henry Orient,* which covered the Manhattan adventures of a pair of imaginative teen-agers, played by Tippy Walker and Merrie Spaeth, with a crush on a concert pianist named Henry Orient (Peter Sellers). The film might have been even funnier if the entire performances of two more experienced hellraisers, London's Hermione Gingold and New York's Barbara Nichols (that un-*Loved One*), had not been cut to salve the Hall. The latter actress, wrapped in a towel, had a shower-bedroom scene that went down the drain. And Miss Gingold informed me: "I had a 'cameo' in the last scene of the picture. By then, Henry Orient had come down in the world to playing piano in a brothel. I was the madam—a character part, dahling—and came on to greet everyone in there. To play my girls, the studio had recruited several Miss Universe contestants from all over the world. Afterward, when the film was booked into Radio City, the producers were told by the Hall, 'I say, but we can't have that ending in the brothel. Our family trade, you know.' The countries that had loaned us my girls were rather disturbed as well when they found out their young ladies had wound up in such a place. Finally, they threw out our business and had a whole new ending made—without us—that satisfied Radio City Music Hall."

The footage of these ladies remained out for all *Henry Orient* bookings.

Although less immediately traceable to Music Hall machinations, Disney's *The Happiest Millionaire* (1967), the filmusical about the Biddles and the Dukes, opened there without a couple of filmed musical numbers. The most unfortunate cut was Greer Garson's only song, "It Won't Be Long 'Till Christmas," a duet with Fred MacMurray who played her husband, the eccentric Biddle patriarch of pre-World War I Philadelphia. All the major players had songs except Mother Garson. Mr. Mayer would have been aghast.

Familial togetherness figured in a major sequence cut from *The Carpetbaggers* (1964), the Joseph E. Levine–Paramount money-grubber that gave us the first facsimile of Jean Harlow by Carroll Baker, whose nipples were just the opposite of Harlow's perfectly swell inch-long mammary antennae. In the ending that the paying public saw, George Peppard and Elizabeth Ashley, as his estranged wife, were reconciled in her office. Actually, a whole sequence in which Peppard and Ashley then returned to the family mansion, daughter Victoria Jean and family retainer Archie Moore had been dropped. And, in the film's only sign of good taste, so had a nude shot of the reedy Miss Baker, since known as the blonde bomb, or the bomb blondesell.

The Levine–Baker *Harlow,* breathing hard on the heels of *The Carpetbaggers* (but not hard enough), was without at least one scene upon release, thus weakening the characterization of young featured player Mary Murphy. A prominent—and occasional lead (*The Wild One,* etc.)—actress, Miss Murphy was assigned the role of right-hand woman to studio chief Everett Redman (Martin Balsam—and actually supposed to be L. B. Mayer), who could have been either Ida Koverman, Mayer's secretary, or Kay Mulvey, studio publicist and real-life friend of Harlow's, or a composite of both. (She was more likely representing Miss Mulvey, since Balsam mentioned she was getting $500 a week, and it has been written by Hedda Hopper that Mrs. Koverman labored 25 years for Mayer at her starting salary of $250 a week. Besides, Kay Mulvey was youngish and Miss Koverman well into middle age.) Miss Murphy was given a nondescript name—even Jean Harlow's films were given phoney titles—and she appeared in only one consultation scene with Mayer and Harlow's impotent husband, Paul Bern (Peter Lawford), whose real name was used. Miss Murphy was seen from such a distance in this brief scene that she was practically unrecognizable. Her billing was pretty good, and there is a still that shows her and Balsam, Raf Vallone, and Red Buttons conferring, probably upon the crisis of Bern's suicide. Levine, finding the film overlong, probably told his cutters in the manner of Mike Todd on Elizabeth Taylor's *Raintree County* to chop anything but his Star, with similar results.

Neither *The Carpetbaggers* nor *Harlow,* incidentally, were at any time prospects for Radio City Music Hall. Although—the times they are a-changing.

16. THE HIGH COST OF CUTTING

The money involved in producing the omitted scenes is something to ponder, too, as Charlton Heston would be the first to tell you.

In March 1965, *Variety* reviewed Heston's *Major Dundee,* a Cavalry–Indians tale, and noted: (1) "*Major Dundee* would benefit by a good 20 to 25-minute snap-up, especially of sequences having virtually no bearing on the main plot"; and, later on (2) "Three editors are credited, which may account in part for film's lack of continuity through too many cutters." So, *Major Dundee* needed pruning—but at the same time had had too much of it.

Star Heston dispelled some of the confusion the same week when he told a columnist the story of a star's supreme sacrifice for art. He was that star, and it all happened when certain scenes to be shot in Mexico for *Dundee* were eliminated from the script to keep from paying overtime. Heston offered Columbia Pictures his entire salary of $200,000 to cover the cost of putting the scenes that he felt were vital back in. (It was mentioned that Heston got much more than the sum per picture, but, he said, "This was an old contract.") The offer was accepted, which for some reason surprised Heston, and the scenes were filmed. Now he had just learned that producer Jerry Bresler had cut them all.

When Heston gave back his salary, someone asked him, "Do you think this will set a precedent with other actors?" "No," he answered. "In fact, it won't set a precedent with me, either." *Now* more than ever.

Dundee director Sam Peckinpah (who had gained notice a short time before with his low-budget but critically acclaimed Western teaming old-timers Joel McCrea and Randolph Scott, *Ride the High Country,* was so upset he vainly tried to have his name removed from the credits. "It wasn't the picture I made," he asserted, charging that the producer fired him from the movie following principal shooting. "They held no previews of the original picture as made and no one ever saw the film or got a chance to judge it until after cuts were made that destroyed it," snarled the director whom Heston afterwards labeled "A feisty little tiger, all tension."

Peckinpah added that producer Bresler had promised that Peckinpah would be "on the picture through the cutting and two previews," but alleged that he was taken off when he objected to the 20 minutes of cuts ordered by Bresler. The director also had deferred 70 per cent of his salary to help lower the budget, initially set at $4,500,000, to $3,000,000. According to Peckinpah, it wound up costing the former, anyway, because among the shooting problems was the complete re-shooting of second-unit footage "done first without following the script."

A review of the film in England by Tom Milne indicated that the cutting of *Major Dundee* went even further there. Milne wrote: "The distributors, disheartened perhaps by the vitriolic reactions of American critics, appear to have washed their hands of the film; my second viewing of it at a London press screening found two scenes missing (one of them vitally important) that had been there the day before. The story doesn't quite end on this note of distress, though: the last quarter of the film may be cut to ribbons, but the first 90 minutes are magnificent."

That same year, another Heston epic, Universal's *The War Lord,* had a less spectacular joust with the cutters; but there was one line omitted following the critics' screenings that robbed audiences of a good laugh.

Said scribe William Wolf: "The night I saw it, the audience stayed respectful as long as possible through the customary battling in 11th century Europe and such lush lines as 'I need you as I need bread, sunshine, fire in winter.' But then the laughs began merrily erupting. What turned the tide was the precious moment when, after a bloody orgy of battle and bastion-storming, virgin bride Rosemary Forsyth looked demurely at war lord Heston and said she was sorry for causing so much trouble."

It was the latter line of the new Miss Forsyth's that was cut when the film was released, forestalling the damn-busting laughter that followed its emission at previews.

Again Heston suffered, but this time mentally rather than monetarily, over the damage done *War Lord* by the studio. "John Collier (who wrote the screenplay with Millard Kaufman), director Franklin Schaffner and myself planned it as a simple love story, contrasted with an examination of the witchcraft rituals of the middle ages. But Universal saw it differently—as a minor league *El Cid,"* Heston related. The studio had insisted on building up the climactic siege scene which, Heston felt, ruined the intimacy of the story. "And John Collier, who is an accomplished medievalist, had written some fine sequences of witchcraft, of a Bergman-like complexity. The studio boss in charge of the project was a Roman Catholic. When he saw the witchcraft material . . . well, most of it wound up on the cutting room floor." Heston was further disturbed when some critics praised Schaffner alone for the rituals left in (such as the Druid wedding) when all had been designed by Collier.

Although *Darling* made another modestly talented female newcomer named Julie Christie a major international star and 1965's Best Actress Oscar winner, her name didn't mean too much to the producers at the beginning. As fellow Britisher and co-star Laurence Harvey tells it, "I worked hard to find backers for *Darling* because nobody wanted it. But then my best scenes were cut out—the ones explaining my character. They were 'too shocking.' " Since the released film was practically a compendium of every contemporary social and moral ill, sick joke, and sordid dramatic device, Harvey's omitted scenes must really have contained—to borrow from the old French joke—the one hundredth way.

England's Arthur Treacher, the American screen's "perfect butler" from the early '30s until the fall of elegance in the '50s, and who found a whole new career in the '60s (in his 70s) as the urbane, disarmingly, sometimes alarmingly no-nonsense second banana on *The Merv Griffin Show,* lists the Jean Harlow–Lee Tracy *Bombshell* (also known as *Blonde Bombshell*) among his first films. And then again, he doesn't.

"In 1933 I was called to MGM to audition behind a sheet," Treacher told me. "There were about 12 of us back there. I was No. 3, I think. We had to say 'Hello, London calling . . .' One of us would be the 'voice off' in the scene where this had to be said. I was chosen by the director for the job in the picture, which was to be a day's work for me. (Jolly glad I was to have it, too.) But Miss Harlow and Mr. Tracy were sick or something—I don't know what was wrong with them, although Mr. Tracy had a reputation for tippling—and they weren't showing up. So my one day's off-screen work stretched into 32. Then, when I saw the completed film, I found the entire business I had worked on was cut."

As producer on most of his films (many of which he also wrote and directed, with taste and literacy if varying commercial success), Albert Lewin feels he had "a lot of control over my pictures, but there are still some cutting experiences that make me wince."

One occurred with *Pandora and the Flying Dutchman* (1951), starring Ava Gardner and James Mason. Early in '66 it was shown with several other Lewin films in a tribute to the retired filmmaker by New York's Gallery of Modern Art, under the aegis of Raymond Rohauer.

"The museum showed the TV print, and that was hacked up," Lewin rightly grumbled. "In my agreement with Romulus Films' John Woolf, I controlled the original cut on *Pandora* only for the first release. So when the film was re-released and then leased to TV, it was cut further and greatly damaged. The worst cuts are in the early exposition and creation of atmosphere. I went to a lot of trouble and expense to get the right mood and establish Miss Gardner's character. Marius Goring, the English star, did me a favor and took the small role of a fellow who commits suicide over Ava. It was only two days' work, and he didn't even get credited. His whole part has been cut. The Flamenco troupe I used in the beginning is gone, too, and so is a beautiful song Dorothy Parker wrote, 'How Am I to Know?', that is sung by Ava."

Lewin said that he had leased it to TV and would get it back in a few years "for the Western Hemisphere—I don't have control over the Eastern Hemisphere. The negative cutouts have been preserved, and I hope to restore the film. I've been told that the picture will be very valuable."

More serious was the case of *Saadia* (1954), for the public got *no* chance to see this MGM film as originally adapted, directed, and produced by Lewin, with Cornel Wilde, Mel Ferrer, and Rita Gam.

"It was the theme in *Saadia* that intrigued me, not the story: the conflict between medicine and witchcraft," stated Lewin. "My arrangement with Dore Schary was that I would shoot it in Morocco, which I did, and edit and score it in England. I was supposed to bring back a complete picture. But TV had thrown Hollywood into a panic. I began getting frantic notes about the budget and finally I had to come back and cut it at the studio in Hollywood.

"I showed it to Dore. Now, the character of the sorceress was tremendously important because she illustrated the theme. Wanda Rotha was impressive in the part, stole the picture in its first form. Dore objected to the emphasis on her. He pointed to her elaborate, fiery death scene and said, 'That dame goes down like the Titanic! She's only a character woman, Al.' He reduced her part—her death is now merely indicated—in favor of the love story, which I had thrown in merely as a sop to the public."

With its many TV showings, the most well-known film written (or adapted) by Lewin is probably *The Picture of Dorian Gray* (1945), although he has said *The Moon and Sixpence* (1943) "made more money than all of my films put together"—*Dorian* was not a big commercial success.

And *Gray* almost didn't get finished. "I was way over budget," Lewin confessed, "and some of the MGM brass wanted to stop the filming. But L. B. Mayer came back from a trip and saw the footage I'd shot and said, 'Al, you're going to finish this film. Don't let them ruffle you!' Without L. B.'s intervention, I don't think I'd have been able to complete *Dorian Gray*," a film in which, incidentally, Greta Garbo had thought of making her comeback—in the title role, played by Hurd Hatfield.

Lewin further recalled: "I was mostly in charge of the cutting of *Dorian Gray,* with one major exception. For a party scene hosted by Dorian, I hired some Javanese dancers I knew who were starving in Chicago and really needed the work. I felt they would lend the right exotic touch to the scene. So they came out and filmed—

it was quite a fine dance, all about the temptation of Buddha. But the preview audience laughed at one of those sideway head-turns as executed by lead dancer Devi Dja. I fought for the number, begged producer Pan Berman to take the film to a big first-run house in San Francisco—since most of the money was in the big first-run, why take it to Pomona, I pleaded? It was one battle I didn't win. Most of the number was cut. I took a trip to Chicago to explain it to the dancers."

In 1935, Samuel Goldwyn writer George Oppenheimer says he received temporary surcease from worry over his difficulties with a trying boss when the "genial and stimulating" Thornton Wilder—with *The Bridge of San Luis Rey* already to his credit—was brought West to work on Goldwyn's remake of *The Dark Angel.* According to Oppenheimer, Wilder's contribution to the story of a man (Fredric March) blinded in the war who tried to conceal this fact from his sweetheart (Merle Oberon) "was a brilliantly conceived and written sequence that took place in a school for the blind. It was filled with Thornton's special quality of compassion together with an extremely suspenseful episode in which the blind man is taught courage and confidence in the face of danger. When *The Dark Angel* was released, the sequence had been cut."

Bing Crosby was frank when he told me about the cutting of a major scene from *The Road to Bali* (1952), the only one of the Crosby–Bob Hope–Dorothy Lamour *Road* series photographed in color.

"The dance director had prepared an elaborate choreography, with Lamour and the two of us doing quite a dance up and down the temple steps.

"I worked very hard on this, because I wanted to get it right, but Hope was occupied with a variety of other projects, as usual, and didn't make himself available for the practice sessions.

"The day we shot, we ran through the number once, and Hope turned around and looked at me in consternation and bewilderment. 'You traitor,' he said. 'You rehearsed.'

"Well, we shot the scene, but as you might imagine, it was a shambles, and of course got the scissors. I might add that I was grateful because I wasn't too good in it myself.

"I believe it cost about $100,000, but it went down the drain."

Not entirely, Bing. The scene turned up some time later in a special anniversary tribute to Paramount Pictures on (where else?) Ed Sullivan's TV show.

Peter Bull related his experience on *Doctor Strangelove, or How I Learned to Stop Worrying and Love the Bomb* (1964) with probably the wildest single sequence never to get in a finished film.

"I suppose the most bizarre film in which I've ever played was *Doctor Strangelove,*" he said. "Every day for five weeks, about 60 actors were summoned to the same set, which represented the War Room at the Pentagon. It was a sensational design, by Ken Adams, and the ebony floor was kept so fantastically polished that we were none of us allowed to wear shoes (apart from on actual 'takes'). We were supplied with cloth flop-abouts. The set took up the whole stage and one wall was given over to a vast and intricate map, which lit up, when required, to show the positions of aircraft around the world.

"The climax of the film, as originally conceived, was to be a mad custard-pie mélée. Indeed, right at the beginning of the War Room sequence you will observe a long and elaborate buffet, on which piles and piles of cakes are established. Toward the end of the script, as shot, all the personnel went berserk and started hurling them from one end of the studio to the other. The film ended with Peter Sellers as the U. S. President and me (as the Russian Ambassador) sitting on the floor, waist-deep in custard pies, making castles out of them and singing 'For He's a Jolly Good Fellow.' The 'he' we were referring to in this case was that macabre Dr. Strangelove (Mr. Sellers again, of course)."

Continued Bull: "This section of the film took nearly a fortnight to complete and must have cost thousands and thousands of dollars but [director] Stanley Kubrick decided, when he came to cut the film, that it was completely at variance with the rest of it, and, though apparently sensationally funny and effective, it just didn't fit in. So it was scrapped. It must have been agony for Kubrick but his integrity is such that I bet he was right."

Bull went on to detail a cleaning woman's disbelief when handed the custard-crusted clothes, plus the "extraordinary" look of the corridors, lavatories and dressing rooms, "as if some creature from Outer Space, constructed rather loosely from a lot of vegetables, had been cruising around."

Much less successful, critically, was Kubrick's next project which *did* deal with Outer Space, MGM's *2001: A Space Odyssey.* Kubrick was still working on it a couple of years after major photography had been completed; and before it opened, Martin Balsam, who had gone from his '65 Best Supporting Actor Oscar for *A Thousand Clowns* to provide the voice for *HAL,* the computer, found his voice replaced by Douglas Rain's upon release in 1968.

Originally shown at three hours (with intermission), almost 20 minutes were soon cut, adding confusion to the considerable boredom that still remained. Vanished were the computer's asking for permission to repeat the message from mission control telling of its own malfunction; parts of the scene in which Keir Dullea removed the faulty communications unit; the computer's turning off the pod's radio before killing Gary Lockwood (thus puzzling the audience when Dullea asks HAL if he has been able to establish radio contact yet), and many visual cuts and shortening of scenes.

In 1961 20th Century-Fox produced its sequel to the surprisingly good *Peyton Place* feature, calling it *Return to . . . ,* and building toward a climactic fire (a leading character was carefully established as a careless smoker) that was to put a match to everybody's problems, particularly Mary Astor's. Although the finished print of this surprisingly bad film (which also wasted Eleanor Parker) contained no such holocaust, there are Fox stills indicating that such an expensive cut had been filmed, then taken out. No picture ever needed a burning more.

June Havoc, whose steady stream of snappy portrayals—some leads, many supporting—throughout the 1940s helped to make that period a part of the movies' Golden Age, was interviewed by me during her 1966 run on Broadway in the all-star revival of *Dinner at Eight,* which she stole. Havoc was giving an hilarious, astonishingly resourceful performance as the dizzy, social-climbing dinner hostess, and looking even better than the *Early Havoc* (the title of her remarkable autobiographical remembrance of marathon dance contests past) of Hollywood's *Gentleman's Agreement, When My Baby Smiles at Me, The Story of Molly X,* etc.

In '52, related the erstwhile "Dainty June" of her sister's autobiographical *Gypsy,* Havoc went to England to make a film called *Lady Possessed,* James Mason's first venture as producer, which was released here by Republic.

"I starred opposite James Mason, whom I *love,* and one scene called for him to beat me and beat me," grimaced the actress with the permanent pucker. "It took many separate calls because we were so realistic we could never quite finish it as I would be too bruised and battered. So after about six returns to it and the very finish where he threw me down a long staircase, it was at last completed. Yes—it was cut!"

The now fabled special effects in the 1936 Gable starrer (with Jeanette MacDonald and Spencer Tracy), *San Francisco,* brought unintentional laughs from the audience at the first preview. The earthquake sequence was a marvel of spectacular invention, but the viewers could not swallow the supposedly grim scene in which Clark, pushing through the aftermath looking for that brave Jeanette, was felled by a huge brick wall—only to rise unmarred and move onwards. Gone with the shot.

Some movies have achieved their costlier highlights with scenes cut and borrowed from other productions. Lana Turner's *The Rains of Ranchipur* (1955) got its smashing rains in color and CinemaScope via the earlier Myrna Loy version, utilizing blue filters for the reprised nighttime deluge. However, in 1961 *Atlantis, the Lost Continent* used footage from four sequences of 1951's *Quo Vadis* plus some of a sacrificial sequence in Lana's *The Prodigal* of '55—so it all evens out.

This kind of scene stealing can be dangerous, though. In the Paul Newman–Joanne Woodward comedy, *Rally 'Round the Flag, Boys* (1958), directed by Leo McCarey, the second shot in the opening sequence was lifted out of another small-town story, *Good Morning, Miss Dove* (1955), and the star of that picture, Jennifer Jones, could still be seen crossing the street. A similar celluloid swatch measuring about ten feet and used in Marlene Dietrich's *The Scarlet Empress* (1934) proved to be "the straw that broke the camel's back" for director Josef von Sternberg. As he tells it: "This short scene showed an enormous number of Russians swarming through the streets to hail the birth of a male heir to the throne of Russia. The crowd scene was not mine but came from Ernst Lubitsch's *The Patriot,* and had been woven so skillfully into the dissolves of my scenes that it was thought that I had indulged in wasteful extravagance by using such large numbers of players for so short a scene. And Mr. Lubitsch, not recognizing his own work, charged

Harlow *(Carroll Baker variety) opened without the above scene with Mary Murphy, Raf Vallone, Red Buttons, and Martin Balsam.*

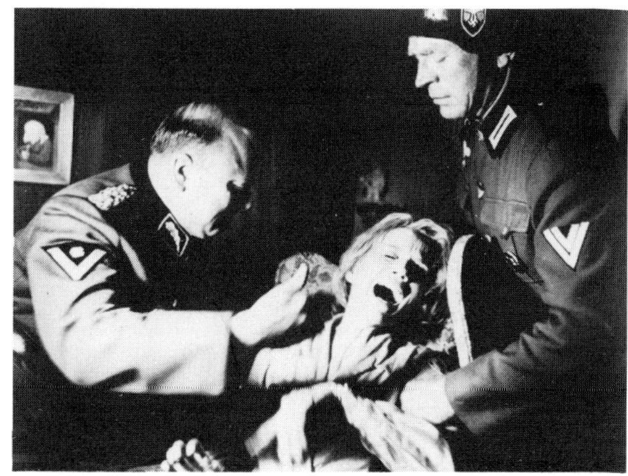

Eva Marie Saint's interrogation was not carried to quite this extreme by the time 36 Hours *had finished editing.*

Ethel Griffies found her grandmother part (represented here with Roddy McDowall, left, and Terry Kilburn, right) cut when The Keys of the Kingdom *opened.*

Barbara Nichols in The Loved One *was reduced to "extra" duty when her scenes (like this one with Robert Morse) were omitted at release time.*

The phenomenally successful The Sound of Music *lost about a third of its footage in Munich: the scenes (like the one above with Christopher Plummer, Peggy Wood, Julie Andrews, and the "Von Trapp children") that showed Nazi villainy.*

The highlight of Edie Adams' role in Love with the Proper Stranger, *a strip number with specially composed Elmer Bernstein music, wound up on the floor—as did most of her clothes.*

me with willful waste and disregard of costs, a charge that echoed and reechoed, never to stop."

One of the more awaited films of the 1940s was the Ingrid Bergman–Charles Boyer *Arch of Triumph* (1948), from the Erich Maria Remarque novel. It was severely edited—Ruth Warrick's important role was almost completely cut—and was a dismal flop. Largely because of the financial bath it took on this production, the recently formed Enterprise Studios folded. Sweden's Ingrid as Joan Madou, walking the studio's expensive French streets but of several different national descents, didn't fare too well, either: she reportedly signed to make the picture for 35 percent of the profits (although another story had her receiving $17,000 a week—as well?—during the many weeks of filming). Admitted director Milestone: "They originally wanted a film four hours long because *Gone with the Wind* came out just before. When we finished, we had a film three and a half hours long. They suddenly decided to have a short film because the bottom fell out of the market. So they cut it almost in half. I don't think you can start out with a script three hours long and end with a finished product half that length. It is bound to suffer."

A word about the other end of the pole: the practically imperceptible cut, one in a much later Ingrid Bergman picture, *The Yellow Rolls Royce* (1965). In one scene Bergman, this time an American widow (from Minnesota), helped bombed-out Yugoslavians during a 1941 Nazi raid. We saw the explosion, then Bergman and partisan friend Omar Sharif removed a child from a demolished building, period. But there was also a still photograph MGM made available (nicely captioned and all) showing the pair comforting an old man in the rubble while a woman handed Bergman makeshift bandages. This apparent latter part of the scene was cut from the film. There was so much else still going on in that scene that even a viewer confronted with a still of the missing bit right after seeing the movie (as I was) was not at first sure whether the old fellow's administerings were in or out.

It seems safe to say that kind (or size) of snip occurs in nine out of ten films, maybe ten out of ten.

An even briefer example of this most prevalent species would be the eye-wink cut made at the climax of Universal's *Mirage* (perhaps the most muddled melodrama since *The Big Sleep* 20 years earlier), in which sweet and lovely Diane Baker shot repulsive and villainous George Kennedy. A still issued and used in the advertising showed Miss Baker recoiling in horror as she fired the gun; but in the released film we saw Kennedy receive the bullet, then our first glimpse of Miss Baker with a gun, smoking, of course, but *after* the shot had been fired. (There were much more inciting discards in this production. In one of his columns, Jack Shafer wrote: "Walter Matthau [costarred with Gregory Peck and Baker] recently lost an argument with director Ed Dmytryk over cuts Mr. D had made in the movie *Mirage*—but it was a beauty of an argument that developed repercussions all the way to the Board of Directors!")

Illness has caused the scrapping of scenes, as well as players, on occasions too numerous to mention.

Vivien Leigh had to quit *Elephant Walk* (1953) when she had a nervous breakdown and was replaced by Elizabeth Taylor, but Vivien was still visible to the eagle-eyed in several of the Ceylon-locationed long shots, at the airport, and in the drive to the plantation, particularly. Practically unheard of is the amount of footage which was kept of Anne Bancroft's role as an Indian in MGM's *The Last Hunt* (1956) after she fell off a horse and was replaced by Debra Paget. It appeared that Miss Bancroft got through all the location work, for she was astonishingly recognizable in most of the outdoor scenes throughout, while Miss Paget did mostly studio emoting. Bancroft—with only a couple of close-ups of Miss Paget—even did one whole scene herself: the rather lengthy one in which Robert Taylor shot the young Indian brave by the river's edge. Needless to say, Bancroft got no billing for this abortive performance in a picture which could have been very important to her during the early stages of her film career when her parts were primarily in B films. *Last Hunt,* while no world-beater, was at least a respectable A with Robert Taylor and Stewart Granger. But Bancroft did have the distinction of providing one of the screen's all-time freak performances. She may have been too unknown at the time *Last Hunt* was originally released to be easily recognized, but there is no doubt today—even on the small TV screen—that it is Anne Bancroft who keeps popping up during the unreeling as, according to the credits, simply "Indian Girl."

Also in the 1950s, I got the chance to observe first hand just how much time, effort, and money can go into a scene (or scenes) eventually junked. I was assistant threater editor for the Newark *Evening News* at the time, and part of my job was doing theatrical pieces for the Sunday coloroto section every other week or so, mostly interviews with celebrities stationed in or visiting the New York area.

When I heard that my then favorite, Jane Wyman, was coming in from Hollywood to film scenes for a picture called *Miracle in the Rain* in Manhattan, I knew I had to interview her. Jane was somewhat less excited; in fact, she had issued an edict: "No interviews." I couldn't believe such unreasonable sounds actually had come from the sweet lips of *Johnny Belinda's* mute mom, and I arranged with Warner Brothers to be on the set, hopeful of a bone or two from the lady. "The set" was Central Park, where the company—including Van Johnson and character actor Halliwell Hobbes—already had commenced about a week's shooting. Naturally, my paper didn't know I was hanging around the set so much that I got an "extra" part in a scene between Jane and the now deceased Hobbes; they'd have told the unwilling Wyman to go pound her dusty Oscar. But I wanted to interview this "great"—I'd done enough spreads on local New Jersey boys in New York choruses. After several days in the park, the company moved on to night shooting in St. Patrick's Cathedral, where I finally wormed my story out of a mighty tight-lipped, one-time Hollywood scatterbrain turned screen royalty.

The Wyman–Hobbes scene on the park bench (which took scads of retakes because of a quirky Mother Nature, plus the venerable Hobbes' difficulty remembering lines), with yours truly in the background, was cut from the movie, however, and I was left with only a few stills as proof of my movie debut, to say nothing of a somewhat jaundiced view of my favorite actress. Still, I was better off than Jane. *Miracle in the Rain* practically forced her to try her own TV series, which, in turn, practically forced her out of show business.

But to hell with me and fate, Janie. You still have your performances in *Johnny Belinda* and *The Yearling,* two of the best acting jobs by a woman in two of the best movies of all time, to sustain you.

MGM's *How the West Was Won* (it was won by sprightly pioneer gal Debbie Reynolds, to believe the picture) was a multipart saga of how the trick was turned, although it was clear in the finished product that one part (or more) was missing. There were parts called "The Plains," "The Civil War," "The Outlaws," etc. But near the end Carolyn Jones came on, unexplained, mysterious, dark of hair and skin, as the simple, makeup-aged wife of blond and bland frontier marshal George Peppard, then much older than you last saw him. You just knew that earlier he'd probably been involved in a little race prejudice, early West style. You recalled that blonde and bland Hope Lange had filmed an episode as the saloon hustler daughter of buffalo trapper Henry Fonda, but her entire role was cut from the picture—considerably diminishing Fonda's footage, which was only a fat "cameo" to begin with.

While Miss Lange didn't turn up in *HtWWW,* Carroll Baker did, also blonde and bland as Peppard's mother, and how much can an audience take? But you couldn't help wondering if Peppard had had a romance with, maybe, fallen angel Lange but given her up for the hardier, healthier Indian (or Mexican) charms of the Jones girl. No one's talking, but it had to be something like that—a segment possibly called "The Prejudice"?

Although it was lively entertainment, no motion picture was ever first-run in theaters with a more obvious chunk missing than *How the West Was Won.* Amazingly, it went on to win 1963's Best Editing Oscar!

When Ken Murray brought his home movies, some dating 30-odd years back, to a Broadway theater in '65 under the title *Ken Murray's Hollywood,* he featured some set-side *How the West Was Won* footage. He included a shot of himself being made up for his role of a 72-year-old prospector in the film and urged everyone to see the epic when it came around again. Murray neglected to mention that his performance had been cut from the film.

Yvonne Mitchell, the fine English actress of Broadway's *The Wall* and the British films *The Divided Heart* (1954), for which she won England's Academy Award, and *Woman in a Dressing Gown* (1956), which earned her the Berlin Film Festival Award, recounted some interesting experiences with Dame Discarde in her autobiography, *Actress.*

Several years ago Miss Mitchell journeyed to the Italian island of Ischia—long before Elizabeth Taylor and Richard Burton dallied there and made headlines while sidelining with *Cleopatra*—and did a picture for Lux Films called *Children of Chance.* Directed by Luigi Zampa, the film was made in two versions: the English, with Miss Mitchell and Patricia Medina, and the Italian, with Gina Lollobrigida and Yvonne Sansom. The conditions were extremely difficult for Miss Mitchell for several reasons, one being that she spoke no Italian, and Zampa, who spoke no English but directed through an interpreter. To further complicate matters the Italian scenes were always shot first, and the entire unit always expected Miss Mitchell to copy her Italian counterpart, Miss Sansom.

"As she is a large and beautiful blonde, and as I am small and dark, I naturally felt that my sort of prostitute was not her sort. She played the part with a disdainful sway of her hips; I wanted to play it as a gay little urchin," the actress recalled.

Miss Mitchell's *Children of Chance* originally ran four hours but was cut down to an hour and 20 minutes in England. The hero was no longer even in the film, and the whole thing now made little sense.

"The story was not there," regretted Miss Mitchell. "Just a jumble of scenes, one following the other, without coherence. The little Ischian children's voices had apparently been dubbed in Rome, to save the expense of bringing the film at that stage to England, and as Zampa did not understand that urchin faces needed urchin or village voices, and as the only English children in Rome were ambassadors' offspring and the like, what appeared on screen were poverty-stricken and dirty orphans, speaking with highly cultured English children's voices."

Miss Mitchell noted that while the Italian version of *Children of Chance* was winning a prize at the Venice Film Festival, the English version was lucky to be shown for a few days at the Astoria in Charing Cross Road.

The Divided Heart, while it had its snips, met a far better fate and became an international award winner. It was the true story of a Yugoslav baby taken by the Nazis during World War II from his parents and adopted by a young German couple. Nine years passed and his mother (Miss Mitchell), who had been in a concentration camp, located the boy and wanted him back. The ending had the real mother winning the boy, but the film closed with a scene not originally intended to end matters. The final scene of the picture was cut, "where the boy showed his mother conjuring tricks on the train journey. It was a good scene in itself, but not such a good ending as the penultimate one, in which the boy assumed responsibility of his mother by quietly taking charge of the train tickets."

Miss Mitchell also wrote that about a fifth of what one sees in the rushes will be used in the finished film.

Simultaneous shootings of the same story for two different markets is not as uncommon as one might at first think, incidentally, although it is done almost exclusively nowadays in other countries. (Years ago, before dubbing techniques were perfected, it was a fairly regular practice for Hollywood to make several versions of the same story for foreign markets, each with different, foreign supporting casts, and sometimes different leads.) *I Mognoli,* an Anita Ekberg–Jack Palance time-waster, was directed in '60 by Leopoldo Savona in a three-hour-plus version, while the American print (released here in 1963), directed by American expatriate André de Toth, was an hour shorter.

In a class by itself is the case of Samuel Goldwyn's *The North Star,* directed by Lewis Milestone with Walter Huston and released by RKO during World War II. A pro-Russian picture (they were our allies then) written by Lillian Hellman, it depicted the resistance of rural Russia to the Nazi hordes and was called the first serious attempt to portray Soviet Russia on the American screen.

A few years back the film was re-released to theaters as *Armored Attack,* which was not the worst of it: it was drastically cut, featured an off-screen narrator whose classroom tones bridged the gaps, and carefully boomed in to talk over any left-in national references by the characters who were now victims not of the Nazis but of Communist oppression! ("Somewhere in Eastern Europe, a people betrayed by their leaders were preparing to fight . . .") Little more than the action interludes remained. The really unique aspect of it all is that the factions behind its re-editing and re-issue owned up to its slaughter like the good Americans they were by inserting with the credits the practically unprecedented confession that *Armored Attack* was an abridgement of a film called *The North Star.*

Now censorship is quite another problem (for another book). We all know the havoc it has caused with some films. It—and the insertion rather than the omission of a scene—even helped to end the career of one of the screen's all-time great stars, Greta Garbo.

But before we get to it, let me join the queue and get in a few personal words about Garbo. I've always thought she was something of a fraud.

God and Garbo fans forgive me if I'm wrong, I've never believed the Sphinx-like Garbo, the dark-glassed, hair-in-the-faced, vant-to-be-aloned (okay, *let*-aloned), shy, reclusive Garbo was the real Greta Gustafsson. Call it heresy, but I've always felt that the image of Garbo as an eccentric loner started mostly as a publicity gimmick to give her screen personality more mystique. And as we know, a lie told often enough sometimes winds up being believed by the prevaricator himself. I believe this has happened with Garbo. She has lived this lie for so long that it and perhaps other personality problems have become the masters of this sensitive woman, despite rumblings way down deep of the Garbo who initially owned "the face of the century."

I could be wrong. I don't know Miss Garbo, nor is there any concrete evidence that my theory is true. (I do have a friend who shops in the same East Side Manhattan store where Garbo buys her periodical one egg.) Still, I have encountered her in New York on (so far) two fairly recent occasions.

The first time: 1964. Slender and dressed pretty much as she might have in *Ninotchka* back in the '30s, she was headed for a gift shop on 57th St., talking an enthusiastic blue streak to a lady-friend and moving that large Swedish bulk a hell of a lot faster than she ever seemed to in pictures. Her face was as firm as it ever was, although many tiny wrinkles had moved in.

The second time: 1965. It was a rainy Friday afternoon and I had finished office chores and bee-lined for a bill of two Orson Welles reissues at the New Yorker, *Citizen Kane* and *Magnificent Ambersons.* I arrived near the end of *Kane.* When the lights went up at the end prior to the next showing of *Ambersons,* I observed that there was only a handful of people in the theater—and that a few rows in front of me (very close to the screen) sat a fidgety Greta Garbo. Wearing dark glasses (which I think she kept on during the movie), a cape, and a green turban that she kept adjusting and tucking her hair under with long fingers, the lady moved around in her seat quite a bit while the lights were up, even turned around to look at the house a couple of times. She looked for all the world like a very lonely woman who was dying to be recognized. But she had established her impenetrable image too well, even for a doubter like myself to attempt penetration. I should have liked to have introduced myself to her, told her she was nicely cast in *Queen Christina*—but I couldn't quite dispel the vision of a flushed out Garbo sprinting off into the storm.

In her own time, the legend got up and left half-way through *Ambersons,* apparently unrecognized by anyone as the theater started to fill up with evening patrons.

Ironically, both *Kane* and *Ambersons* were made about the time Garbo's career was coming to a close.

With the arrival of the 1940s, and the diminishment by spreading war of Garbo's important European boxoffice, MGM decided to turn the actress into an "oomph" girl for home audiences in a comedy called *Two-Faced Woman.* George Oppenheimer, who worked on the screenplay, said that director George Cukor, furthermore, got the idea to refute the myth that Garbo had big feet by having co-star Melvyn Douglas praise her tootsies and then, in a bedroom scene, lift up one of her feet to reveal its beauty. "At first preview," continued Oppenheimer, "Garbo's bare foot looked larger than legend and elicited one of the loudest and rudest laughs I have heard in a theater. The scene was promptly cut out of the film."

The picture, which was improvised much of the way and dealt with a plain wife who tried to entice an indifferent husband by impersonating her own glamorous twin sister, opened in November '41, and was immediately condemned by the National League of Decency; the Most Reverend Francis J. Spellman, Roman Catholic Archbishop of New York; the police amusement inspector of Rhode Island; the Catholic Interest Committee of the Knights of Columbus of Manhattan and the Bronx; and Australia, among others. Garbo, who had always tried to avoid playing "bad womens," had said, "No mamas, no murderesses," and who wasn't so crazy about doing the picture in the first place, was shocked, and was heard to say, "they've dug my grave" and "they're trying to kill me"—meaning MGM.

The studio then "cleaned up" the film mainly by putting in a scene which, paradoxically, cut out the heart of the story: a telephone call that apprised the husband (Douglas) of his wife's masquerade, so that when he chased her around he supposedly knew what he was getting into all the time. Ludicrously, the rest of the picture still played as if he did not know the sexy sister was really his wife and failed anyway. Garbo has refused to make another movie (although she did film some tests under camerman James Wong Howe for *La Duchesse de Langeais* later on, and wouldn't the buffs like to get hold of this celluloid?).

On today's screen, however, the telephone call would have been cut *out.* And probably is, on some TV *Early Show* somewhere (which is yet another book).

INDEX